The Black Aesthetic Unbound

The Black Aesthetic Unbound

Theorizing the Dilemma of Eighteenth-Century African American Literature

APRIL C. E. LANGLEY

The Ohio State University Press • Columbus

Library of Congress Cataloging-in-Publication Data
Langley, April C. E.
  The Black aesthetic unbound : theorizing the dilemma of eighteenth-century
African American literature / April C. E. Langley.
    p. cm.
  Includes bibliographical references and index.
  ISBN-13: 978-0-8142-1077-2 (alk. paper)
  ISBN-10: 0-8142-1077-5 (alk. paper)
1. American literature—African American authors—History and criticism.
2. American literature—African influences. 3. American literature—Colonial
period, ca. 1600–1775—History and criticism. 4. American literature—
Revolutionary period, 1775–1783—History and criticism. 5. American litera-
ture—1783–1850—History and criticism. 6. Aesthetics, Black. 7. Wheatley,
Phillis, 1753–1784—Criticism and interpretation. 8. Equiano, Olaudah, b. 1745.
Interesting narrative of the life of Olaudah Equiano. 9. Aidoo, Ama Ata, 1942–
Dilemma of a ghost. I. Title.
  PS153.N5L35 2008
  810.9'896073—dc22
                                2007019590

This book is available in the following editions:
Cloth (ISBN 978-0-8142-1077-2)
CD-ROM (ISBN 978-0-8142-9157-3)
Paper (ISBN: 978-0-8142-5660-2)
Cover design by Janna Thompson-Chordas
Type set in ITC New Baskerville by Juliet Williams

CONTENTS

PREFACE

To plan to write a book about the way in which three different continents have impacted the literature of a people, captured, enslaved, transported, and oppressed by the very same three continents, was never my intention. The seeds of this book began at a time when I could scarcely imagine theorizing the dilemmas into which I had been born as an African American woman. Years after Langston Hughes's "Theme for English B" freed me to express my black and beautiful self, and long before the day I stood up in my fourth-grade class and dared to give my teacher and fellow classmates a lesson in black history for which I was promptly and physically removed from class, I knew how it felt to be a problem. Literally, decades before I was first introduced to Jeremy Bentham's Panopticon, in an Introduction to Graduate Studies course, I knew firsthand the internal prison he described. *The Autobiography of Malcolm X, Giovanni's Room, If They Come in the Morning, The Spook Who Sat by the Door,* and *Black Boy:* With few exceptions, my first experience of literature was with black United States literature written during the era of the Black Power movement—the period between the mid-1960s and late 1970s. This literature offered wisdom of the ages, as it foretold everything, knew from whence every ail sprang, and provided the curative texts to fix the world that came crushing down on me—a disenfranchised young black woman growing up in (sub)urban "ghettos" from New York City to Los Angeles.

As a result, when I later encountered Fyodor Dostoyevsky's *Notes from the Underground,* I could not help but notice how much it reminded me of Ralph Ellison's *Invisible Man.* When I read William Faulkner's *As I Lay Dying,* I thought immediately of Toni Morrison's *The Bluest Eye.* It was the way Morrison just let her characters be and how, because of what seemed to me at the time a more natural or realistic way of narrating things, her characters interconnected while separate histories unfolded, and each from a different character's point of view. This way of inviting a reader into the lives of each character from different vantage points was the quality I thought made Faulkner's writing seem so like Morrison's. When I read Mark Twain's *The Tragedy of Pudd'nhead Wilson,* I couldn't help but notice that the voices of Tom, Chambers, and Roz echoed an ironic humor that seemed similar to the sentiments of a character with which I was most familiar—Langston Hughes's Jess B. Simple. It mattered not that the white canonical texts preceded the black ones. To my mind I could only wonder in amazement at how these white writers managed to capture what I would later understand as a black aesthetic. The more I read these canonical white and black texts and the more comparisons I made between them and many others, the more I began to realize that my earliest experience of literature had not been a conventional one. Years later, an English professor would refer to this way of reading and understanding literature as backing into the canon.

Perhaps the only exceptions to my unconventional engagement with literature were two works that I had been weaned on since a small child—the Bible and key plays in the corpus of William Shakespeare. Nonetheless, I maintain that my experiencing of literature was quite traditional for black children growing up in New York City in the 1960s— during a time when everything was racial and political and nearly every text—by a white or black author—was meant to convey some underlying message about freedom from oppression. We—young black people—were in the middle of a revolution that in the words of Gil Scott Heron "would not be televised." We had witnessed the repercussions of the deaths of two great martyrs—Martin Luther King Jr. and Malcolm X—and had witnessed the suppression and violence against those organizations and persons who resisted being silenced and restricted. The most vivid manifestation of the Black Power era was seen in the imprisonment of Angela Davis, an image that only served to further drive home the point that to be young, gifted, and black carried with it a great responsibility—to save the race.

All this to say, that race mattered and it mattered that black people were not merely the great-grandsons and -granddaughters of slaves. It mattered that black people were a people with a history beyond the transatlantic triangular trade, beyond their enslavement, colonization, and emancipation in the United States, the British colonies, Britain, and other western European colonies and countries. For it was in this historical moment of the 1960s that I, like other black people, discovered my geographical, historical, and philosophical roots in Africa. Thus, as we metamorphosed from Negroes, Coloreds, and blacks, we were transformed into African Americans—a people with history, land, and ties to ancient cultures and civilizations, whose universal contributions to all civilizations represented a force with which to be reckoned. Romantically, I was Eulalie,[1] and years later I regretted that I did not discover Christina Ama Ata Aidoo and other African writers when I was a child—it most certainly would have mattered and in ways that might have changed my life forever.

Three decades later—as a scholar of African American literature—I continue to grapple with the same dynamic forces, this time neither looking for nor expecting full reconciliation. Consequently, I have had to admit that the only way to recover with more honesty and clarity a heritage that black people in the 1960s, 1970s, 1980s, and indeed 1990s had been claiming for themselves is to directly confront (in the twentieth century) the glaring impossibility of such an undertaking. This project represents my attempt to hypothesize about how to break out of such historical impasses—located ironically in the tension between verifiable realities of slavery and colonization of people of the African Diaspora, throughout the Black Atlantic, and the attendant psychoses that have resulted in romanticized responses to post-emancipation and postcolonial conditions.

Thus, I have had to address some very personal and political questions about what it means to be African, American, and the descendant of Afro-British Americans in the United States of America. Because of my love of literature and my somewhat naïve faith in the value of all forms of literature for humanity, I wanted to begin my literary journey at the beginning and close to home—all of them real and imagined, in the United States, somewhere on the African continent, and throughout the Black Atlantic. I have made three critical assumptions: First, because the black experience literally and figuratively encompasses Africa, Europe, and America, we cannot continue to operate as though only two of these locations matter—Europe and America. The continent of Africa matters significantly. And, to conflate Africa within a limited framework of African America, Europe, or America is to risk rendering Africa as nonexistent—and even (especially) metaphorical and abstract renderings matter. Second, although African American identity is inextricably tied to Africa, it is both dishonest and irresponsible to superficially offer Afro-America as a stand-in or representative for Africa. We must not conflate Africa with Afro-America—one is not equivalent to the other. Third, because the narrative of the black experience is laden with as much fiction as are narratives of the Western worlds' encounters with African worlds, which translate sometimes rather loosely into the narrative of the unnamed but nonetheless white experience, we must recognize the ways in which distortions and romanticizations of truth from either direction function similarly—and we are all culpable, though to be sure, not always equally so.

This, the boundless recovery of an invented but nonetheless real Africa, is the dilemma I am willing to face, the journey I am willing to undertake, and that for which I gladly and freely plunge into the mythic and literal Atlantic to recover what is mine. This is my sojourn—I am returning—to recover Africa from African America, to return myself to myself. The call to acknowledge and deal with *The Dilemma of a Ghost* has long since been issued and addressed. This book represents a visible manifestation of an inward and ongoing response to the question . . . What is African in African American?

ACKNOWLEDGMENTS

First, I want to thank God for giving me the strength and wisdom to know when to follow my own mind, when to take the advice of others, and when to be still and calm through the many years and the daunting process out of which this book was produced. "I can do all things through Christ which strengtheneth me" (Philippians 4:13).

Beyond that, I am indebted to a great many grants, libraries, scholarly societies and organizations, mentors, friends, colleagues, and family for their financial support, resources, conversations, debates, inspiration, encouragement, prodding, and faith, including the following for their generous funding of research, travel, and resources on three continents (Africa, Europe, and North America): American Association of University Women Dissertation Fellowship; Howard University: English Department, Afro-American Studies Resource Center, Afro-American Studies, Sterling Library and Staff, Moorland-Spingarn Research Center and Staff. I am especially grateful to professors Eleanor Traylor, Victoria Arana, Sandra Shannon, and E. Ethelbert Miller for generously extending encouragement and a research home to me; University of Missouri-Columbia: Office of Research (Summer Research Fellowship, Research Council, Board, and International Travel Grants) College of Arts and Sciences (Junior Faculty Travel Grants), English Department, Women's and Black Studies (Travel Grants), Ellis Library, Center for Arts and Humanities (Travel Grants); University of Notre Dame: English

Department, African and African American Studies Program, Hesburgh Library; Washington University in St. Louis: African and Afro-America Studies Program Post Doctoral Fellowship, English Department, John M. Olin Library; West African Research Association, West African Research Center (Dakar, Senegal) and Baobab Center. I also thank the following students, librarians, staff, and research assistants for their contributions: Danielle Roth and Josh Lubatkin (work-study students WUStl), Sharon Black (staff support UMC), Dorothy M. Long, Victoria M. Thorp, Mrs. Joyce L. Rose (departmental secretary Afro-American Studies–Howard), Jean Currie Church (Chief Librarian Moorland–Spingarn Research Center Staff), Anne Barker (Humanities Librarian UMC), Raye Mahaney (Department Secretary–WUStl), Adele Tuchler (administrative assistant–WUStl), Abdou Karim Sylla (research assistant, Dakar Senegal). Special thanks are due to Sandy Crooms, Eugene O'Connor, the anonymous readers, and The Ohio State University Press for their hard work in publishing this book.

I offer my deepest gratitude to the following scholars, former professors, and colleagues for the profound impact they have had on the thinking, development, and articulation of a great many ideas brought forward in this study: Carol Anderson (for the "aesthetic" conversation and years of mentoring), JoAnne Banks-Wallace (for being my guide through this rough journey and shedding light on those things I could not or would not see), Boubacar Barry (special thanks to you and Madame Barry for opening your home and library to me), Jacqueline Vaught Brogan, Joanna Brooks (my scholarly sister and friend—thanks for reading proposal, chapter drafts, and the entire manuscript at many stages and listening to me talk through my ideas, for John Marrant's *Journal* and allowing me to stand on your shoulders!), Leslie Brown, Brycchan Carey, Angelo Costanzo (for asking difficult questions early on and your meticulous reading of chapters in this book), Garrett Duncan, Stephane Dunn (for reading an eighty-page chapter twice and reminding me that trailblazing is worth the risk!), Gerald Early, Christopher Fox, Dolores and Jerry Frese, Rosemary Guruswamy, Glenn Hendler, Peaches Henry (for refusing to let me give up, demanding that I write with clarity, and for losing hair from reading "muddled" early versions), Clenora Hudson-Weems, Eileen Julien, Anthonia Kalu (with love and reverence for my scholarly mother, African sister, and living ancestor for mentoring, teaching, motivating, encouraging, intellectually and spiritually feeding and finishing what Dr. Peters started; sharing your home, family, and most of all wisdom on everything from grad school seminar to tenure process and child rearing), Joycelyn Moody, J. Cameron Monroe, Carla Mulford, Mungai Mutonya, Christopher Okonkwo, Hugh Page, Timothy Parsons (for talks, materials, and encouragement on West African research), Erskine Peters (my mentor and ancestor, the one who made me stay on this path when other roads were easier—I will always miss you), John Saillant (for offering practical advice on my research), Wilfred Samuels (for blazing the path and for generously reading my earliest versions of Equiano and offering important criticism, being accessible and responding when I have most needed your help, thanks for helping me to stay on the path), Sandra Shannon, Donald Sniegowski (for encouraging and inspiring my love of African literature and for the dissertation advising), Zabelle Stodola, Leigh Swigart, Joseph Thompson, Dorothy Tsuruta (the first of my professors to put me on this scholarly path by introducing me to Lucy and Phillis and the one who encouraged and inspired me to pursue a Ph.D.), Robert Vinson, Wendy Wilson-Fall, Rafia Zafar (for teaching me how to be a good scholar and colleague, introducing me to so many wonderful people, and "capturing the captivity"), and Ewa Ziarek (for unearthing the underlying question). Though they are not in any way responsible for any errors, omissions, faux pas, or oversights that may be found in this book, the best of this work could not have been possible but for their influence, ideas, and generosity.

Last, but certainly not least, I want to thank my family for their unconditional love, support, and sacrifices all these many years as I traveled and sometimes lived months at a time away from home and spent countless hours at my computer, especially to my love, my husband Jimi for his tireless and unrelenting support—truly "the wind beneath my wings." On every page your blood, sweat, and tears mixed with mine make this our book. To my mother Alga Brown—thank you for the patience and the comfort that only a mother could offer during those times when I might have thrown in the towel and for reading as well as listening to pages of "scholarly" work and forcing me to make things clearer. To my god-daughter Danielle April Winston, thank you for DQ, laughs, and lots of love. To my sisters Diane, Peaches, Stephane, Susie (Bettye), and Wanda, I thank you for "feeding me" with your spiritual and nurturing gifts—for taking care of me and reminding me to take a break, and to Aunt Sandy for always opening her heart and home in D.C., VA, and South Africa. Thanks to my Uncle Carl for reminding me to "smell the roses" and for my mother-in-law Bettie Mack Langley who always had a kind word to say and smile to give me. Thanks to my spiritual family: Pastor Carolus Taylor, Charliss Taylor, Friendship Missionary Baptist Church, Pastor Anthony Pettus and Macedonia Missionary Baptist Church. To the entire Langley, Brown, Sanford, Henry, and Dunn family I extend my eternal love and gratitude, as they gave so much of themselves so that I might be able to complete this work. I dedicate this book to them and to the memory of *thousands gone,* which include Erskine Peters, Luther Brown, Evelyn Persons, Dollie Hanson, Laverne Elder, and Lucy Johnson.

Historical and Cultural Recovery

Eighteenth-Century Scholarship

and the Politics of Visibility

Black Aesthetic Unbound

The Black Aesthetic Unbound ("Unbound") rearticulates the early black aesthetic that operates alongside the European-American colonial literary traditions by recovering suppressed African worldviews in the earliest American literature. Two central themes unite this study. First, it draws upon the concept of *dilemma* as developed in Ghanaian playwright Christina Ama Ata Aidoo's 1964 play, *The Dilemma of a Ghost,* which dissects the problematic relationship and historical disconnections between Africa and African America in the fictional marriage of a West African man and African American woman. Second, it invokes the notion of a *Black Aesthetic Unbound* to expose how theoretical attempts to free black texts from white envelopes have created yet another dilemma for early black texts—that of proving that the texts are representatively black enough. Rather than attempting to free the eighteenth-century black text from either its literary or literal black or white self, "Unbound" liberates additional African lenses through which Afro-British American literature in the eighteenth century might be interpreted.

During the era of the slave trade, more than twelve million Africans were brought as captives to the Americas. With them they brought memories, ideas, beliefs, and practices, which forever shaped the histories and cultures of the Americas. However, even the expanding and exciting field of early African American literature has yet to sufficiently confront the undeniable imprints of West African culture and consciousness on this early black writing. This book offers a sustained study of the relationship between specific West African modes of thought and expression and the emergence of a black aesthetic in eighteenth-century North America. It explores how Senegalese, Igbo, and other West African traditions provide striking new lenses for reading poetry and prose by Phillis Wheatley, Olaudah Equiano, Lucy Terry, James Albert Gronniosaw, John Marrant, and Venture Smith. In so doing, this work confronts the difficult dilemma of how to use diasporic, syncretic, and vernacular theories of black culture to inductively think through the massive cultural transformations wrought by the Middle Passage.

Influenced by more than five decades of African-centered scholarship, John Charles Shields and Paul Edwards located the critical link between African aesthetics and African American literature as early as the 1970s. During the 1980s, Houston A. Baker Jr., Henry Louis Gates Jr., and Mae Gwendolyn Henderson developed theories based on African and African American vernacular and aesthetics in *Blues, Ideology, and Afro-American Literature* (1984), *The Signifying Monkey: A Theory of African American Literary Criticism* (1988), and "Speaking in Tongues . . ." (1989). By the late 1990s, Chikwenyne Okonjo Ogunyemi and Anthonia Kalu developed culturally specific West African and gender-based theories in *African Wo/Man Palava* (1996) and *Women, Literature and Development in Africa* (2001). Paul Gilroy's *The Black Atlantic* (1993), Helena Woodard's *African-British Writings in the Eighteenth Century* (1999), and Wilfred Samuels's extensive critical work have informed early Afro-British aesthetic studies. Most recently, Vincent Carretta's controversial work, which argues on the basis of newly recovered documents that Olaudah Equiano was born in South Carolina, not Africa, underscores the importance of establishing an eighteenth-century black aesthetic that is not solely dependent on locating Africa through fixed geographical, historical, or cultural locations.

"Unbound" traces one of the most culturally diverse historical periods of African American literature—the eighteenth century—through its triangular engagement with the languages, cultures, and experiences of Africa, Europe, and North America. It does so first by exploring the paradoxical implications of the multiple positions of Africanity in early Afro-British America, both real and imagined. Next, by drawing upon the immensely eclectic and interdisciplinary range of scholarship available—across disciplines from one side of the Black Atlantic to the other—I locate elements of a developing eighteenth-century black aesthetic. Finally, this book offers new ways of incorporating existing Western and Afro-Western critical tools alongside new Africanist ones to relocate Africa (both real and imagined) within African American literature.

The *Black* Aesthetic

Long before current scholarship could begin to forge new paths in black American literature, it often did so by bracketing, castigating, and worse yet exiling early black aesthetic critics' African-centered scholarship to an intellectual and cultural nomad's existence. As a result, the significant impact of the work of scholars such as Addison Gayle, Hoyt Fuller, and Amiri Baraka (Leroi Jones) toward the foundation of what we now laud in progressive interdisciplinary movements has not been fully appreciated. Understandably, it is fitting to invite them back to the table, to participate in a meal they not only helped prepare, but also one for which they supplied many of the essential ingredients. Notably, texts such as Dudley Randall's *The Black Poets*, Abraham Chapman's *New Black Voices*, Stephen Henderson's *Understanding the New Black Poetry: Black Speech and Black Music as Poetic References*, and Leroi Jones and Larry Neal's *Black Fire* are representative of a range of black literary history, major themes, and conventions of black aestheticism.

These critical foundations have been defined and articulated in one of the most fundamental studies of the work of the early black aestheticians, Addison Gayle's *The Black Aesthetic*. Drawing upon historically powerful literary antecedents from Pauline Hopkins to Richard Wright, the scholars represented in this groundbreaking collection—many political icons, some reaching near-demagogue status during the era of what has come to define black activism and nationalism, the late 1960s and 1970s—constructed a frame of reference for identifying, analyzing, and evaluating black art and culture, thus defining an aesthetic dimension of black or African identity that remains with us today. These black artists, scholars, activists, and innovators unapologetically and diligently created the contexts and carved the necessary spaces within which to name, create, and celebrate blackness. Their words announced the cultural wars between blacks and whites already centuries in progress. More important, they articulated in distinct black voices the sociopolitical and historical implications of those wars. They refused to be silenced, even by one another, and indeed many of the early debates remain at the center of today's discussions of black literature, aesthetics, politics, art, music, and nearly any subject or issue which impinges on the conditions, lives, and experiences of black people.

Paradoxically, while these early black aestheticians spoke representatively in a diversity of voices, which inaugurated a context within which to celebrate as never before the language, the sensibility, the art, politics, psychology, sociology, history, and the meaning of black existence, they regrettably left effectively silenced other black voices. In so doing, they forfeited a rich cultural heritage of black aesthetics, which they dismissed as being irrelevant and steeped in white culture. If it is true, as Hoyt Fuller claims, that "the new black writers have decided that their destiny is not at the mercy of the white man" (346), it is also true that their destinies are tied to other equally oppressive dilemmas. As Fuller amply identifies, black people are burdened with negative images of themselves upon which myths about black inferiority are erected. Further, compounding this dilemma faced by these new writers as inheritors of the black aesthetic is the necessarily "vast" gap between "white and black interpretations of those values" (330) which underlie their divergent yet intersecting experiences in a racially divided world. As Larry Neal argues in "The Black Arts Movement," the onus is on the black writer to create through her literature a new "symbolism, mythology, critique, and iconography" (257). Importantly, this new aesthetic must speak to and for the global and local issues affecting the "first" and "third" worlds inhabited by people of African descent.

This book addresses the implications of black aesthetics for eighteenth-century black writers, who at best have been tolerated and condescended to, and at worst exiled and otherwise banished from the canon of "real" or "authentic" black literature. To that end I would like to offer three extensions of a bridge from the eighteenth-century Afro-British American authors in this study and their literary and cultural descendants who consciously constructed the black aesthetic. First, the existing cultural traditions that constitute the basis of the black aesthetic are present in the diverse worldviews and ways of knowing brought forward in the earliest black literature. Second, the "desire for self-determination . . . nationhood . . . the relationship between art and politics; [and,] the art of politics" (Neal, 257) are of primary (not secondary) concern to eighteenth-century black artists. Moreover, I contend that without their deliberate attempts to craft a humanity and positively alter and affect first their own black consciousnesses through a "reordering of

Western" aesthetics, they would have been unable to effectively prick the conscience and raise the consciousness of a white slaveholding and oppressive society. Third, while there can be no doubt that it would have been impossible for these early black writers to write solely for, and speak to, black people and their concerns, as the fundamental project of the twentieth-century black aesthetic has insisted upon, we should not assume that these eighteenth-century writers were not consciously aware of the need to alter a reality—symbolically or otherwise—that did not correspond with their own experience of black humanity.

In "'Total Life Is What We Want': The Progressive Stages of the Black Aesthetic in Literature" Reginald Martin elaborates on the critical contexts, concepts, and historical factors impacting formations, and attempts to reformulate black aesthetics. He explains that the "elucidation of the term black aesthetic will only come with the acquisition of a clear understanding of what it meant to its originators, its progressive stages, and where the term uncomfortably rests in the world of literary thought today" (49). Part of that reformulation will also require us to relocate eighteenth-century black writers as an important (albeit uncomfortably situated) stage in the development of a black aesthetic.

The Scholarship of Visibility

The dilemma for contemporary scholarship on eighteenth-century literature by black English-speaking authors,[1] though not unrelated to the very predicaments faced by the early black authors themselves, is not quite the same. Like them we (scholars) mourn the loss of an Africa buried under a palimpsest of European and Anglo-American ways of knowing. Further, we remain similarly moored to methods of unraveling and celebrating cultural hybridity and diversity that produce equally troubling structures and systems. However, unlike our eighteenth-century literary predecessors, we are bound in different ways, constrained and compelled through distinct historical and aesthetic moments that oblige us to disentangle the very quandaries left by these early black writers.

Significantly, as studies of the past ten years make clear and visible, the scholarship around eighteenth-century Afro-British America is caught in a web of contemporary criticism, theory, and history that undermines attempts to unconditionally recover the literature of this period from the white and black envelopes that continue to enclose it. Not surprisingly, the conditions of recovery are complicated by remnant proscriptions from all corners. Importantly, much critical work has been done of late to uncover problems, debates, and conflicts associated with the historical, cultural, and literary knowledge that impacts Afro-British America. Consequently, such scholarship confronts predicaments—some deeply imbedded and others lingering just beneath the surface—in a way that enables us to more clearly extract meaning from hidden texts of Africa, Britain, and America present in this early black literature. This tendency in current scholarship to engage formerly bracketed impasses in the study of early Afro-British American literature has forged new and expansive paths for scholarly advances in the field. Thankfully, these significant advances and inroads in early black historical and cultural studies have made possible work such as mine. Indeed, discernable changes in early black literary studies can be marked by an unbounded approach that discloses issues that have been traditionally excepted, deferred, underanalyzed, or (un)consciously omitted.

To be sure, while not wholly representative of the field of eighteenth-century black literary studies, the work of Rafia Zafar, Katherine Clay Bassard, Joanna Brooks, David Kazanjian, Phillip Gould, and Vincent Carretta offer much to my rendering of an unbinding of the black aesthetic through a theorizing of the dilemma of self and identity in the eighteenth-century Afro-British American literature. Principally, their scholarship provides key points of entry into some of the most heavily debated issues in a relatively small but far-reaching and diverse area of study. Consequently, each of these scholars cracks interdisciplinary windows that I more fully open throughout this text. Each identifies an aesthetic, or contributes to the location of a crucial component of an existing or developing aesthetic, operating in the worlds and works of eighteenth-century Afro-British American authors. It is therefore fitting that I introduce this book, in the tradition of the literary ancestors to whom it is dedicated, by an invocation of these scholarly muses. More to the point, I want to acknowledge the critical space their work has left for my own. While I have both agreed and disagreed with them on more than a number of critical occasions, their engagement with the multivalent ghosts that haunt eighteenth-century Afro-British American literature has troubled my own theorizing about the literature. Not surprisingly, their innovative and controversial literary and cultural work—as well as the wealth of scholarship they carry forward in their work—highlights the strength of early black literary studies.

Surveying the critical paths they have laid, I attempt to map out how and what their scholarship makes visible about the impingement of intersecting forces—from Africa, England, African America, and Afro-

British America—on early black writers and their texts. Further, I reflect on diverse dilemmas each scholar confronts as she or he attempts to unearth complex nationalized historical realities alongside equally problematic racialized political strivings. While I have resisted the impulse toward any superficial categorization of this body of scholarship, I have located a common thread. Because their work necessarily exposes the irresolvable gulfs and divides created as a result of the transatlantic slave trade, like the writers they study, these scholars have all participated to some extent in an invention of Africa.

Similarly, not unlike the eighteenth-century Afro-British American writers whose works they study, these scholars find themselves in a catch-22 situation. At least two impossible scenarios present themselves: First, in exposing the very obstacles that impede complex contemporary analysis of Afro-British American literature, one risks rendering (by default) Africa invisible. Second, one's attempt to correct the first scenario—by replacing or renaming a previously displaced Africa—risks arrival on a slippery slope toward origins, roots, and essentialism. "Unbound" offers yet another scenario, one that neither brackets nor wholly defines an African self in early black literature. Rather, I submit Africa—invented, imagined, and real—as a visible manifestation of the dilemma these writers faced and the means by which they attempted to reorder tricontinental identity. Clearly, the critical playing field is anything but neutral: visibility is a political move—intentional or not. Far more exciting and valuable than any attempt to reconcile the two scenarios—caught between the need to theorize Western ways of knowing and the desire to actualize African ones—is what we produce as a result of such critical confrontations. Notably, in their decisions to unmask black captivity, to spiritually interrogate divine interventions, to raise Lazarus from the shadowy depths of American Awakenings, to mourn what and how history remains, to aestheticize the poetics and narrative economies of commercial and cultural conversion, and to reauthenticate documents, these scholars have identified and thus contributed critical strands to the uncovering of an eighteenth-century black aesthetic.

Out of a seemingly "whitewashed" eighteenth-century black literature Zafar uncovers black aesthetic elements: masking, capture, and renaming. Specifically, black American writers donned masks as self-consciously empowering moves to inscribe and rename the terms of their humanity. Moreover, by "capturing the captivity" these early black writers "changed permanently the meanings of the genres they appropriated" (10). Equally important, Zafar's scrutiny of how identity politics was conflated with the politics of canon formation exposes "race" as a gatekeeping mechanism that codes blackness in such a way as to render an eighteenth-century black text white. Drawing a line between Jeffersonian politics and twentieth-century black aesthetic criticism, she exposes how DuBoisean double consciousness was misapprehended, the effects of which have been to misname and displace the earliest black American literature. Problematically, writers like Wheatley have been subsumed under the racialized, nationalized terms of one historical period (eighteenth century) and the politics (or politicized aesthetics) of another (post-1960s and 1970s Black Aesthetic, and Black Arts Movement). Behind the "contemplative girlish countenance [that] announces . . . then, as now, that Wheatley has resolved to take on the ghosts and models of European culture" (38), is a mature and equally determined poetic voice confronting "then as now" the specter and symbol of Africa.

Bassard locates Wheatley's Africa within the discourse of African Americanism and the language of survivorship, exposing early black women's works as viable instruments and channels through which foundational strategies for the assumption of pre-emancipation agency can be analyzed. In doing so, she unpacks a great deal of historical, theoretical, cultural, and discursive baggage as she confronts aesthetic and cultural processes that both enable and provide obstacles for early black women's writing. In particular, Bassard's "practice of reading black women's intertextuality"—what she terms "spiritual interrogations"—stands prominently on the concept of divine authority as being undergirded by the interrogative rather than the imperative mood. Thus, subjectivity, agency, and racial and gendered configurations of culture are expressed as a kind of divine dialogue that produces power through a regeneration of knowledge about black women and their texts. This textual matrix contains, transforms, releases, and regenerates the very power it describes, and thus enables birth and rebirth, through poetic narrative recovery and revision. Looking out beyond her frontispiece, ready to do battle with American, European, and African ghosts, we are reminded of Wheatley's transformation by means of spiritual interrogations—a call to spiritual and cultural conversation. Transformed by looking inward, Wheatley now has a subject in view, and that subject is her own spiritual and African self.

Brooks highlights the significance of this type of Christian conversion as that which links the spiritual and cultural self—as both a personal and communal event reinforced through personal testimony and reenacted in spiritual resurrection of an entire community, through her attention to the prevailing "tropes of revival and resurrection . . . [in] the story of Lazarus" (10). In so doing, she points to the way that black writers like Wheatley used existing religious "formulas such as conversion, revival, and resurrection" to confront internal and external crises resulting from the "alienating and mortifying effects of slavery, colonialism and racial oppression" (9). Consequently, the "physical performances of death and rebirth" that "signified" individual, communal, and cultural transformation as manifested in the Lazarus figures provide a key to unlocking early black writers' engagement with African and other (nonwhite) discourses. Despite claims of "literary 'whiteface'" (14), black and Indian texts speak as much to one another, and their own respective black or Indian communities, as they do to white communities. More important, an "understanding of how race was lived and how racial identities were formed in the eighteenth century" (14) provides a clear map and a progressive strategy for theorizing the dilemmas presented by issues that define, recover, and reconstruct race.

Kazanjian argues for a reorientation of established methods of dealing with trauma, and the traumatic circumstances to which such concepts of loss are affixed. Namely, loss is viewed as an abundant social process rather than an individual pathological one (ix). Mourning is thus constructed as a political agent doing battle with an unsettling and essentializing history (2) that underscores the irresolvable nature of loss—the "mourning without end" (3). Thus, it is mourning itself, rather than the lost object, that signifies a recurrent and self-producing object to be mourned. Such a focus enables a consideration of how African writers construct imaginative realms that function as literal spaces of conflict resolution and analysis—developing corrective and survivalist strategies through which imagination can be used to provide practical solutions for changing current conditions. Considered thus, the imagination, like loss, mourning, and melancholia is seen as an equally valuable tool, but for different purposes and to different if equally important ends. Beyond merely bringing the past to history (or history to the past), one must also acknowledge that mourning not only recovers what remains but mourning also affixes itself to historical fragments and vestiges—like barnacles that adhere (are moored) to the bottom of a ship.

Affixed to antislavery writing and its aesthetic product, the commercial jeremiad is a genre that reverses the terms under which Africans were deemed savages and barbarians in comparison to the supposedly more cultured and civilized white men and women. Gould invites dialogue about the implications of an antislavery discourse which "effectively made 'beasts'" of slave-trading "Europeans and Americans"—whites (19). Gould's attention to what this literature reveals about the eighteenth-century Anglo-American world and its relationship to nation, race, and commerce lays bare important secular tensions that existed on both sides of the Atlantic. Less about ending slavery than justifying commercialism, sentimental rhetoric about the barbarity and viciousness of the slave trade was to define—by negation—a more civilized commerce. Concurrently, antislavery literature projected a simple and unaffected guise for the enslaved African whose innocence was juxtaposed against callous unremorseful man stealers. In so doing, he demonstrates yet another dilemma faced by eighteenth-century Afro-British American writers, the double-edged sword made evident in their simultaneously negative and positive varnishing of dual self-images, and the subsequent questions such polishing invokes about issues of black literary agency and empowerment. As such, Gould invites a productive revisiting and expanded understanding of the way signifying languages are liberated.

Carretta's call to contemporary scholars to confront the "powerful conflicting evidence" (xv) that the recovery of Equiano's baptismal and naval records demand, highlights the dilemmas posed by any attempts to recover Africa in eighteenth-century Afro-British American literature. Namely, because these documents contradict Equiano's narrative claims to an African birthplace, through their authentication of him as an American-born South Carolinian, those who privilege Equiano's account of his pre–Middle Passage African experience must justify their continued reliance on his narrative in the face of other—officially sanctioned—forms of evidence. Further, Carretta's claim that "the author of *The Interesting Narrative* was an even more profoundly self-made man than [Benjamin] Franklin if he invented an identity to suit the times" (xvii), while it reinforces and validates an African man's claims to agency, is based primarily on the fact that he was not in fact African by birth, but rather by invention. Clearly, Carretta's biography offers compelling evidence that must be grappled with, but the evidence, like the argument it implicitly makes about African identity, must be grappled with as well. Specifically, equally impenetrable are the codes and multiple paradoxes in which eighteenth-century black texts such as Equiano's are enshrouded. One great paradox remains: To be a "citizen of the [African] world" (367) an African-descended person must continually engage the dilemma of a ghost.

Historical and Cultural Recovery

Without early black history and cultural studies the work I undertake would be impossible. Indeed, the historians whose work informs mine exhibit a shared interest in compiling, presenting, and analyzing a body of knowledge about the African continent as a means to enable viable connections between the slavery era of black American history and its pre–Middle Passage origins. Thus, these scholars have enabled a direct challenge to the bracketing of seemingly irresolvable cultural gulfs and divides among Africa, Europe and the West, and the North American colonies. In particular, the pioneering and trailblazing efforts of Sterling Stuckey, Mechal Sobel, Michael Gomez, and Craig Wilder have yielded viable maps for African recovery—despite the tensions inherent therein. Importantly, their unapologetic historical and cultural recovery of Africa emboldens my own efforts to interrogate what is African in Afro-British American literature. Moreover, their work, which rigorously reconstructs Africa and African ways of knowing[2] through a variety of archival, primary, and secondary sources, is part of an ongoing project of imagining Africa through new—and necessarily African-centered—lenses.

Sterling Stuckey locates the origins of Afrocentrism in pre-emancipation slave culture by identifying the wealth of sources from which African-descended people were able to draw, the extent to which they were conscious of indigenous African practices and ways of knowing, and how early blacks used such knowledge to survive and resist their conditions under slavery. In particular, Stuckey's sketches of African religious practices, rituals, and such cultural practices as dancing, drumming, placing of hands on the dead, singing, and shouting spirituals, burial rituals, and especially the symbolic and practical use of the circle and the ring are critical to understanding the seeds of an early black aesthetic—with both the forms and the rituals they accompany sharing equal importance. Hence, "for the slave, the retention of important features of the African cultural heritage provides a means by which the new reality [sacred and secular] could be interpreted" (24). Such an articulation of the powerful influence of African aesthetics in spiritual and secular contexts is critical to unbinding a black aesthetic that may reveal eighteenth-century black writers' assumption of yet another level of agency and aesthetic self-sufficiency through their reconnection with Africa.

Mechal Sobel's exploration of the independent nature of relationships between blacks and whites in American culture troubles the space of reciprocity. In so doing, she points to one of the dilemmas faced by attempts to reconnect with African ways of knowing—the vexing problem of how to capture cultural reciprocity and interdependency while acknowledging ideological and political extensions of power that are both facilitated and restricted by models of shared cultural influences. Sobel points to such coded assemblages as time, work, place, space, death, causation, spirituality, nature, naming, family society, and ancestors as evidence of how black and white colonial America attempted to construct a coherent world in the face of such irresolvable and volatile forces as slavery. Like the transplanted Africans of different ethnicities who invented African cultural and political identities to meet this and otherworldly needs, eighteenth-century Virginians (and by extension all of the British-American colonies) created a cultural identity shaped by three continents—Africa, Europe, and North America. The question of how Africa influenced the West suggests serious implications both for how we view black intertextuality and how we interpret Afro-British American appropriation of Anglo-British-American ways of knowing.

Michael Gomez utilizes sources from anthropological archives to runaway slave notices to expose "this basic dialect—the adoption of an identity forged by antithetical forces from both without and within the slave community—[as] itself emblematic of the contradictory mechanism by which the African American identity was shaped" (12). This way of viewing identity informs an understanding of early black literature as necessarily marked by deliberate confrontation with seemingly irresolvable and incompatible African, British, and African American structures of meaning. Such a perspective has important implications for the analysis of Afro-British American literature that begins long before the critic, editor, or amanuensis enters the conversation. Namely, early black writers maintained African cultural retentions by refusing to be fully acculturated by "coercive" forces from without, by subverting dominant culture through "reinterpretation" and constructing a composite of racialized African identity based on ethnic fragments borrowed from within. Importantly, these fragmented representations of Africa contradict totalizing narratives that distort and monolithically construct Africa. Thus, Gomez unpacks discrete and invaluable elements of an eighteenth-century black aesthetic.

Recovering Afro-British-American agency in Pan-African nationalism as one of the early manifestations of collective black consciousness, Craig Wilder calls attention to African-descended people as active agents in their own history. Rather than "conflate or dissect the histories of peoples of African descent," his work troubles static notions of universal African "collectivism" (3). Essentialism, neither celebrated nor vilified, is constructed as an inevitable consequence of the transatlantic slave trade. Confronting the catch-22 situation of blacks as simultaneously victims and culpable agents in their own enslavement, Wilder resists engaging history as the story of "what was happening to them" (3). Instead, he presents a historical narrative of Africans in the New World from the perspective of "what they were constructing for themselves" (4). As a result, he complicates simplistic views of the connection between black oppression and unity. More importantly, Wilder compels the scholar to confront dilemmas posed by reconnecting with African ways of knowing. Early blacks had to sift through shards and remnants of Africa, not merely as signs of an irretrievable universal or particular African identity, or as a purely black reaction to white victimization. Quite the contrary, blacks acknowledged and celebrated what slavery was unable to wholly divest them of—their African cultures—however fragmented.

Chapter Summaries

Chapter 1: "The *Dilemma of a Ghost:* Early Black American Literature and Its Mournings/Moorings" analyzes the displacement of Africa in prevailing theories of African and black American literature, historicizes the dysfunctional relationship between Western- and African-centered theories, and outlines my integrative approach to reading an eighteenth-century black aesthetic back into black American literature. Drawing upon twentieth-century West African playwright Christina Ama Ata Aidoo's *The Dilemma of a Ghost* (1964), this chapter argues that themes of loss, horror, reconciliation, restoration, and harmony are central to the literatures of the African Diaspora. Further, I explain how a syncretic blend of Senegalese poetics and an Igbo duality discourse are used as organizing structures for theorizing the dilemma of eighteenth-century Afro-British American literature.

   Chapter 2: "What a Difference a 'Way' Makes: Wheatley's Ways of Knowing" highlights the dilemma involved in attempting to rewrite both the spiritual and political histories upon which enslaved and nominally free African-descended people, especially African-descended women, have been constructed. Wheatley's choice of form and subject matter reveals a complex matrix of signification and syncretization: the poet's choice to take on—especially in the neoclassical and elegiac forms—the simultaneously sacred and profane suggests a very sophisticated under-standing of the conventional history of the use and development of both forms, and in multiple contexts. This chapter's reading of Wheat-ley's "Niobe" poem reveals an eighteenth-century Afro-British American aesthetic steeped in spiritualization of the secular and secularization of the spiritual.

Chapter 3: "Kaleidoscopic Re-Memory in Equiano's *Interesting Narrative:* Shifting the Lens to Replace the Landscapes" argues that the question of "What is 'African' in African American literature" emerges in the consideration of an imagined or invented Africa in the context of *The Interesting Narrative of Olaudah Equiano or Gustavus Vassa, the African written by Himself.*[3] I identify African ways of knowing that underlie Equiano's vision and his relationship to the selves and the societies he inhabits: the concept of *chi,* its related Igbo concept of duality, *mbari,* and the complementary discursive mode of *palava.* Thus, I use the model of the Owerri Igbo *mbari* problem-solving structure as one way of theorizing the dilemmas that face Equiano's attempts to use his life story to both reclaim an authentic Igbo heritage and recount a narrative of progress in the New World. In so doing, Equiano's narrative defines an eighteenth-century black aesthetic that is both submerged in and emerges from the *Dilemma of a Ghost.*

Chapter 4: "Reading 'Others' in Eighteenth-Century Black American Literature: The Promise and Dilemma of New Ways of Reading" con-cludes this study by revisiting the dilemma of the unanswerability of the question of what is "African in African American." Applying both the African and Afro-Western elements outlined in chapter 1 to brief read-ings of the works of Lucy Terry, James Albert Gronniosaw, John Marrant, and Venture Smith, this chapter offers conclusions about the prom-ise and dilemma of a culturally specific reinterpretation of Africa that recovers a nonstatic and dynamic African cultural and critical presence. Thus, in the spirit of Sankofa, *The Black Aesthetic Unbound* is pleased to carry forward what remains, that which has been both glaringly present and absent, Africa.

Rather than presenting new cultural connections between African American and African knowledge bases, I have tried to shed more light on those cultural connections which already exist on both sides of the Atlantic. Throughout this work I try to avoid uncritical assumptions that cultural traditions which are shared in common between Africans and African Americans are a given. I hope to have avoided a reliance on one way of understanding what "black is" or "ain't." I have also tried to ground my interpretations in the literary and life texts of the eighteenth-century African-born (or descended) British-American writer, and where authentication was not possible, I have identified that as an area for future research.

Finally, I have tried to resituate black intertextuality within a mode of self-talk or intratextual dialogue in order to privilege, as does Henderson, "the other [within]" (119). My understanding of "other" is neither wholly grounded in, nor dependent on, Western philosophies of other/self dichotomies, regardless of their critical strengths. Rather, I have acknowledged useful aspects of the Western and African-centered interpretive strategies I appropriate, while remaining grounded in a duality discourse that both mourns and is moored to an Africanist *palava*. I have shown that using intratextuality or self-talk precipitates simultaneous ongoing and continuous dialogue between women, children, men, and between the ancestors in this world and the other. It is in this way that what we have come to understand as the black aesthetic may be unbound. And, as a result, perhaps this newfound aesthetic freedom, modeled in and emerging from an Africanist *palava* tradition, will allow sufficient room for an imaginative space through which African, American, and Afro-British American ancestors, living and dead, might pass.

ONE

The Dilemma of a Ghost

Early Black American Literature and
Its Mournings/Moorings

The ghosts of the dead ancestors are invoked and there is no discord, only
harmony and restoration of that which needs to be restored.

The Dilemma of a Ghost[1] (Aidoo, 33; Prelude)

From eighteenth-century Afro-British American works like Olaudah
Equiano's *The Interesting Narrative* to twentieth-century West African
playwright Christina Ama Ata Aidoo's *The Dilemma of a Ghost*—first performed in Ghana in 1964—themes of restoration and harmony are central to the literatures of the African Diaspora. Ultimately, the critical
import of Aidoo's play is its attention to motherhood, the double bind
of victimization and agency, marriage, naming, cohesive and fractured
Africanness, unreconciled strivings, memory, myths of the wayfarer, the
been-to, motherless children, ancestors, prodigal sons and daughters,
routes and roots, slavery, freedom, black and white, lightness and darkness, fruitfulness and barrenness, and life and death itself. These are
themes that are captured in the concept of mourning/mooring. The
dynamic thrust of this work resonates throughout history as it responds
intertextually to the call of eighteenth-century Afro-British American
writers who first stood at the junction of the transatlantic triangle, caught
between worlds that represented equally binding personal, communal,
political, and aesthetic dilemmas—all related to self and identity.

Mourning/Mooring

Mourning/mooring signifies a range of figurative and literal expression used to describe the dilemma posed by inescapable cycles of conflict and accord. As a symbol, the metaphor of mourning/mooring captures the phenomenon of an imagined but nonetheless real state of lost African consciousness. Further, mourning/mooring suggests the deep sense of loss that pervades African consciousness in its attempts to reconnect with African ways of knowing,[2] or the traditional systems of knowledge based on African worldviews that cohere and transform over time and space. Indeed, from displaced African to disenfranchised and marginalized Afro-British American, the black writers in this study underscore the point that their New World survival depends on successfully utilizing and adhering to nearly every aspect of their mourned African and non-African worldviews—fragmented or not—as these shards provide valuable tools with which to endure.[3]

Mourning and mooring are posited as interrelated terms utilized to render explicit the constructed nature of Africa in African American literature and literary theories. My linking of these terms signifies simultaneously on both the method and motives for such refitting.[4] Mooring denotes the process of being anchored or secured to a particular grounded position. A ship or other type of sea vessel is considered moored when it is anchored to or in a particular place. Unlike being docked—stationed at a specific place for a short time—when a ship is moored, it is secured firmly in place and is not likely to move for a long time. Correlatively, moor connotes the imbedded negativity affixed to the term as universal signifier of racial, social, and geographical darkness. This association with darkness speaks to the interrelatedness of mooring with mourning.[5] Hence, the attachment to African values grounded in indigenously derived origins that mooring is meant to suggest is attended by a profound sense of loss that its complementary term "mourning" invokes.

Mourning denotes a sorrow over the loss of someone or something very dear or a longing for that someone or something. This inward mourning is usually manifested by some visible physical sign. There are representations of mourning in all forms of life: Animals "pine" and plants are said to grieve figuratively when they "droop" or "hang down." For early African Americans, singing certain types of spirituals was considered a visible sign of mourning not only for the loss of a loved one in physical death but also for the loss of their freedom and their familial ties as a result of slavery.[6] The implicit comparison between questing for and identifying with a seemingly unrecoverable African consciousness and the immeasurable sense of loss and displacement that mourning connotes in my use of the term "mourning/mooring" is manifested in eighteenth-century literature through the integration of fragments that signify African worldviews.

Hence, my use of the slash signifies a reciprocal and fluid relationship between the two terms. Indeed mourning/mooring calls attention to our[7] reliance on and negotiation of fragmented but nonetheless integrated interpretive strategies to construct and therefore interpret black American literature. Because interpretive renderings presume the existence of certain values and systems of knowledge, the translation of the texts and contexts associated with such literature insists upon our reliance on those structures and ways of knowing that are both indigenous and exogenous to the cultures that transmit these literary modes of expression.

The Dilemma of a Ghost

The Dilemma of a Ghost is a play about the marriage of Ato Yawson and Eulalie Rush, young people from two different cultures, countries, and continents—black American and continental West African, United States and Ghana, North America and Africa—who meet and marry while attending college in the United States. The play opens with a curious prologue by a mythical narrator—The Bird of the Wayside—whose cryptic poem and dialogue narrate the history of and foreshadow problems that befall the Odumna clan (Ato's family). A significant aspect of the family's history has to do with sacrifices that have been made by Ato's family to send him to university in the West and the expectations the family has upon his return.

Certainly, the family understood that such forfeitures as their land and "family heirlooms" (70; Act 3) were investments in the security and wealth of the entire Odumna clan. At the very least, the community expected that Ato's return would "mean the paying off of all the debts" (41; Act 1). However, as the Wayside Bird[8] reminds us: "The Day of Planning is different from the Day of Battle" (2). The reality of this difference is evident when Ato returns home with an (unannounced) American wife, who is referred to as a "Black-white woman[, a] stranger and a slave" (53; Act 2).[9] Moreover, it is believed that Eulalie's habit of spending all their money "buying cigarettes, drinks, clothes and machines" (73; Act 4) is the reason the family remains in debt.[10] Even more appalling to his family is the fact that Ato has completely disregarded the traditional role of family in one's marriage. Ato's mother, Esi Kom, laments that "these days one's son's marriage affair cannot always be one's affair" (79; Act 4). Either unable or unwilling to comprehend her grandson's apparent amnesia concerning traditional customs and behavior, Nana insists that "it may be so in many homes. Things have not changed here" (79; Act 4). To the contrary, much indeed has changed, and in their very home. There can be no doubt that Ato's actions make clear that he views marriage and childbearing as a matter of personal rather than communal concern.

More problematic is his failure to properly fulfill his responsibility as cultural interpreter and mediator. His failure to explain the cultural significance and importance of childbearing to Eulalie, even after she repeatedly questions him on this subject, coupled with his refusal to admit to his family that he and his wife have decided to "postpone having children" (37; Prelude), create a complicated situation for all parties concerned. Believing his wife to be barren, the entire family (including his mother, sister, uncles, aunts, and grandmother) appear at the apartment of Ato and Eulalie prepared to "wash her stomach with [medicine]" (81; Act 4) and perform ritual libations and offer prayers to ward off evil spirits who are preventing conception. Once again, even when presented with the opportunity to set the record straight, rather than admit his deliberate and egregious violation of cultural taboos, he lies. Ato responds to their questions by repeatedly insisting that nothing is wrong. Consequently, Ato's been-to[11] cultural ambivalence and amnesia are exposed, as the gap between his American wife and his African family widens. Moreover, for Eulalie, this failure to explain to his family why she and Ato haven't had children is the final straw that exacerbates already existing marital conflict. The tensions within their marriage escalate into violence after a heated argument, during which Ato slaps Eulalie after she refers to "his people" as "narrow-minded savages" (87; Act 5).

Upon hearing about their fight, Esi Kom chides her son harshly for failing to deal fairly with either his wife or his family, warning that he has offended the ancestors by abusing this motherless child. Ultimately, it is Esi Kom who embraces Eulalie and accepts her into the family, and by extension the African community. Not surprisingly, it is Ato who is left standing in the middle of the courtyard, like the ghost at the Elmina Junction, not knowing which way to go.

Throughout this five-act play Aidoo uses the metaphor of the ghost differently to expose the sense of lostness that pervades not only issues of family and marriage at the local level, but also the global dilemma of cultural divides between continental Africans and African-descended people throughout the Diaspora. Like the problems that trouble the marriage of Ato and Eulalie, intercultural, familial, and intracultural impasses are grounded in conflicting views of history from both sides of the Atlantic. As the worlds within the play microcosmically collide, characters are revealed through ghostly visitations with their former selves, their ancestors, or the imaginary realms within which they attempt to reconstruct missing pieces of their fragmented worlds. For example, Ato's confusion about his proper place upon his returning home to Ghana is exposed through a recurring dream about "two children in the courtyard singing [a] song about the ghost who did not know whether to go to Elmina or to Cape Coast" (62; Act 3). The boy in the dream is a "ghost of Ato's former self" (29; Characters) and the crossroads at which the "wretched ghost" (61; Act 3) stands—Elmina and Cape Coast—are both former European (Portuguese and Dutch) settlements and slave-trading forts in this region of Africa.

Likewise, Eulalie is haunted by conversations between "the voices of her mind" (54; Act 2) and her dead mother. Sadly, these spectral voices do little to comfort one who mourns the loss of "someone she loves and knows to tell things to and laugh with" (55; Act 2). Instead, these otherworldly voices remind Eulalie of the sacrifices and suffering of a mother whose "hands [were] chapped with washing to keep [her] in College" (55; Act 2), the inability to "make a family out of Harlem," and her disgust with "the whole of the States. . . . Congress, Jew and white trash, from Manhattan to Harlem" (55; Act 2). Even the reminder that she has returned to the "very source"—the Africa of her dreams—is of little comfort, as the "rumble of [real African] drums" (56; Act 3) contradicts her exotic African fantasies. However, it is the veiled conversations between two village women—under the mantle of harmless gossip[12] about Ato, Eulalie, and the entire Odumna clan—that most vividly capture the dilemma of a ghost. Uncannily echoed are such societal predicaments as barrenness, fertility, prosperity, poverty, and, most tellingly, the antagonistic and seemingly infertile marriage of African and Western cultures.

Therefore, both in her creation of characters and in her depiction of the contexts in which such characters and worlds confront one another, Aidoo's ghosts echo similar forces at work in the Africa and

Afro-America of the sixties—the historical period in which this play is written. Civil disobedience in the form of riots, sit-ins, school boycotts, rent-strikes, the formation of activist organizations such as the Student Non-Violent Coordinating Committee (SNCC), black nationalist organizations from UNIA Garveyites to Nation of Islam Muslims, as well as increased student activism on college campuses such as NYU, the passage of the Civil Rights Act of 1964, police brutality and judicial abuses, are only some of the historical events that mark the literal landscape of Eulalie's Harlem. Like the 1960s Afro-American worlds of political unrest and cultural maladies from which Eulalie retreats, Ghana, too, is plagued by apparitional forces that signify struggles to maintain cultural and economic independence.

This newly independent national is dealing with failed political expectations, unemployment, overwhelming taxes, and a troubled African leadership—most strikingly manifested in such figures as Kwame Nkrumah (Ghana's first leader after its independence in 1957). Supported by funds raised from a poor Ghanaian family to send him to the United States to study at the university, and embraced by black Harlemites during his meager years in the United States, the dilemmas that aspects of Nkrumah's complex life reveal are explored in the imaginary life of Aidoo's Ato.[13] Consequently, the relatively limitless problems unearthed in *The Dilemma of a Ghost* are made possible through both the dynamic structure and the multidimensional characters in Aidoo's dilemma tale. Indeed, the list of paradoxes, quandaries, and mind-boggling predicaments are revealed through the fertile soil in which Aidoo plants the numerous seeds of discord, harmony, and irresolvable tensions her characters and their worlds confront.

Thus, in *The Dilemma of a Ghost,* Aidoo's first play, the lack, want, failed expectations, and barrenness that weigh down the figurative world of ghosts in the play are not coincidentally those that also trouble Ghanaian and Afro-American society. Ato, Eulalie, the Odumna clan, people of the village, the community, the Wayside Bird, and the ancestors find themselves embroiled in chilling and alarming economic, cultural, and national crises. Put simply, Aidoo's *Dilemma* provides a model for locating, unbinding, and articulating a black aesthetic that spans historical, geographic, political, inter- and intracultural divides, and, most importantly, one in which both continental Africa and the African Diaspora are equally troubled and considered—though necessarily from different cultural and critical landscapes.[14]

Like Ato, the early black authors in this study remained ambivalent at times about what it meant to be an African. Like the Wayside

Bird, white-black woman Eulalie, the Odumna clan, and the developing African diasporas throughout the Black Atlantic, they, too (eighteenth-century black authors), mourned/moored their African, British, American, and Afro-British American selves as they attempted to recover, invent, and rename a place for themselves within a newly constructed Africa. Like Eulalie, they conversed with voices that beckoned them to an imagined African homeland. Like Esi Kom, we bring them—however problematically—back to our community.

Paradox of Mourning/Mooring

The restoration to which Aidoo's *Dilemma* draws our attention in her play is neither as easily recognizable nor as attainable as it might seem. For African-descended peoples the concept of cultural reconciliation and recuperation of what was lost during the horrific era of transatlantic slavery—before, during, and after the Middle Passage—requires bringing up the dead to invoke the living. Thus, the ghosts of these enslaved, disfigured, maimed, displaced, and misnamed African peoples summon celebratory memorializing and re-memory of lost origins. Paradoxically, however, the ghosts of these African ancestors also dredge up and invoke sorrow and madness at those things that are wholly unrecoverable. Accordingly, the struggle to mitigate such overwhelming loss, and in a manner that loss itself neither names nor paralyzes African people, is a taxing and complicated one. For one thing, the invocation of ghosts, and the ancestral fragments and connections they offer to an otherworld, entails a complex braiding of multiple and fractured knowledge and interpretive strategies. For another, such weaving also—more often than not—compels Africans to reenter the Middle Passage, the place of rupture, metaphorically, figuratively, physically, psychically, and most of all cautiously. Herein rests a menacing dilemma. Such a return not only requires inhabiting deep and inconsolable spaces at the initial sites of devastation. Middle Passage reentry also entails confronting and further confounding an already difficult and frighteningly complex web of terror. In so doing, one risks entering a maze from which one may not wholly emerge.[15]

From these abysmal and unbounded depths eighteenth-century black American literature has emerged, bequeathing a historical legacy that continues to rise.[16] The distinctive and unmistakable imprint of the Middle Passage can be seen in early black writers' expressed attempts to document their historical quests and yearnings for simultaneous connection and disconnection with and from Africa, Europe, and Afro-British America.

In fact, the paradox of collective yearnings for and objectification of seemingly unrecoverable African ways of knowing is an unconscious theme underlying many central motifs in early black American literature. Henry Louis Gates Jr. explores a simultaneous yearning and objectification in his articulation of one of the oldest literary motifs, the talking book trope. The talking book illustrates the underlying desire for lost African orality in the call for a speaking text that starkly contrasts the black slave's need for literacy. Because orality is simultaneously absent and present in the written text, the book mocks literacy. In Gates's terms, the talking book "reveals . . . the curious tension between black vernacular and the literate white text . . . the *paradox of representing*, of containing somehow, the oral with the written" (*Signifying Monkey*, 131–32; emphases mine). I emphasize the *paradox of representing* in the passage above to underscore the inextricable and problematic link between interpretation and representation for black writers.

One of the earliest dilemmas faced by Afro-British American writers was the problem of representing themselves, and since written expression was an important mode of representation, they necessarily confronted the conflict that the disconnect between orality and literacy posed for oral people in a literate world. First, they externalized or objectified both written and spoken language—demonstrating their awareness of the need to contend with this problem. Second, rather than merely mocking (or attempting to contain) the written within the oral, or its converse, they represented both forms of communication as desirable and necessary bridges between the different worlds—African and non-African—in which they lived. In so doing, early black writers symbolically engaged and acknowledged aspects of both worlds to which they were moored even as they mourned their limited access to either.

Hence, in addition to its metaphoric use, mourning/mooring doubles as a concept which highlights the unifying potential of engaging and theorizing the dilemma of self and identity in early black American literature. Specifically, this term suggests a doubled intertextual relationship in the notion of link and loss—or what might be termed an intratextual integration. For not only is there a link between the literature of these displaced Africans and their homeland, but also, more importantly, that link is directly attributable to a sense of loss of African consciousness. This sense of loss is amplified as Africans attempt to negotiate their lived experiences in a world that is completely contradictory to many principles contained in African worldviews, whether on the cosmological or material level. These early black writers' manipulation of Western language reveals an understanding of Western worldviews as well as an awareness of the tension and the contradictions between African worldviews and their lived experiences in the New World.

The works of Phillis Wheatley and Olaudah Equiano provide exemplary models and positions (Senegalese and Igbo) from which to view the competing contradictions inherent in the integration of African consciousness into early Afro-British American literature. To begin with, for each of these writers African consciousness suggests an awareness of one's self as fundamentally African and essentially human.[17] What is more, both Wheatley and Equiano assert this Africanness as a necessary stage in their development as Christians and as colonial American citizens. Africa occupies a critical space in the rhetoric, reason, and roots (routes) of each of these eighteenth-century authors—in the various ways he or she has constructed or imagined it. Certainly their respective works, though to different degrees, confront the ethical impasse one reaches when trying to integrate multiple identities, cultures, and philosophies into a single mode of being or persona. Such integration is especially difficult when one is African, and thus seemed by Westernized standards not entirely human.

Furthermore, these writers were expected to symbolize the quintessential Afro-British American Christian—noble in African birth, British-American by acculturation, education, and association, and Christian by spiritual and cultural conversion. As a result, they had to proceed cleverly and cautiously in their attempts to expand upon such limitations. However, their works suggest they managed to rise above such limitations largely because they embraced what Robert Ferguson has referred to as "the problematics of the unknown and indeterminate in revolutionary America." Necessarily, Afro-British American writers of the American Enlightenment have dealt with "the first dilemma . . . [of] knowing where one stands" (33). They understood what their human rights were whether or not such rights were acknowledged by others. Further, they understood the moral (and religious) ground on which they stood.

Despite claims by black aesthetic critics like Amiri Baraka and Addison Gayle that early writers such as Wheatley and Jupiter Hammon attempted to transcend African elements of their multicultural identities, black writers rode the changing tides of racial and national contradictions, making the invisible visible by the mere fact of their refusal to be invisible as Africans or Afro-British Americans—confronting in their respective works both the practical and abstract elements of the oppressive societies they inhabited. As a result, the parameters of both Christianity and the Enlightenment were extended to include Africans. Accordingly, their literary labors were arduous and fraught with irresolvable problems, both ontological and epistemological.

Consequently, early African American literature manifests visible signs of mourning, both the many *thousands gone* in the Middle Passage and the cultural connections that have been displaced and misplaced as a result of the transatlantic slave trade. Eighteenth-century black writers James Albert Gronniosaw (1770) and Venture Smith (1798), who appropriated the concept of Noble African Savage to assert their humanity based on a royal African lineage, attest to this Afrocentric mourning. When I speak of Afrocentric mourning or being moored to dysfunctional Western ways of knowing, I intend to draw attention first to the historical intractability and permanence associated with early black Americans' unproductive assimilation of such ontologies and epistemologies. Next, I mean to focus on the link between physical and metaphysical states of enslavement because slaves are moored both to their masters and to their masters' ways of knowing—both the physical material world and the underlying knowledge systems that attempt to construct and define these worlds.

Theorizing the Dilemma

In order to comprehend the vast conundrum faced by African-descended writers and narrators, it is useful to reflect on their diverse employment of and engagement of *dilemma:* (a) as a model for individual and communal cooperation; (b) as a means of describing the unique problem of simultaneously being neither African, nor British, nor American in colonial British America; (c) as a structure through which the complexity of blackness can be critically examined, extended, and represented; (d) as a symbol, signifier, and mediator of irresolvable linguistic expressions of sameness and difference; and (e) ultimately, as vehicle for successfully translating, navigating, and transforming the complex institutions (religious, educational, military, familial) that impeded their cultural recuperation.

Leon Felkins's description of a game known as the prisoner's dilemma provides a useful structure for considering the possibilities of *dilemma* as reconciliatory model:

The Prisoner's Dilemma is a short parable about two prisoners who are individually offered a chance to rat on each other for which the "ratter" would receive a lighter sentence and the "rattee" would receive a harsher sentence. The problem results from the fact that both can play this game—that is, defect—and if both do, then both do worse than they would had they both kept silent. This peculiar parable serves as a model of cooperation between two or more individuals (or corporations or countries) in ordinary life in that in many cases each individual would be personally better off not cooperating (defecting) on the other. (http://perspicuity.net/sd/pd-brf. html)

By extending the prisoner's dilemma to encompass the unique situatedness and sociohistorical context of a different but related category of captive/prisoner—enslaved Africans—we are able to explore critical implications of community mourning/mooring in the formulations of an eighteenth-century Black Atlantic worldview and the parallel development of an eighteenth-century black aesthetic. To begin with, a prisoner is not a slave, at least not as constituted in Felkins's model of the prisoner's game. Though both prisoner and slave share the unenviable condition of being captives, and therefore subject to their respective masters' authority, the prisoner belongs to a community of guilty persons who have been tried and convicted of crimes against his or her former community—namely, society. A prisoner, who was formerly constructed as a member of a community, is now reconstituted as a member of another type of society. The enslaved African shares no such guilt or conviction. In fact, the enslaved African was not even considered a person (human being) as such. Rather, African slaves were constructed outside humanity, and therefore considered "naturally" outside any community of humans (free or imprisoned). I want to emphasize the point that no crime has been committed, except of course if one counts that of the slaveholder, who has stolen property—that is, the systematic, "legal" removal of bodies from Africa to the New World during the historical period of the transatlantic slave trade. Although it might be argued that at least some eighteenth-century Africans who came to the New World were first slaves or prisoners of war (in Africa) who were sold by former Old World (African) masters, for a variety of reasons, including crimes against their former community, such qualification does not negate the extreme and fundamental difference between prisoner and slave.

For, even if the enslaved African were guilty of crimes against his or her African society so heinous[18] as to warrant his or her subsequent permanent removal, the societies into which enslaved Africans were forcibly immigrated did not admit them as members or citizens. This is so primarily because their enslavement, unlike the prisoners to whom Felkins refers, is both permanent and inherited. Moreover, even those blacks admitted as nominal citizens were subjected to codes and laws that bound the free and enslaved African as captives by degrees. The prisoner in Felkins's model, though problematically so, is constructed as somewhat of an active agent who has been afforded the opportunity to legitimately escape the condition of imprisonment.

For the enslaved African no such choices exist. Even when opportunities for agency and pro- or re-action are allowed (as exceptions) the authorizing agents may rescind or violate any offers extended without cause or reason. Perhaps the most glaring difference between the prisoner and the enslaved (or nominally free) African is the condition under which freedom is extended—as a condition of inheritance. For example, one's freedom could be determined from birth depending on (among other things) the condition of one's mother—whether or not she was a slave. Moreover, as a condition of being actual property, rather than a human captive, a slave could be willed as an inheritance upon the death of his or her master. Of course, a slave could also be manumitted, as some were, by a master's legal bequest, as both freedom and slavery were inherited. This unique aspect of the difference between those legally and illegally incarcerated emphasizes the multiple layers of complexity of dilemmas African Americans engaged. Actually, eighteenth-century Afro-British American writers often made use of such legal convolutions and employed them as strategies for (literal and figurative) escape and survival. In order to do so, they necessarily cooperated with and defected from all communities, those they imagined, constructed, and therefore mourned, as well as those in which they were imagined and constructed, and thus those to which they were also moored. Thus, if one substitutes prisoner with slave, the dilemma is even more complex as a model for individual and communal cooperation.[19]

Unbinding a Black Aesthetic

James Baldwin[20] addresses this type of complexity straightforwardly in an interview (Spring 1963) with Kenneth Clark. Here, Baldwin recalls his response to his mother's question about whether his "teacher was colored or white, and [he] said she was a little bit colored and a little bit white. But she was about your color." Using this description of his elementary school teacher as a smooth segue into an elaboration of the DuBoisean conundrum, he offers:

> As a matter of fact I was right. . . . That's part of the dilemma of being an American Negro; that one is a little bit colored and a little bit white, and not only in physical terms but in the head and in the heart, and there are days . . . when you wonder what your role is in this country and what your future is in it. How, precisely, are you going to reconcile yourself to your situation here and how you are going to communicate to the vast, heedless, unthinking, cruel, white majority, that you are here? And to be here means that you can't be anywhere else.

Hence, Baldwin underscores the position (and positioning) of African Americans as directly within a political, psychological, and physical/geographical quagmire. Specifically he argues that to be "here" (in America) is to negate the possibility of being "elsewhere" (especially Africa). He points up the physical, mental, and emotional risks involved with any attempt to reconcile, represent, or otherwise reconnect with selves that are both foreign and indigenous. Even more problematic is the fact that both the foreign and the indigenous self have different meanings in different locations.[21]

However, it is in Baldwin's *Notes of a Native Son* that we are most starkly reminded of the dilemma faced under such paradoxical and unwieldy ontological circumstances. Here, Baldwin argues that the very misrepresentations we hope to unmask and critique through signification we risk reinstating—and larger than life. Baldwin uses the character of Bigger Thomas as created in Richard Wright's *Native Son* as an example of one type of ghostly dilemma that threatens to haunt the American imagination. Such representations, Baldwin argues, thwart African Americans' attempts to reconstruct very distinct and particular knowledge about their multiple and complex American identities. In order to do so, though, Baldwin traces Bigger's socioliterary antecedent in the figure of Uncle Tom—Harriet Beecher Stowe's literary re-imagining of an enslaved black man—a composite figure based loosely on a fictionalized Josiah Henson—in her *Uncle Tom's Cabin*.[22] In the same breath that Baldwin indicts Stowe's thorny sentimentality he casts serious doubt on Wright's "more enlightened" stance. "*Uncle Tom's Cabin*—like its multitudinous, hard-boiled descendants—is a catalogue of violence" focused on "unmotivated, senseless" brutality. Conceivably, if Stowe left "unanswered and unnoticed the only important question: what it was, after all, that moved her people to such deeds" (14), then Wright was equally culpable. Tragically, "in overlooking, denying, [and] evading his complexity—which is nothing more than the disquieting complexity of ourselves—we are diminished and we perish." Exposing the gaps left by his literary predecessors, Baldwin reasons: "Only within this web of ambiguity, paradox, this hunger, danger, darkness, can we find at once ourselves and the power that will free us from ourselves" (15). Baldwin's strategic location of black identification and empowerment within the realm of darkness is telling. Baldwin's own evocative and almost insentient insistence upon rendering black life in its fullness and complexity announces the critical and apparitional impasse that belies confrontations of self and identity in African American literature before, during, and after this (early 60s) historical moment.

Pointing to the failure of history to account for and acknowledge such obstacles and constructions, Theresa Singleton contends that "many archeologists recognize a message of Langston Hughes's poem 'I, Too': you cannot fully understand the European colonial experience in the Americas without understanding that of the African."[23] Thus, Singleton's use of a literary reference to signify the response of African American archeology to catastrophism[24] (7) illuminates the interdisciplinary nature and interrelatedness of the archeological and literary project of recovering Africa. Catastrophism refers to the "belief that all vestiges of African culture were destroyed during the Middle Passage and subsequent enslavement." Singleton argues convincingly that catastrophism is largely responsible for "the reluctance to accept the possibility of African origins for African American culture." Expressly "eager to suppress racist arguments that people of African descent were innately inferior to Europeans, antiracist scholars, including many blacks, embraced catastrophism['s] [argument] that black Americans, deprived of their African culture, had fully assimilated into American culture" (7).

This articulation of the relationship between the European and African colonial experience in the Americas is particularly significant to reading early African American literature because the incorporation of previously misplaced African ways of knowing recovers Africa within a framework that acknowledges the problems inherent in outdated catastrophism and unproblematized Africanism. Africanism is a term coined by anthropologist Melville Herskovitz to denote "survivals of African traditions and beliefs" in black American culture (*Myth,* 7). Singleton observes, as have others, that this attempt to identify "the presence of . . . African-derived cultural traits" can be problematic because "the archeological search for 'Africanisms' [whose] . . . primary purpose is to recover ethnic markers . . . [does] not examine the social complexities that affect why [they] emerge, persist, or change" (Singleton, 7–8).[25] Clearly, such challenges to "Africanism" identify it as a valuable term to be problematized, extended, and more critically employed in analyses of African Diaspora cultures.

Grounded in and defined by contradictions that have been repeatedly directly, indirectly, and euphemistically applied to nearly every facet of black existence, the location of Africa invokes the condition of a pure dilemma as an irresolvable thing that should be wholly avoided. Yet "dilemma" insists upon immediate engagement, especially at times when such action seems either impossible or undesirable. The term announces itself as a deterrent to any action, as it forewarns us that attempts toward resolution or reconciliation of any issues embroiled in a dilemma will be fruitless. Further, consequences associated with attempted actions (whether proactive or reactionary) promise to sink one further into a quagmire of irresolvability. However, it is because African-descended existence is more often than not teeming with conflict that confronting rather than sidestepping problems—and at the most unlikely time or place—is so valuable. In fact, rather than creating impediments for resolving problems, such a method of dealing with problems actually offers strategic loopholes,[26] however problematic.[27]

Even more telling is the way in which the ultimate signifiers of a pure dilemma can be evaluated through the synonymous relationship between the terms used to underscore the competing premises of a horned syllogism. Put crudely, it is the way in which polar opposites, extremes, or any type of dichotomous relationship are referred to as "as different as *black* and *white.*"[28] John Sekora exposes the predicament of the earliest Afro-British American autobiography in this way. When "white sponsors compel a black author to approve, to authorize white institutional power[, then] the black message will be sealed in a white envelope" ("Black Message/White Envelope," 502). Thus, Sekora underscores the very perverse racial dilemma that impacts eighteenth-century ghost writing and the equally problematic contemporary critical attempts to unseal the envelope and reread its contents.[29]

Moreover, the changing goals of African American archeology "from the study of a forgotten people to the study of the formation and transformation of the black Atlantic world"[30] (Singleton, 1) parallels the progress made by literary studies during the past two decades.[31] Namely, both disciplines have been actively engaged in landscaping and remapping the critical terrain of African spaces within African American culture and literature. Necessarily, the literary project of releasing an eighteenth-century black aesthetic from the confines of static, monolithic, and unproductively essentialized historical and cultural mourning/mooring is methodologically conceived within a similar frame of reference. Singleton's archeological space enables the exploration and interpretation of the "extent [to which] African American culture is derived from African heritage" (7).

This study widens and unveils existing critical spaces for rereading and rewriting Africa into Afro-British America through its interrogation of eighteenth-century black authors' engagement with coexisting dilemmas posed by the diverse African, British, and Afro-British American cultures and histories that construct Afro-British American literature. In so doing, I argue that scholars' critical engagement with the complex and conflicted situatedness of African cultures within early black American literature requires a systematic analysis of the underlying philosophical and political question: What is "African" in African American literature?

Predictably, the dilemma associated with depicting an autobiographical self, recovering the biographical elements of an African life in narrative, as well as the compelling obstacles concerning black self and identity are all related to the metaphors of mourning/mooring. In discussions, scholarly, political, artistic, and otherwise—across the African Diaspora about and by Africana people—this sense of the unrecoverable, that which one simultaneously wants and yet resists reclaiming, remains at the center of the resolvability of issues related to African identity. Take, for example, the current debates among African scholars about the significance of language and its relationship to naming and identifying Africa and Africans.[32] The most central question of "What is Africa?" that underlies considerations of who can be deemed authentically African is relevant to locating the persistent dilemmas facing black writers that both antedate and postdate the authors in this study, as such questions impact, and are extended to: what is African literature? Or, what is an African author? Not surprisingly, even questions about what constitutes an African language are matters of grave concern. Further complicating such issues are questions about how African languages can be said to more truthfully and more fully express a range of African cultural, aesthetic, and sociopolitical phenomena. Moreover, the question of how interruptions and Western intrusions into the development and maintenance of African languages and consciousness have come to frame African worldviews has been engaged and in such a way that the whole notion of Africa demands careful and critical reinterpretation. That is to say, how does the question of Africa and its exploration, categorization, and archivalization both mask and unearth the peoples it claims to represent?

Notably, what are the connections between Igbo, Yoruba, Wolof, Fulani, Gikuyu, and other indigenous African cultures and communities that are both troubled by and reinvented to meet the demands of Western identification? Winthrop Jordan (among other scholars) argues that white and Western identity is constructed against black and African identity. Whiteness is defined by its negation of blackness. If this is so, then as the needs to reidentify—based on historical phenomena and social conditions—evolve, change, or otherwise manifest themselves in the actual lives of black and white people, the need to rewrite African identity remains a constant. Clearly, there is a need to confront the problems posed by perpetual attempts to colonize, enslave, and otherwise order mechanisms through which African-descended people attempt to represent collective and particular identities. At the same time, there is a need to resist, complicate, and otherwise unpack strategies and paradigms of appropriation—African and non-African—that remain at odds with the very purpose of cultural and historical self-recovery and identification they claim to uphold.[33] For example, attempts to recover an African self through the locating of black difference in vernacular language or other structures of knowledge represent only the first stage in bridging the gap between Western and African ways of knowing. Additional critical work must be done to provide adequate frameworks for understanding how intracultural and intercultural existence is mediated.

Further, as scholarship has more than sufficiently argued, a mere inversion of white universals by black particularized universals only threatens to further embed African identity and knowledge within dysfunctional and damaging structures. Ironically, such seemingly radical reversals often result in the exploitation of blackness in the service of whiteness. Metaphorically speaking, black presence is emended, manipulated, appropriated, and cast into white presence. Elizabeth Fox-Genovese employs the metaphor of statue to capture the concept of casting black identity into white presence, with her probing question: "What if my statue is not myself?"[34] Not surprisingly, even when one does attempt to utilize existing white structures to recapture fragmented elements of black ones, the problem is not as obvious as the "fitting of a square peg into a round hole." Rather, the dilemma is discovering what constitutes squareness and roundness, and, more significantly, in what contexts. Tragically, factors that affect black representation are so broadly situated that what at first seems liberating can in effect be paralyzing. Attempts to recover and reimagine Africa—especially within the historical moment of the invention of America—risks a return to the very static, encased, and frozen markers that originally named Africanness in order to project Americanness.

Paradoxically, then, American identity is defined (among other things) by a newly created and simultaneously negated African identity. Not surprisingly, this newly emerging African identity refuses the terms and designs of its ordering.[35] Knotted in unbreachable and unbreakable boundaries, both Africa and America are questing toward more fully integrated and conscious knowledge of their respective political and cultural identities. Even the attempt to unravel the meaning of cultural and political identification seems to impede any progress as it insists upon an immovable sense of memory as knowledge upon which to substantiate itself. As in, if only Africa could remain African long enough for Africans to recollect and make sense and use of its remains. If only America could become America. If only the inherently constitutive components of America could be located and ordered quickly enough to settle once and for all: what it means to be American. Embroiled in the struggle for political, social, economic, and human suffrage, new identities are framed and identified, and new ideologies and ways of expressing them are enabled. Problematically, new tools have yet to be fashioned which enable concomitant coping mechanisms.

Importantly, the aesthetic of black presence and absence first comes to be articulated in the published writings of black authors, narrators, poets, and thinkers of the eighteenth century. Not unlike those who will come after them, such aesthetic delineation—conscious or unconscious—is not created in a single cultural, racial, social, national, political, or generational vacuum. Neither is their black aesthetic meant to be dislocated, e-raced, or otherwise subsumed under universal and mainstream structures. For, as much as the aesthetics of eighteenth-century blackness names (and unnames) through its appropriation of neoclassical secular and Judeo-Christian sacred texts and scientific and natural subtexts, eighteenth-century black writers reimagine and recollect their identities through a refashioning and reconfiguration of such texts and subtexts alongside culturally specific and syncretized African ones.

African-centered analyses, such as those put forward by Henry Louis Gates Jr., Houston A. Baker Jr., and others, encourage a consideration of how and in what context Africa is signified and focus heavily on the African ways of knowing that underlie the cultures and histories brought forth in the literature of early displaced Africans. Despite attempts to disengage them from African-centered worldviews, early black Americans remained moored to ways of knowing that validated their claims to African and Western humanity. This continuity is present in African ways of knowing whether they are indigenously derived or synthesized through integration with Western ontologies and epistemologies.[36]

Therefore, the incorporation of indigenously derived African ways of knowing into the study of eighteenth-century black American literature contributes syncretized models of interpretation that negotiate meaning and knowledge about the abstract and material existence of real people in various vernaculars, languages, utterances, and silences in African and African American cultures. This approach to reading literature is important, because these historical, social, political, and aesthetic hermeneutics interrogate the construction of African identities in the invention of Africa. [37] As Anthonia Kalu argues, more importantly, they bear witness to "the African writer's efforts to synthesize a transitional culture" based on "an understanding [of] the complementary relationship between ancestral and Africanized western knowledge bases" ("Oral," 37). Such efforts presuppose the impossibility of arriving at discrete, pure, or wholly African ontologies and epistemologies and assume that "What is 'African' in African American literature" is also what is Afro-Briton and Afro-American.[38] That is, African worldviews are necessarily cosmically diverse in their formulation and implementation, because structures that mediate the multivalent mass of cultural identity formations (such as those characterized in Senegalese and Igbo national and cultural identities) are inherent in the African ways of knowing that underlie African worldviews. Although slavery and colonization have figured less prominently in the cosmic diversity of African worldviews, their contribution to the hybridity of worldviews across the Atlantic has been significant.

In order to theorize the way in which dilemma functions as a viable tool for eighteenth-century black writers as they inaugurate—consciously and unconsciously—a black literary tradition and a history of the history of black ideas, I adopt and adapt paradigms and methodologies from scholars such as Chickwenye Okonjo Ogunyemi, Erskine Peters, Lisa McNee, Anthonia Kalu, and others. Their readings of culture and literature illustrate the broadening scope of African American studies in its rigorous attempts to integrate African ways of knowing into the fields of literary and cultural criticism. Without continuing attempts to discover diverse ways of analyzing and theorizing early black American literature, scholars and theorists will find it difficult, if not impossible, to articulate and appreciate the complexity of not only black American literatures but also that of the cultures and peoples these literatures represent. Necessarily, theorizing such literature and its cultural groundings demands a theorizing of these underlying dilemmas out of which such writings are born.

It is therefore necessary to move beyond engaging dichotomous arguments about ownership, influence, and cultural warfare in the field of literary and cultural studies, implicit in the question of What is "African" in African American literature, by exploring the extent to which such arguments frame and influence contemporary readings of early black American literature. Further, it is fruitful to explore the need for self-interrogation and investigation by scholars and critics of black American literature, for such self-examination necessarily leads to questions concerning the impact of scholarly work on the imagining of Africa.[39] As critics consider more carefully what kind of Africa is being constructed through literary analyses, both African- and Western-centered readings will exhibit more complex and thoughtful expressions of African identity, history, and cultural values in African American literature. Theorizing the *dilemma* rather than being bound by its limitations contributes to a "restora[tion] [of] the historical consciousness of the African peoples" (Cheikh Anta Diop, xv) through its approach to locating African ways of knowing in the earliest black American literature.

African modes of articulating the self and society based on an understanding of African historical consciousness exist simultaneously within a conscious knowledge of such binary Western ontologies and operate outside frameworks that characterize "typically Western" epistemologies, exemplified in Cartesian modes of philosophical discourse based on the *cogito*. One can see the dynamics of an African worldview or consciousness operating in the functional indeterminacy of Yoruban deities (i.e., Esu), in the complementary registering of blackness and humanness in the music and language of the Negro spirituals and the blues, in the multiple uses and users of the *lappa* (a versatile dish), and in the commonplace fluctuation between vernacular and formal African and Western forms of expression. This expansiveness and diversity in African American literature can be seen most clearly in its intertextuality or call-and-response. Scholars' readings[40] of these distinct aspects of African literature have resulted in the development of specialized methods of inquiry that simultaneously re-member and recognize Western and African-derived influences and their respective ways of knowing. Their work is important, because it facilitates a more global and therefore more illuminative reading of early black American literature.

Abiola Irele highlights the integral relationship between African ways of knowing and African literatures:

> The great fortune of African writers is that world views which shape the experience of the individual in traditional society are still very much alive and continue to provide a comprehensive frame of reference for communal life. The African gods continue to function within the realm of the inner consciousness of the majority of [West African] societies, and the symbols attached to them continue to inform in an active way. It has thus been possible for our poets in particular to evoke them as a proper, and indeed integral element of their individual imaginings. (*The African Experience in Literature and Ideology*, 196)[41]

Irele's assertions regarding postmodern African writers is particularly relevant to eighteenth-century Afro-British American literature's construction of Africanness and contemporary scholars' reading of it. It bears repeating that eighteenth-century black American literature manifests an awareness of the contradictory relationship between African worldviews and the lived experiences of Africans in the New World. In his pioneering work, "The Poetics of Ascent," John Shields points to the African origins of Wheatley's American self.[42] He notes that "Phillis Wheatley . . . brought with her . . . a teeming repository of her African experience." Moreover, Shields suggests that Wheatley "retained elements of her syncretized African faith, if not always consciously, at least just beneath the surface of her creative imagination" (53–54). Less explicitly, Mukhtar Ali Isani's African-centered rereading of Wheatley's concern with "the state of Africa and the welfare of the African" ("Gambia on My Soul," 57) demonstrates her access to a comprehensive frame of reference for communal life that can be located in the "metaphysics of the irreducible" (53). Moreover, Wheatley's "genteel but biting" critique in her "Letter to Samuel Occum" of the "Words and Actions [of America] . . . so diametrically opposite" (67) exists within a framework of African consciousness which privileges an interrelated rather than a differentiated relationship between interpretation and representation. Ironically, the dilemma is that the great fortune of the African writer's access to African ways of knowing has caused a great ontological hardship because of the incongruous and dysfunctional relationship (in the early African writer's mind) between African and Western epistemologies.

This ontological hardship is evident in the tension between the mourning of imagined indigenously derived African aspects of one's self and the mooring of one's imagined self to Western-influenced ontologies. Paul Gilroy argues that "notable black American travelers, from poet Phyllis [*sic*] Wheatley onwards, went to Europe and had their perceptions of America and racial domination shifted as a result of their experiences there. This had important consequences for their understanding of racial identities" (17). Gilroy's point about contradictions in Western worldviews (e.g., "race" in America vs. Europe) illustrates the reciprocal influences of Africans' and Europeans' experiences in Africa, whether real or imagined. Surely, for "notable black American travelers" such as Wheatley and Olaudah Equiano, the experience of Senegambia and Benin (Africa) preceded the experience of England (Europe). These African experiences may explain, at least in part, why—as Angelo Costanzo observes—"eighteenth-century [black] narrators had a closer connection to Africa that bespeaks a particularly African view of spiritual life" (25). Moreover, such African spiritual connection attests to the way African spirituality remained with African-descended people long after their forced physical removal from Africa. As Robert Farris Thompson in *Flash of the Spirit* has pointed out, this African spiritual consciousness continued to function in concert with black American Christian values and identity. And it is this Afro-spiritual presence that we recognize in the work of eighteenth-century African American writers.

Clearly, eighteenth-century Afro-British American writers were as conscious of national and racial identity constructions as are contemporary literary scholars. Early black writers' awareness of the dysfunctional epistemologies that limited their existence in freedom and slavery stemmed from their connections to African ways of knowing and the contradictions between their African worldviews and Afro-British experiences. That these displaced Africans and their texts managed to survive by reconnecting with and rearticulating their fragmented African ontologies and epistemologies alongside Western ways of knowing proves the importance of integrating African ways of knowing into a reading of early black American literature. More important, such integration is also illustrative of their employment of the diverse dilemmas as strategic and aesthetic vehicles for reconnection and disconnection with their African, American, and Afro-British American identities. Approaching early black writers' works in this way will enable a recovery of suppressed African worldviews in the earliest American literature. Even as I suggest that African consciousness has to be recovered, I want to argue that it has not been entirely lost. I want also to suggest the extent to which early African Americans sought to identify their African worldviews through an embracing of the *Dilemma of a Ghost*—their mourning/mooring.

In *Moorings and Metaphors: Figures of Culture and Gender in Black Women's Literature,* Karla Holloway manipulates the concept of mooring as connoting a "deliberately fixed" perspective and place. Both Holloway's perspective and the recovery of African American woman's interpretive space are based upon "cultural ways of knowing as well as ways of framing that knowledge in literature" (1). While Holloway's focus is on primarily twentieth-century black women's literary tradition, her assertions concerning the value of "establish[ing] a dialogue between theorists of language and literature" (21) as well as the significant attention she directs to the concept of "loss [that] characterized the colonial era" (20) of black American history parallels issues taken up in this study about the interconnectedness of the twin concepts mourning/mooring. Indeed, Holloway's investment in—and her "deliberately fixed" (1) perspective on—"ancient [and unnamed, but nonetheless metaphorically 'African' women's] spirituality" (1) exposes the dilemma faced by subdominant discourses that attempt to negotiate simultaneously empowering and disempowering Africanisms that have been historically moored to dysfunctional ways of knowing.

As a result, Holloway's attempt to dislodge productive elements and fragments of woman-centered and African-centered theories to posit "an Afrocentric interpretive model for black women's literature" (22) requires a strategic sidestepping to avoid overessentialized and totalizing structures that threaten to disembody African women. Hence, Holloway confronts a seemingly static and therefore nonexistent space of black *elsewhere* as a necessary step toward diluting disempowering and dysfunctional epistemologies of race and gender—and through equally volatile fragments of African woman's spirituality. Moreover, such discourses illustrate the extent to which systems of interpretation and analysis which seemingly continue to (re)invent a romanticized Africa do so, in fact, because such romantic links remain necessary cultural bridges.[43]

Put simply, to read early black American literature through an analysis of the ways eighteenth-century Afro-British American authors embraced dilemmas is to (re)read and participate in (re)reading literature in three central ways. This approach to dilemma speaks to, reads, and identifies traces and markers of African ways of knowing in eighteenth-century black American literature. The dilemma is first theorized through a (re)reading of early black American literature and its writers as a talking book[44] in which the author through his or her literature talks back to the critic. In this way the dilemma posed by the imaginary veil between a critic and her text are revealed as such, and thus the theory is freed to engage a literary work as one that speaks about some aspect of the author's unique experience as similarly imagined, but nonetheless real, in his or her historical situatedness. The meaningful dialogue that occurs between the African author and the critic by way of the literature draws attention to the consistent internal dialogue between Afro-British American texts and their African, British, and Afro-British American audiences.

Structurally, the dilemma is momentarily and productively suspended, rather than resolved, in order to approach a text by having a conversation with it, not merely about it. Thus, the critic expects the author and her literature to speak even if her mode of expression requires translation. Moreover, while the dialogue is always productive it is not always harmonious, because the author and the critic do not always agree. Confrontation of and engagement with the horns of the dilemma function in the same manner as *palava*—a consensus is often achieved in the space of disagreement or difference.[45] Having a conversation with an eighteenth-century slave narrative, for example, means that the critic attempts to address questions the narrative poses by repeatedly interrogating the multiple and diverse vistas from which the author speaks. Often the critic is required to converse or speak in different and unknown tongues in order to shed light on the author's unique experiences, for example, as a displaced African in the New World.[46] Fundamental to the critic's demand for a more contextualized rendering of black American experiences is an approach to theorizing the dilemma of Africa through the achievement of meaningful dialogue that always leads back to Africa.

Though dialogue implies a verbal conversation between a listener and a speaker alternating roles as necessary for meaningful communication, in black American cultural contexts speaking and reading are orally and aurally integral. To "read" someone is to analyze his or her actions or reactions in a given situation at a particular historical moment.[47] One is also considered to have been read when one has been told off or chastised for having what has been discovered to be maliciously deceptive actions and motives. This way of reading suggests a direct confrontation of an indirect action or motive. Thus, to apply this type of approach to a reading of early black American literature one must be aware of an author's simultaneously implicit and explicit modes of expression. Such a rendering requires a critical reading of a black text in light of its author's use of direction as well as indirection to signify and/or simultaneously make a direct statement. It is not merely a question of whether or not "the shoe fits" as in "if the shoe fits wear it" (Gates, *The Signifying Monkey*, 83). Rather, reading as a form of translating, mediating, and imparting the literal and figurative meaning of an experience in black American literature is a direct address to the person wearing the shoes. This integrative aspect of reading literature through such a dilemma suggests interesting emendations to Afro-Western synthesized ways of knowing such as signifying.

The ongoing cultural, historical, and literary dialogues in which early black American literature participates constitute a significant factor in countering totalizing representations of the African experience in the Americas. As such, early black American literature through its counter-discourse becomes an interpretive site for (re)reading Africa in America. In this way, the literary recovery of Africa is possible through a rein-tegration of African consciousness into strategies of critical inquiry. While such strategies make possible the location of imbedded African contexts within self-narrating Afro-British American texts, the exposi-tion and analysis of African and Western ways of knowing should not be entered into lightly. Necessarily, we must acknowledge that modes of critical analysis do not operate exclusive of their aesthetic, cultural, sociohistorical, political, or philosophical influences. Therefore, it is important to identify ways that transformative strategies both construct and deconstruct boundaries; both enable and disable transition between static and fluid interpretations of Africanness, African Americanness, and Americanness.

Moreover, focusing on attempts to silence African voices and African ways of knowing permits a negotiation and mediation of and between binary Western constructions and African texts, which attempt to speak, read, and significantly interpret (in) their own modes of cultural expres-sion. Language is a key mode of cultural transmission for the black American writer because language, through its semiotic relationship to literature and culture, links black Americans to seemingly misplaced African worldviews. As I have argued earlier, the concepts of link and loss operate symbolically and simultaneously as anchors and connectors between early black Americans and the African ways of knowing that underlie their misplaced African worldviews. Eighteenth-century writers such as Equiano and Wheatley were ontologically sustained by their discovery, early on, that mooring themselves even metaphorically to the shared experiences of Africans throughout the Diaspora anchored them more deeply in the cultural and historical foundations of the African ancestors they mourned. Importantly, attempts to locate such epistemological groundings through reconnection with the earliest threads of intertextuality in the tapestry of black American literature and culture remain critical to uncovering early Afro-British American aesthetic fragments.

African Ways of Knowing

My approach to early Afro-British American literature employs diverse expressive modes and interpretive strategies. In particular, I enlist certain tools and methods that will enable me to underscore the simultaneously incongruous and metonymic relationship between mediating forms of knowledge by and about Africans. This crisis of self-representation that early Afro-British American writers confronted required them to invent and recover ways of knowing that both centered and decentered Africa. Like these early writers, I have had to appropriate, integrate, and challenge strategies and modes of articulating the theoretical and political dilemmas imposed by ontological and epistemological Africanness. In so doing, I have realized both the transformative potential and the abortive essentialism that attend any recovery of Africa.[48] As both a bridge to and a marker of the logical boundaries of African-centered scholarship, mourning/mooring establishes that which is problematic as potentially invaluable and productive. As interrelated terms, mourning/mooring mark(s) particular historic and geographic spaces of African American identification and uncovers problems associated with attempts to connect with African consciousness. [49]

Further, the tenuous relationship between loss, link, and African ways of knowing which frames my examining of the dilemma of self and identity in eighteenth-century Afro-British American literature retains both the empowering and unproductive ideologies, but only in conjunction with indigenously grounded African ways of knowing. In this way, mourning/mooring structures and reinforces the integrative aspects of this text's approach to reading early Afro-British American literature. As such, this logical grounding contributes to a systematic study that is necessary to "facilitate consistent and viable participation of people of African descent in the reinstatement of Africa's and Africans' contribution to modern advancement" (Kalu, 282). In some sense, mourning/ mooring can be seen as a kind of reverse middle passage in the journey toward Africa for displaced Africans in the New World. This is the logic that governs the ways in which I manipulate the varied and diverse expressive modes and interpretive strategies that express African ways of being in early black American literature.

AFRICANIST *PALAVA* STRUCTURE

The discursive structure that governs my translation and engagement of the multiple modes of expression voiced in African ways of knowing is grounded in the concept of an Africanist *palava* as outlined by Ogunyemi. *Palava* refers to "interpretation, both as textual analysis and as translation from one language to another . . . [and] misinterpretation through misreading or misunderstanding [that] generates *palava* or quarrel. The [role of the] critic as interpreter [is to] attempt to set the record straight, to resolve disputes through illumination to make a text more easily understood, especially as most are written in the language of the colonizer" (Ogunyemi, 96). One example of the kind of textual illumination made possible by an Africanist *palava* can be located in a rendering of Wheatley's "Niobe" from an African-centered lens. Specifically, the young African woman poet troubles the multiple contexts within which divinity and motherhood can be interpreted by her diverse employment of neoclassical forms to effectively translate from African to Greek mythology. She conveys some startling recoveries and reinvention of Africa in her signification of images of water and life through the image of the goddess Leto (Latona), patron goddess of mothers, whose daughter Artemis (Phoebe) is depicted in classical portraits with her bow and quiver, as well as her water jug and bowl. For one thing, given Wheatley's reported memory of the pouring out of water by her own African mother, such translations suggest the poet's consciousness (mourning/mooring) of similar West African traditions. Such goddess traditions can be seen in contemporary Nigerian women writers. For example, in her novel *Efuru,* Flora Nwapa, the first published Nigerian woman author, invokes the image of the childless mother in the Igbo deity Mammywata, a postmodern barren goddess of water. Aidoo echoes a similar theme in *Dilemma,* as the Ghanaian mother Esi Kom embraces the African American motherless child Eulalie. As can be seen, the strategies for translation, interpretation, and representation of black aesthetics are boundless.

Therefore, it is critical to translate the problematic or misinterpreted components of a text in order to complicate the multiple meanings imbedded in conversations between the speaking text and its African and Western contexts. Such a method seeks not merely to resolve disputes, it seeks to unpack and interrogate the strands of disharmony. Neither is such an approach meant solely to illuminate perpetual conflict within an author's text by a constant misinterpretation and distortion of the multiple expressive modes, methods, and interpretive strategies that constitute the competing dilemmas to which a text is mourned/moored. Rather, I intend to enhance my interpretation of and conversation with early African American literature by using a "greater variety of ingredients [for] a more zestful and rich [*palava*] sauce" (Ogunyemi, 100). In this way, "palava sauce as text . . . forms part of a revisionary tradition . . . [which produces] a counter discourse" (101). *Palava* is to discourse as reading is to signification. Just as the *palava* registers harmony in a necessary and productive but discordant tone, reading exposes an indirect action or motive through direct confrontation. Most importantly, the epistemological structure designated by *palava* is inextricable from the ontological logic of mourning/mooring, which negotiates simultaneously empowering and disempowering discourses of African-centered ways of knowing.

The logic and structure that govern this way of reading encourage continual critical self-interrogation of the ways and extent to which, as a critic, I, too, am participating in the invention of Africa. Hence, the self-referential nature of this approach demands that I use theoretical approaches, which reflect a diversity and vastness of African worldviews. The diversity of tools in my methodological approach is important for three reasons. First, they are diversely employed as communicative devices for translation and expression of African ways of knowing. Second, they emphasize the range of connotative functions that each of the African ways of knowing I employ suggests. Third and most important, they signify the legitimacy of these African ways of knowing as systems which mediate and facilitate literary analyses from the perspective of multiple constructed African worldviews. Together these approaches participate in the integrative and recuperative process of signifying what is African in African American literature. In his articulation of this process of recuperating Africa in African America, Gates insists that "whatever is black about black American literature is to be found in [an] identifiable black Signifying (g) difference (*The Signifying Monkey*, xxiv). However, as I confront the dilemma of naming, claiming, and strategically resituating blackness or Africanness, I attempt to unburden critical voices from such limiting expectations. Not only is such a way of rendering (figuratively or otherwise) what is, essentially speaking, black or African in African America irresolvable, it is irreducible. To face this dilemma head-on is to free—to release and relocate—the black aesthetic.

Having presented the rationale, the logic, and the structure of a dilemma-driven method of reading eighteenth-century Afro-British American literature, I will briefly describe below the various approaches I employ in this study. They are signifying, speaking in tongues, *palava, taasu,* and *mbari.*

SIGNIFYING

Signifying articulates a discrete and distinct black vernacular voice located simultaneously within early African American folk traditions and indigenously derived Yoruba African cultural origins. Specifically, signifying unites the figures of the Yoruban god of indeterminacy, Esu Elegbara, and the African American trickster, the Signifying Monkey, to create a theory of African American literary criticism. Esu's indeterminacy is central to the complex role of mediation between representation and interpretation, literal and figurative in speech, writing and reading, and divinity and humanity. Signifying's indeterminacy is also integral to the complex role of simultaneously implicit and explicit (re)creation in its dual gendered and genderless embodiment. Not only is the double-voicedness of Esu apparent in the physical characteristics, the doubled lips, pictured in varied depictions of Esu (and Signifying Monkey), but also in the various and varying myths that support the diverse roles enacted upon her/his metaphysical and physical being. Most importantly, the very nature of the indigenous myths of the origin of Signifying underlies the cultural diversity imbedded in the structure and form of African American literature, as it signifies on the interrelatedness of language and meaning in its oral and written form and content.

SPEAKING IN TONGUES

In the same way that black signifying suggests intertextuality in its proffered meaning, speaking in tongues suggests intratextuality in its deferred meaning. "Speaking in tongues" is Henderson's "trope for both glossolalia and heteroglossia" (123). She notes that speaking in tongues assumes two very different but related meanings of this term—the ability to speak unknown tongues and the ability to speak different tongues. The Old Testament suggests a dialogics of difference and the New Testament a dialogics of identity, with both meanings being privileged in black women's writing. Henderson performs an interlocutory function by interpreting the tongues of white male critics, white and black feminist critics, and finally the Bible (Scriptures). She "propose[s] a theory of interpretation based on . . . the 'simultaneity of discourse'" which allows for a move away from the "'absolute and self-sufficient' *otherness* of the critical stance in order to allow the complex representations of black women writers to steer us away from 'a simple and reductive paradigm of "otherness"'" (117; emphasis in original). In order to translate the meaning of tongues in an African-centered woman's context, Henderson juxtaposes Bakhtin's model of "conflict" and Gadamer's model of "the potential of agreement" to signify "a form of self-relatedness" (120) that is crucial to her "notion of difference and identity underlying the simultaneity of [black women writers'] discourse" (120).

Mourning/Mooring *Palava*

Simultaneously curative and creative, a syncretic blend of Senegalese poetics and Igbo duality constitutes a framework that interprets Afro-British American literature within more culturally specific African-centered contexts. Admittedly, such elements are not meant to wholly represent Africa or African ways of knowing as such. Rather, my use of a Senegalese poetic and Igbo duality represents one fraction of the possibilities enabled by such an approach. Methodologically, structurally, and imaginatively linked to African-centered frameworks, such theorizing embraces and engages rather than suspends and forecloses new knowledge about alternative views and insights into our understanding of the literary and cultural history of Africans in America.

Africanist *Palava*

Palava, a homophone and feminine version of palaver, which refers to a kind of chitchat or empty talk between disparate people, signifies meaningful conversation that both quarrels with and builds bridges between such communities. As a strategic method for interpretation, *palava* enables scholars to translate critical fictions and facts through multifaceted interpretive mechanisms that are simultaneously commonplace and universal. Specifically, *palava* is a vernacular theory based on a woman-centric vision of literature and is governed by the language of the commonplace as signified by the *lappa,* which is a piece of cloth used primarily by women but also available for use by men. This vernacular language makes use of both the practical (unisex) uses of *lappa,* and the theoretical concept of *palava* that signifies the underlying complementarity and consensus necessary for the participation of both men and women in cultural and national re-creation. Therefore, because palava is grounded in indigenously derived African ways of knowing, it functions as a viable structure through which African worldviews can be interpreted in Afro-British American literature. Ogunyemi's description of the fabric *lappa* and its vast uses demonstrate *palava's* universality and invite us to think critically about its symbolic textual ubiquitousness. "The simple two or three yards of fabric is versatile: it can be used as a dress, a blanket, a pillow, a curtain or screen, a mattress or sling, a wall decoration, or an *aju* to cushion and protect the head from the load it carries" (4). Thus, the *palava* as a concept functions analogously to the fabric *lappa.* That is, the language of *palava* is adaptable in its embellishment, indirection, and direction; in its simultaneous conveyance, displacement, translation, transmission, sustenance, inspiration, effect, and communication of African culture and African ways of knowing. Importantly, *palava* simultaneously integrates and disintegrates as it breaks down false or dichotomous boundaries—especially those of race, class, and gender.

Thus, *palava* as both organizing structure and an interpretive strategy facilitates ideological, linguistic, and spiritual remappings of African ways of knowing onto African cultural landscapes.[50] Necessarily, the *palava* negotiates the different and unknown critical tongues of psychoanalysis, feminism, womanism, poststructuralism, and identity theories that construct identities only to silence them. *Palava,* through its insistence on maintaining ongoing dialogue with theoretical, historical, and literary texts, adapts existing interpretive strategies such as speaking in tongues in order to redirect the discursive desire (and thus resist the tendency) to rewrite our stories onto other(s). In doing so, *palava* counters dysfunctional dominant and subdominant rereadings of black American literature. Further, such agency is recovered by directly confronting unconscious and conscious attempts to enslave early black writers' physical and spiritual texts and contexts.

AFRICANIST *TAASU* AND SENEGALESE POETICS

"*Taasu* is a form of praise poetry that [Wolof Senegalese] women perform at family events . . . *Taasu* mark the subject positions of an individual agent, but also provide a discursive space for negotiating relationships between participants at these events during and through the exchange of gifts" (McNee, 25). My use of this interpretive strategy is particularly relevant to engaging the difficulties associated with poetic and autobiographical intersections of race, class, and gender in eighteenth-century Afro-British American contexts, from African perspectives and aesthetics. The use of Senegalese poetics provide a valuable link for reconnecting with African knowledge bases. *Taasu* is thus a West African Senegalese Wolof way of knowing that provides the foundational grounding for what I term Senegalese poetics. Operating with a structure guided by a Senegalese poetic means allowing culturally specific Senegalese forms such as *taasu* to take precedence when considering such elements of an English-language poem as the worlds it creates, the depth of characters and their interactions in those worlds, as well as the view or frame of reference from which the poet orders all the elements at play in the world of the poem.

Indeed, an equally, perhaps even more, empowering reading of agency in eighteenth-century black women's writing is made possible through a recentering of the African female principle in our critical apparatus—reading, for example, Wheatley's work through the lens of *taasu*. In her groundbreaking work *Selfish Gifts*, Lisa McNee emphasizes the critical import of *taasu*, through which "autobiographical discourse becomes autobiographical exchange" (25). What is significant about the *taasu* as a viable structure for interpreting and analyzing the works of early black women writers like Wheatley is that this African autobiographical poetic (in form and content) is particular to women. Indeed, *taasu* are "richly allusive, context-specific works that can best be understood if we consider their social function as well as their internal textual tools for creating meaning" (25). However, even as we approach *taasu* in their context-specific spaces, we must be careful not to oversimplify, conflate, or otherwise relegate these culturally specific African women's songs to solely privileged gender spaces as happens in many traditional feminist readings of early black women's texts. Indeed, the kind of freedom that this poetic form permits women to exercise through the execution of selfhood more fully occurs within multivalent contexts—some taboo, others quite conventional. Moreover, such freedom and self-exploration happens in the context of communities and histories that must simultaneously be remembered and recovered. Thus, viewing conventions of eighteenth-century black poetry through the structural lens of *taasu*, with a view to imagining the poet Wheatley in the context of *taasukat* and griot traditions (writing and recording the history of Africans in the New World) permits us to theorize about how an Afro-British American aesthetic informed by indigenously derived African ways of knowing makes a difference in the way history is written and recovered.

However, because eighteenth-century Afro-British American poetry like Wheatley's is equally informed both by other West and West Central African traditions—imagined and real—and Afro-Western synthesized poetics, my use of the term "Senegalese poetics" refers rather loosely to forms of writing, formalized interpretations of literature, and cultural interventions that privilege a synthesis of culturally specific African ways of knowing such as *taasu* and alongside a more generalized (but equally rich) composite of Afro-/Afra-Western ways of knowing. Therefore, I integrate West African Wolof *taasu,* Nigerian *palava,* African American signifying and speaking in tongues, as well Afro-Western biblical reinterpretation and other available symbolic structures of meaning such as Sankofa, griot, and Bird of the Wayside. Together, these constitute a Senegalese poetic. Doing so reveals the literal worlds, people, and circumstances that inform eighteenth-century Afro-British American aesthetics. What this way of approaching this literature suggests is that given precedence, African ways of knowing will draw back a curtain that has for far too long been covering what is behind African works such as Wheatley's—Africa.

AFRICANIST MBARI AND IGBO DUALITY

While *mbari*[51] generally refers to a physical structure built to honor Ala (an Igbo earth goddess), I utilize *mbari* as a metaphor to redirect attention to the African aesthetics that privilege (like the *mbari* structure) what is both good and bad in a society. As both a figurative symbol and once viable method of conflict resolution, this structure functions as a means to locate areas and issues that require attention from the community. Since needs and issues within communities shift and evolve over time, *mbari* as a physical structure is necessarily temporary. Further, it allows alteration, correction, and invention, and as a result it provides a functional structure through which aspects of Africa can be celebrated and recuperated and through which unresolved conflict can be addressed, if not wholly resolved.

Like most Igbo structures, *mbari* operates within a duality discourse—what scholar Anthonia Kalu (following Chinua Achebe) refers to as the "tendency . . . of things to exist in pairs" ("Women and the Social Construction," 283). Equally important to duality are such concepts as divine intervention, fate, luck, and destiny, which are reordered through an understanding of the role of *chi* as an internal mediating structure between human and divine purposes. The concept of *chi* (as a god, guardian angel, personal spirit, or spirit double) and its underlying duality, in conjunction with signifying, speaking in tongues, and *palava* provide nonquantifiable paradigms of complementarity based in African worldviews. One example of Igbo duality discourse at work is the kind of dialogue this African way of knowing permits about such seemingly Western Christian tenets as providence and predestination. Thus, Western ways of understanding crucial elements of the formation of self and identity are unpacked through Igbo duality. Such can be seen in the simultaneity of the oral and written in signifying, in the intersectionality and overlap of the symbolic and the material in the *lappa,* in the identification of the interpretive with the prophetic in speaking in tongues, and in the literal and figurative sojourning of the African women and men not only to themselves (as in *taasu*), but also to their mother's and father's houses (*mbari*).

Consequently, *mbari* not only honors and celebrates what is good in a community, but it also depicts those areas of conflict that need to be resolved. As a result, the art is temporary not unlike certain issues that plague or trouble a community. Moreover, as it is a temple of worship, the *mbari* shrine is sacred space that, while necessarily open for human viewing, is restricted to all but the deities for whom it was constructed. Chinua Achebe describes *mbari* in this way: "*Mbari* was a celebration through art of the world and the life lived in it. It was performed by the community on command by its presiding deity, usually the Earth goddess, Ana. Ana combines two formidable roles in the Igbo pantheon as fountain of creativity in the world and custodian of the moral order in human society. An abominable act is called *nso-ana,* taboo-to-Earth" ("African Literature," 1).

Significantly, early black literature like the *mbari* suggests the value of functional structures through which aspects of Africa can be celebrated and recuperated, and more importantly those through which conflict can be creatively resolved. As such, Afro-British American poetic and narrative working out of such binary conflicts as Western/non-Western identity, European/African identity, and master/slave relationships is accomplished through early black writers' creative handling of various rhetorical strategies as well as conventional literary genre expectations. Like the sacred *mbari* house in which all things—past and present—are displayed and into which the builder cannot enter, such works operate from the outside, having already placed within the necessary tools for reconstruction and rebuilding of Africa. At the same time, both the material and the contexts for building—from the inside and outside—are continually being adapted, changed, and developing over time. Specifically, *mbari*, "the cosmic dualism [that] reverberates . . . in the symbolism of *mbari*" (54), is epitomized in the inspiration and method for its construction and reconstruction, its sacred space and secular designs, in its particular (otherworldly and earthly) calls to construct meaning, and through the communal participation necessary for its completion and appreciation.

Early black writers like Wheatley and Equiano can be analogously linked to the artist/builders of the *mbari* in important ways: First, like the *mbari* artists, these writers are "responsible for the . . . creation of an entire new world in general" (Cole, 218). Second, the figurative world of the writer, like that of the *mbari* artist, is "inherently imperfect, as any structure that attempts to summarize the world must be" (219). Lastly, like the *mbari* artists/builders, these writers as well as their works are derived from and belong to the sacred and material worlds and communities out of which they create. It is not only their collective writings or works that symbolically represent *mbari;* it is their lives as well. These early Afro-British American writers and their works are the sacred shrines that pay homage to their African ancestors and their African American descendants.

At the level of critical analysis, viewing their works as literary *mbari* permits an Africanist intervention into the Afro-British American text. This intervention and African way of seeing, like the literal *mbari* house, responds to a divine request—what Bassard terms a spiritual interrogation. This divine request to build an *mbari* house is typically manifested as a significant problem within the community that must be addressed. Marked by such characteristics as cosmic unity, idealized figures, ritual celebrations, and secrets, this shrine to communal conflict and the attendant dilemma as well as cooperation and wealth, the *mbari* is as much a shrine to dilemma as it is to *agbara* (god). "As much a social institution as a religious one. . . . Change is also embraced because *mbari*, the most profound offering known in society, contains somewhat paradoxically, much that is not spiritual" (Cole, 197). Of course this makes perfect sense in terms of Igbo duality, because no one thing ever wholly represents another in its totality. There is, in fact, always more than one way to be—and that simultaneously.

An understanding of the process of building an *mbari* house of the

Owerri Igbo is instructive in considering the implications of deliberately constructed frameworks whose purpose is to overtly and directly confront societal dilemmas. Moreover, the process of the *mbari* is in some respects as important, if not more valuable, to the society in which it is built, than is the actual shrine. However, one point must be made patently clear—the use of this culturally specific African way of knowing (*mbari*) is not in any way meant to signify that any sort of complete or whole rendering of any Igbo culture can be either absorbed or sifted through what is ostensibly a multicultural Afro-British American literary tradition which is steeped as richly in Western textures and structures as it is in African and Afro-Western ones. Igbo-born or not, *mbari* does not authorize us to construct a monolithic African, black American, or essential and Igbo identity out of, say, an eighteenth-century narrator's *Interesting Narrative*.

Beyond the widely recognized dilemma of reconstructing precolonial Igbo histories—especially of the eighteenth century—due in great part to the unreliability of both oral and written sources, which is reason enough alone to dismiss superficial renderings of Africanisms onto African-descended cultures, one must recognize that the history of *mbari*, as practiced primarily by the Owerri region, is also difficult to pinpoint with regard to specific origins prior to 1850. Moreover, one would also have to deal with the inability to locate, for example, Equiano's claimed birthplace in Igboland, and then determine if Owerri Igbo inhabited the region he refers to as Essaka. Add to this quite practical list of reasons even the issue of what a specific locating of Equiano's actual origins in an Owerri Igbo culture at the historical moment of his capture—when he would have learned important elements of such a tradition as *mbari* from his childhood—would add to our understanding of the complexity of African fragments as epistemological shards for a more diverse analysis of this literature.

But, of course, as with *taasu* we are not attempting to use *mbari* as an overlay to assert a one-to-one correspondence between building an *mbari* shrine and writing a narrative such as Equiano's. For one thing, the differences in form, context, and purpose are not analogous. The point of drawing upon *mbari* as an Africanist significatory practice and structure for analysis is to consider how shifts to an African register enable us to theorize the dilemma of eighteenth-century Afro-British American identity. More precisely, the point is to consider how African-centered ways of knowing, such as *mbari* (and, more importantly, the epistemological possibilities it suggests) constitute one method of reconnection. Clearly, when one uses psychoanalytic theory to interpret and analyze the works of Chaucer, there is an understanding that the author cannot in any logical sense be said to have been consciously operating within a structure that such works as Chaucer's predate. On the other hand, because Freud drew from sources in antiquity (Oedipus, etc.) to articulate what he termed phases of the psychosexual self, it is helpful to view a fifteenth-century work through such lenses. There will necessarily be echoes and parallels that lend a level of critical depth to an understanding of the literature and the culture to which we might not otherwise have access.

So, when I use *mbari* as a structure to analyze eighteenth-century Afro-British American literature, I take a step toward reconnecting with traditional African knowledge bases, however problematic. This is precisely what it means to confront the *dilemma of a ghost*.

AFRO-WESTERN WAYS

Signifying recovers submerged voices as necessary strands of thread in the poetic tapestry of the *lappa*. And, in so doing, signifying (re)marks upon each thread as central to maintaining existing African and Western textual patterns and creating new designs. Moreover, signifying through its analysis of both inter- and *intra*textuality illuminates the productive and nonproductive textual dialogues that translate literary meaning based on previously displaced African worldviews. As a result, signifying enables a rearticulation and interpretation of the threads that constitute the fabric of early African American narratives, poetry, epistles, and other genres of literature. To be sure, when a text signifies, it not only brings up the memory of a prior text, but it also remembers a host of other signifiers—authors, actors, folks, and other writings—constituted in contradictory and complementary worldviews.

AFRA-WESTERN SPEAKING IN TONGUES

Speaking in tongues utilizes a self-reflexive critical mode to translate and mediate internal and external dialogue along raced, classed, and gendered lines. In this way culturally encoded meaning is derived by speaking to, about, and in the tongues of black women, white women, white men, and black men, not discursively rescuing black women from white men, white women, and black men—through intersecting and replicating oppressions. Speaking in tongues rewrites dominant political and spiritual epistemologies and broadens this scope of gendered and raced translations. Further, by exposing the simultaneous and necessary revision of dominant and "subdominant discursive order[s]" (Henderson, 121), speaking in tongues exposes attempts to bracket disharmony between (for example) raced or gendered communities. Thus, in concert with *palava,* speaking in tongues enables a gendered critique of racial oppression within "homogeneous and heterogeneous social and discursive domains" (121).

Confronting the dilemmas posed by competing structures of oppression—such as patriarchy and racism—through interpretive unbounded speaking in tongues, enables recuperative readings of African ways of knowing within early Afro-British American literature. It must be noted that what enables the unbinding of tongues is the integration of African ways of knowing—such as *taasu, mbari,* and *palava.* Moreover, such recuperation exposes the dynamic and vital impact of gender in the development of an eighteenth-century black aesthetic. What this type of development suggests is that gender is not a newcomer to the table of interrogated oppressions. Issues related to oppression and suppression of women's texts and contexts have always been a part of *palava* between Africana people. Speaking in tongues involves interpretation, communication, and most of all an ear bent toward the speaking subject. According to historian Michael Gomez, Africans "reinterpreted the dogma and ritual of the Christian church in ways that conformed to preexisting cosmological views" (10). If this is so, then we must pay careful attention to how "reinterpretation" of the Bible facilitated the process of Africanizing Christianity, and, by extension, symbolically translated a Western text into an African one.

Emerging Patterns

The motifs that constitute the approaches I have just described echo three emerging patterns at the heart of theorizing the dilemmas that frame and constitute the eighteenth-century Afro-British American texts in this study.

First, these approaches are governed by an ideology of integration. That is, the mourning/mooring of lost African consciousness, which guides these systems of interpretation, necessarily integrates individual and collective identities—which include women, men, and children. Signaling the real and imagined bases upon which competing and cooperating epistemologies—such as *palava,* signifying, speaking in tongues, *taasu,* and *mbari*—are constructed, an integrative ideology is crucial to facilitating links and unveiling disjuncture between indigenously derived African and Western-derived ways of knowing. Consequently, they are necessarily inclusive, bringing women, children, and men into conflict and harmony with each other. Moreover, ritualistic practices such as the building of the *mbari* shrine and the formal and informal ceremonies that attend *taasu* represent expressive modes that create a cohesiveness that serves and reconnects the community with tradition, ancestors, and intersecting yet parallel African and Western worlds.

Second, vernacular language is the primary mode of transmission of African ways of knowing. One of the more visible signs of mourning/ mooring is the commonplace language that figuratively and literally links cultural loss and displacement in the New World with recovery of fragmentary linguistic survivals from West Africa. The fusion of sacred, secular, political, personal, and vernacular modes of expression trans-lates the experiences of displaced Africans into polyphonic registers and rhythms. Consequently, this interlingual and intercultural dilemma yields an abundant marriage of distinct but complementary interpretive strategies, methods, and modes of expression. If we consider vernacular in the context of a figurative and literal return home, a return to one's mother or father "tongue," we can begin to apprehend the depth of linguistic power that is implied in vernacular. Indeed, the very concept of home for people of African descent points to the necessary negotia-tion, reintegration, and translation of familiar and foreign, sacred and secular, political and personal experiences. Such translation demands our re-consideration (an unbinding) of what and how "vernacular" is expressed through the voices of Afro-British American writers. One does not construct an *mbari* without preliminary conversations that require speech in more than one secret tongue. Similarly, *taasu* as a form of praise poetry is necessarily guided not only by vernacular but by context specific and appropriate languages for each performance, as well as the gift exchanges given in the form of words and other material exchanges. For example, *taasu* permits Wolof women's voices to come forward in a way that frees them from taboos that conflate Senegalese griot tradi-tions with either wholly male or essentialized female and communal characteristics. The reciprocal and practical nature of the exchange of gifts—the autobiographical praise poem that is at once communal and particular—demonstrates the need for translation and linguistic complementarity in the marriage of form and structure.

Third, spirituality is a key component that emerges either directly or indirectly in this approach. In its indirect form spirituality typically emerges as a trope, a figure of speech that is metaphorically linked with physical or spiritual darkness or death. In its direct form spirituality addresses the hermeneutics of an otherworldly self in both African and Western contexts. On a cosmological level, mourning/mooring is manifested as a veiled quest for unrecoverable African ways of knowing, which simultaneously transgresses and transmits foreign and alien modes of expression. None of the African ways of knowing I have been describing, even in the most secular contexts, can function entirely outside the realm of spirituality. However, what seems most striking about *taasu* in this regard are the extremely diverse poles of its ceremonial uses—from something as sacred as a naming ceremony or baptism to *sabar* (women's parties which include taboo dances and songs). Of *mbari* little more can be added except that, like *taasu*, the spectrum of aesthetics from sacred to profane are all open for inclusion in the *mbari* shrine. And, of course, the god (*agbara*) for whom the *mbari* is built is always represented.

If, as scholar Michael Echeruo and others have lamented, "we have yet to develop adequate theoretical tools by which to read our own [African] writing" ("An African Diaspora: The Ontological Project," 7), then it seems reasonable that looking to African structures and significatory practices such as *palava, mbari,* and *taasu,* as well as Afro-Western signifying and speaking in tongues, is part of the process of developing such tools. Alternative modes of analysis and matrices such as these provide the interpretive tools necessary to reach new critical depth in our study of early Afro-British American literature. Clearly, we must permit Africa and African ways of knowing to take the critical "lead" in our analysis and our choice for analytical models of interpretation. Surely, such a way of approaching literature requires a theorizing on multiple levels the dilemmas posed by these new tools and some of the old blueprints. It also requires us to learn new ways of understanding African knowledge bases with which we must necessarily reconnect.

These emerging patterns suggest the value of mourning/mooring as an organic blueprint for fragmentary reconstructions of Africa aesthetics within Afro-British American literature. Ultimately, to resituate, integrate, and recuperate is to journey back across the Atlantic to do battle with historical and contemporary dilemmas and, more radically, to invoke their previously dormant ghosts.

TWO

What a Difference a "Way" Makes

Wheatley's Ways of Knowing

Now *Manto* comes, endu'd with mighty skill,
The past to explore, the future to reveal.

—Phillis Wheatley, "Niobe" ll. 37–38

The epigraph above is illustrative of early African American literature's reconfiguration of literary space into a figurative junction between African and Western ways of knowing. Wheatley, a displaced Senegalese griotte, an eighteenth-century American slave–poet laureate, and a foremother of African American literature, was born in Senegal in (approximately) 1753 and brought to Boston in 1761 via the slave ship *Phillis*, after which she was named. The sickly African girl, who arrived with little more than a cloth to cover her small shivering frame, had "in sixteen months time" attained satisfactory proficiency in the English language, Greek mythology, Greek and Roman history, English poetry, and Latin.[1] Juxtaposing the exploration of the past alongside the revelation of the future, poet Wheatley imagines herself and the seer–poet Manto as simultaneously occupying the traditions of classical Western mythology and West African praise singers. In classical Western (Roman and Greek) mythology, Manto is known primarily as seer or prophet, a priestess, and a poet (rivaling Homer). Therefore, extending Thomas Hale's definition of griot/griotte to include such functions as "genealogist, historian, adviser, spokesperson . . . mediator, interpreter . . . witness, praise-singer . . . [and] participant in a variety of ceremonies" (57), I interpret Manto as a griotte. Notably, beyond her primary role as seer, Manto also functions as ceremonial participant and praise singer in Latona's worship, as she exhorts "the Theban maids" to pay tribute to the goddess. Further, as ceremonial participant, Manto "brings people together with [her] speech" (49), and, as praise singer, Manto "announce[s] not simply of [Latona's] qualities but also [the Thebans'] duties and responsibilities" (48). I take a similar position with regard to the poet Wheatley, whose revision of the Niobe myth, from Book VI of Ovid's *Metamorphoses*,[2] demonstrates her functioning as poet/griotte with comparable and diverse roles. Illustrative of her operating within this West African griot tradition, Wheatley endeavors (through "Niobe") to mediate, celebrate, inspire, translate, and foreshadow the national and natural distress engendered by slavery, indenture, and other oppression in an era of American independence. For, just as Manto is endowed with "eyes [that] could see what was to come," Wheatley is bequeathed a history of experiences of what had been. Manto's prophecy, like Wheatley's poetry, disseminates knowledge about the past and future even as it envisions alternative possibilities within the present historical moment.

Wheatley highlights the dilemma involved in attempting to rewrite both the spiritual and political histories upon which enslaved and nominally free African-descended people, especially African-descended women, have been constructed. The poet engages this dilemma through her multiple ways of knowing—African, American, and Afro-British American. Demonstrating her intellect and poetic genius as well as her political savvy, Wheatley creatively and purposefully interposes African and British-American experiences to reveal the shape and substance of an eighteenth-century Afro-British American aesthetic.

In "Subjection and Prophecy in Phillis Wheatley's Verse Paraphrases of Scripture," William J. Scheick argues that "Wheatley's dual exposure to theological and secular applications of Holy Writ accounts for the compatibility of her religious and her political writings . . . [a] double exposure [which] encouraged her to relate evangelical Protestantism to both Revolutionary patriotism and romance neoclassicism" (123). He maintains that "Wheatley's deliberate application of biblical matter in her verse often registers underground observations about slavery, observations that she evidently believes are supported by the Bible" (124). Scheick proposes that David became a surrogate for Wheatley because of his "ruddy skin" and ascension from servitude, that she may have gleaned knowledge about biblical passages from "popular interpretations" such as Matthew Henry's commentaries, and that in her "vicariously . . . experienced . . . reenactment[s]" (124), Wheatley evinces a "displacement of anger toward [slavery and slaveholders]" (125). These observations provide valuable insights into the poet's subversive employment of biblical paraphrase. John C. Shields adds that in "combining Christian and classical elements, Wheatley [not only] falls within a common tradition," but she also (more importantly) "casts her own practice of such syncretism into her own mode" ("Phillis Wheatley's Use of Classicism," 102). Importantly, Shields attributes this unique "third theological element . . . hierophantic solar worship" (103) to her African origins. Scholar Marsha Watson maintains that the "fusion of pagan and Christian myths in Wheatley's poetry . . . suggests something more complicated . . . Wheatley['s] attempts to rewrite the contemporaneous, received 'wisdom' about her people" (121). The scrupulous attention (of the aforementioned scholars) to the "polycultural"[3] voices in Wheatley's classic works suggests valuable considerations for interpreting "Niobe" as a paraphrase of at least one (Hagar) if not more (Eve, Mary, etc.) biblical stories.

In this chapter I will argue that Wheatley applies what might be termed a *syncretic Senegalese poetics* to her reinterpretations of two concurrently revered and despised mythologized figures of women—Niobe and Hagar. Moreover, I maintain that through Wheatley's use of Afro-British American ways—grounded in culturally specific African knowledge—she is able to travel through and unpack thousands of years of African women's history within an African frame of reference. And, in the process, she suspends time itself. By "suspend" I do not mean to suggest that Wheatley's recovery of mythological and mythologized figures denotes some static recovery of Africa and African women. Rather, I use this term to suggest at least one way in which Wheatley's use of time might be viewed from the perspective of West African measurements of historical time.Wheatley's recovery of Africa is exemplified in the tradition of the Sankofa-Bird, or bird of passage, which constantly moves forward to the future even as it continually looks behind to its past. Not only does this image of Sankofa echo themes of life and death seen throughout the poet's work, but this West African way of viewing time also alludes to the way in which the past is continually brought forward into the present and continued into the future. Further, she signifies the present condition of African-descended people who appear ghostlike to hang above, dangle, or swing backward and forward between worlds fraught with irresolvable dilemmas. In this context, time is both a transcendent and concrete measure of progression and development—numinous and temporal, fluid and liminal. Thus, when I suggest that Wheatley suspends time, I intend to point up the prophetic power of her poetry to simultaneously move beyond (by looking back to the present and forward to the future) and yet capture the present time. She captures time in this way for the valuable lessons it can teach and because such a way of presenting time permits the poet to more strikingly convey her messages and its meaning to her audiences. Importantly, Wheatley invokes parallel historical moments of "distress" from a mythic past to tackle critical concerns in the present. As poet, griotte, seer, and ancestor, Wheatley recovers mythological figures of women, refiguring a history that makes a difference for the very real women they were meant to symbolize, and—equally important—the societies that attempted to hold them and their voices hostage.

Part of Wheatley's unbinding of Afro-British American women's history from its British-American internment is done through her engagement with the dilemmas that American freedom poses for African-descended peoples. Specifically, "Niobe" illustrates her intervention into a newly forming American space, a complex space compounded by multiple discourses of motherhood, gender, lineage, race, and class. To further complicate, and thereby necessarily trouble, this space, Wheatley speaks from a suspended and imagined but nonetheless real position as an American citizen. It is from this position that she depicts her own metamorphosis from victimhood to survivorhood and then to autonomous selfhood. I invoke Bassard's model of survival here as I consider "the matrix of gender and culture in which this discourse of race and racializations occurs" (33).

Suspended thus, above and safely beyond the slave ship and the Middle Passage, Wheatley attempts to unwrite one "discourse of difference" (43) while rewriting another. She engages the dilemma of unwriting herself as a black American slave, and rewriting herself as an Afro-British American citizen. As in many of her other works,[4] the black Christian Wheatley challenges racially motivated views of religious truths and the distortions of biblically based myths upon which American nationhood is established. "Niobe" represents a challenge to the paradoxes she embodies—race, gender, religion, and nation.

Consequently, to re-member "Niobe," Wheatley draws upon a very personal and particular knowledge of violence and oppression. As a young slave girl, she had survived the rupture of kinship and endured the violence of the Middle Passage firsthand. As both a slave and an Afro-British subject, Wheatley complicates American national identity and subjectivity by interrogating the extent to which this new nation[5] and its citizens could truly be considered independent. In fact, with white women accepted only marginally as citizens, and African slaves, both male and female, completely excluded from citizenship, America as a nation could not morally claim true independence. In response to this paradox, Wheatley presents an autobiographical text that speaks both to the independent and dependent aspects of eighteenth-century America. As in many of her other works, the black Christian Wheatley challenges the racially motivated view of religious truths and the distortions of biblically based myths upon which American nationhood was established.

Against such distortions of Africa as a static or impermeable space of "dark abodes"—literally and figuratively—Wheatley's invention of Africa is grounded in an understanding of Africa as a term that signifies and reconstructs as it defines.[6] Rather than assuming an essentializing or totalizing representation, Wheatley assumes, as do many eighteenth-century Afro-British Americans, that whatever is African is also Afro-British and Afro-American. As a result, Wheatley weaves out of "Niobe" an integrative and inclusive myth of early American origins, using not only Western ontologies and epistemologies but fragmented African ones as well. In the same way that traditional etiological myths recapture and recover discrete British origins, Wheatley's "Niobe" reimagines synthesized African origins. More importantly, Wheatley reinvents Africa as a necessary stage in re-membering and resituating herself within the newly imaginable independent America. Countering the delimiting and dysfunctional assumptions embedded in "interpretation[s] . . . based on western unilineal perception[s] [of] African woman as [inescapably and perpetually] oppressed from all social positions" (Kalu, "Those," 81), Wheatley reimagines motherhood, womanhood, humanity, and her own subjectivity within an African-derived context that interpolates her as an "active participant in all aspects of . . . existence" (82). This way of interpreting and relating to herself and her experiences shows Wheatley's awareness of the universal and multidimensional roles that African women play in the development of society. Scholars such as V. Y. Mudimbe and Kwame Anthony Appiah have suggested the limits of African self-invention. Mudimbe exposes the flaws inherent in systems of African-centered "models of analysis explicitly or implicitly, knowingly or unknowingly" that not only "depend on Western epistemological order" but also on the tendency of "Africanists . . . to separate the 'real' African from the westernized African . . . rely[ing] strictly on ['real' Africa]" (x–xi) as the ultimate source of African knowledge.

This troubling of the very foundations upon which knowledge by and about Africans has been invented exposes underlying systems of Western-derived knowledge which effectively silences African voices. More pertinent to my own study in this book is how such theorizing about the dilemma, critical frameworks of representation and analysis, supports my argument about the need to reconnect and reorder (or in Mudimbe's terms "recolonize") the conditions under which we locate black aesthetics and meaning in eighteenth-century Afro-British American literature. Following Mudimbe, I maintain that recovering history within African frameworks derived from "real" and "westernized" African ways of knowing not only reveals how Africa was reinvented by these early black writers, whose texts created new epistemological systems, but also implicates contemporary scholars (including myself) in yet another type of invention of Africa. Appiah broaches the dilemma of the invention in Africa: "[W]hat, given all the diversity of the precolonial histories of the peoples of Africa, and all the complexity of colonial experiences, does it mean to say that someone is African?" (25). Unlike Mudimbe or myself in his critique of African essentialism (the invention of a static monolithic Africa and African structures), Appiah dismisses the viability of African structures of meaning as interpretive lenses for reading early black literature. Nevertheless, Appiah's rejection of topologies of nativism that marginalize the diversity out of which African texts are generated is a valid one. Moreover, Appiah's concerns about the way in which such topologies overstate and misstate the audience to which African writing is addressed points to the shared dilemma faced by the earliest African writers and their modern descendants. For it is this same kind of essentialism which displaced eighteenth-century Afro-British American writers from their African, British, and American mournings/moorings. Ultimately, I concur with Anthonia Kalu, who recognizes the cultural significance of the productive invention of Africa, which in turn enables rereadings like "Niobe." Namely, I extend Kalu's "understanding [of] the complementary relationship between ancestral and Africanized western knowledge bases [that] also facilitates a new reading of the African writer's efforts to synthesize a transitional culture" ("Traditional," 37).

Kalu's analysis applies to several other issues related to the problematic relationship between American independence and Afro-British American identity. Hence, Wheatley's "Niobe" can be interpreted as an attempt to grapple with this dilemma. Thus, she uses her neoclassical myth ("Niobe") to explore the catastrophic repercussions of colonial America's race, gender, and class oppressions. Even more arrestingly,

Wheatley exposes the powerful effects of such manifold excesses of power on the literary and physical bodies of eighteenth-century women and slaves. Unlike analyses of power and agency which depend upon the subverting of primarily dominant Western ontologies and epistemologies, Wheatley's text resituates not only African women's subjectivity, but also cultural hegemony within African-derived contexts.

Pointing to the ways in which Wheatley's work may be seen as a recentering of both African and European women, David Grimsted argues that Wheatley's egalitarian treatment of elegies suggests "a public extension of women's centrality in the private rituals of death" (353). He further submits that "Niobe represented a rare attempt to give fully tragic stature to woman's centrality in the family and in the age's rituals of mourning" (370). Grimsted argues that Wheatley's "personifications of favorable things such as Liberty . . . and Peace are made feminine, while *negative* things like Death and Power are masculine" (370). I agree with Shields, who, countering Grimsted's reading of associations of death in Wheatley's work as negative, argues that the poet's celebration of death is in fact a "reject[ion] [of] transitory life on earth and [her] long[ing] for escape through death" (*Collected Works,* 252).

Bassard's readings of Wheatley's elegies further complicate both views of death in Wheatley's work. Specifically, she argues convincingly that Wheatley expresses her own grief through the "device of having the deceased speak words of comfort to the loved ones left behind [as] a sort of self-ventriloquism" (70). Consequently, Bassard concludes that Wheatley's elegies signal her "desire to speak beyond the 'grave' of separation to those she left behind" when she was "brought from Africa to America" (70). Significantly, if Wheatley brings so much of herself to a genre designed toward literal expression of an objectified grief of another person, then the figurative representations of death in her neoclassical poetry demand equally and introspectively guided interpretations. We will want to look more closely at what gendered personifications and figurations of transitory death tell us about the poet's own view of death. At the same time, we can hardly ignore the poet's desire for either escape or resurrection.

Indeed, addressing the question of why "Wheatley returned to [the elegiac] form so often that it became her primary vehicle for poetic expression" (59), I offer the following. Perhaps such a return can be found in the poet's longer than usual rumination on what might arguably be said to be the longest elegiac expression in Wheatley's corpus. In this extended elegy, "Niobe" mourns the physical death of fourteen children, the spiritual and social death of two others as well as their mothers and fathers, and the geographical spaces they represent—Africa and the Americas. Further, it seems crucial to expand on what might be termed the quintessential moment of self-subscription for a black woman poet, Wheatley's gesturing and signifying of death, power, childbirth, spirituality, war, incest, murder, and slavery, culminating in her own engagement with a discourse of silence or silencing (depending upon one's reading or attribution of the final lines).

If, as Bassard suggests, separation from one kind of community permits an attachment to another, it might necessarily follow that such an attachment permits the creation, but not necessarily the total assimilation, of another kind of community. Thus, Wheatley mourns her African roots at the same time she is moored to European community and ways of knowing. Further, she attaches herself metaphorically to Africa in order to sustain, develop, and survive in America. Indeed, part of her survival depends on her ability to create a viable American community. She brings with her what remains of what she mourns. In the absence of what she doesn't have she creates out of what is there. If, following Bassard, we are to successfully contextualize Wheatley's poems "within the frame of cultural memory" (69), then we must be able, as Wheatley was, to expand our notion of culture. To be sure, culture for Wheatley, while it included Africa, America, and Europe, was no simple matter.

Yet, because "all fixed points are problematical" (Baker, 200), one must understand that women's centrality cannot be mediated solely through death or spiritual (re)birth. In fact, early black poetry such as Wheatley's questions the very grounds upon which such false categories as margin and center exist. That is, through its engagement with different and unknown tongues, Wheatley's poetry translates and mediates converging and diverging registers. As Niara Sudarkasa notes, "The 'public sphere' in most West African societies was not conceptualized as 'the world of men.' Rather, it was one in which both sexes were recognized as having important roles to play" (55). In Ogunyemi's terms, "the erection of borders where they did not exist before is the heretical sign of colonialism and divisiveness. . . . Rupture along gendered lines, rather than a parallel working-together, becomes the colonial heritage" (49).[7] Logically, the erection of borders is problematic whether its intent is to decenter dominant constructions or recenter those perceived at the margins. This is so because a "center-periphery model, where the periphery is totally victimized and disempowered, is not very useful" (49). Moreover, the terms under which one is located or dislocated are rarely assigned by those most at risk. As an enslaved African woman, Wheatley would not have missed the opportunity to poetically critique the unequal power relations of all types, including those between women and men. Such is suggested in Wheatley's juxtaposition of simultaneously powerful and disempowered figures in such works as "Niobe." As a Middle Passage survivor, who mourned the thousands gone (most vividly her mother and father), her work most certainly would have expressed grief and desire to speak to them as well as her own desire to transcend at times this lonely space. However, she could ill afford to retreat to such literal or figurative spaces as those imagined in her creative works for too long. Thus, in the spirit of Sankofa the African griotte sought to bring forward from each space of grief those lessons which were most valuable for her and others.

In terms of Wheatley's Christian ways of knowing, a celebration of death did not signal a disdain for life. Rather, the poet understood that suffering and sacrifice in the material world gave value to the rewards of the spiritual world. The devout Christian Wheatley would not have overlooked the significance of Jesus Christ's physical birth and earthly life; for without these events there could have been no crucifixion, death, or spiritual rebirth. More importantly, as much of Wheatley's work attests, she clearly comprehended the grave significance of The Great Commission,[8] which could only be carried out in the temporal world. To be effective, concepts such as death and spiritual rebirth must be interpreted within an integrative framework that engages the dynamic energy of men, women, and children in such realms. Brooks's *American Lazarus* provides important tools for scholars revisioning death in eighteenth-century black texts. She argues that scholars must address the ways in which writers like Wheatley were "creating from the chaos of colonization and slavery new identities, new communities, and new American literary traditions" (6). Significantly, early black writers like Wheatley had a different relationship to death than whites, one which Brooks poignantly locates in the biblical tradition of Lazarus which "encompasses both death and resurrection" (9). Hence, the "early writings [of African Americans] reflect the imposed discontinuities, cruelties, and mortalities of life under slavery and colonialism, and they demonstrate the drive to claim life from death and meaning from chaos" (9).

Indeed, Wheatley's death corpus exists in a marketplace[9] in which "whole kingdoms in [*Death's*] gloomy den are thrust / and nations mix with their primeval dust" ("To a Gentleman and Lady" ll.7–8). While the celebration of death as a vehicle through which humanity can pass from the ephemeral to the eternal world is meant to assuage and redirect the sentiments of the bereaved in Wheatley's elegies, her own understanding of life and death is rendered with far more complexity. Thus, Wheatley's self-consciousness is revealed in texts such as "Niobe," which put Wheatley's Christian self in simultaneous dialogue with her female, African, and American selves.[10] Although "Niobe" cannot be deemed autobiographical by traditional standards, when interpreted through the matrices of African ways of knowing, Wheatley's poem transposes and redefines the limits which define autobiographical texts. Further, such revisioning by its assumption of creative agency as a literary and cultural inheritance enables us to read "Niobe" as a text that undermines the concept of nation as a stable and natural entity. Thus, "Niobe" critiques the underlying ontologies and epistemologies that construct master narratives or proof texts to establish knowledge about raced, classed, and gendered others. Rather than merely challenging hegemonic control by exposing the effects of its practices, the counterdiscursive narrative of "Niobe" destabilizes hegemonic control by exposing underlying bases that enable supposedly natural and national codes and values.

Before moving to a discussion of the different ways in which Wheatley's work can be seen to destabilize various forms of power, it is necessary to clarify how African *ways* of knowing make a *difference* in our reading of power in Wheatley's poetry. What I have been referring to as a syncretized Senegalese poetics is a synthesis of West African modes of expression and historical transmission—Senegalese *taasu*, Nigerian *palava*, Akan Sankofa Bird, Ghanaian Bird of the Wayside—and African American theoretical models of interpretation—speaking in tongues, signifying. Moreover, no single attribute above will be wholly representative of this African-centered approach to analyzing Wheatley's work.

For example, her public performance of the mythic warring goddesses marks what might otherwise be invisible, the poet's very private "distress" at her own familial—maternal—disconnections. Carrying forward the seeds from an ancient past in her mourning/mooring of political upheavals, social chaos, and spiritual degeneration, her words reflect present crises facing Revolutionary America. Symbolic of the power of myths which are often imbedded in the histories brought forward in West African griot traditions—signified in the Sankofa and Wayside birds—the poet's words can be seen to carry more than one meaning and function, and on more than one level. I want to reiterate that what I am identifying here is a hermeneutic structure that privileges African modes of cultural expression and interpretive strategies—drawn both from culturally specific West African structures of meaning and those structures which represent a fusion of Western and African traditions.[11]

As I hope to demonstrate in my reading of "Niobe," all these elements of a syncretic Senegalese poetic—grounded in both culturally specific West African and African American ways of knowing—provide a new way of seeing Wheatley. In so doing, I argue that we are also able to view Wheatley's revisiting of "Niobe" as her most significantly personal, political, spiritual, and African work. Thus, we free previously bound views of race, class, and gender in eighteenth-century Afro-British American aesthetics. Such a liberating reading will enable us to consider the extent to which Wheatley's use of religion to veil antislavery protests was even more powerfully executed and extended through her longest poem, "Niobe." It will be useful to consider how the poet, who was so well versed in secular classical traditions—identifying with such classical mythological female figures as Niobe, Latona, Aurora, Phoebe, Mneme, and Flora—might also have had some equally important biblical figures of women in mind as she reimagined Ovid's Niobe. While there is no evidence to suggest that she modeled Niobe after such biblical women as Mary, Eve, or Hagar, we can be sure that Wheatley, as a devoutly Christian Methodist, was well acquainted with these holy women from her biblical readings.

Indeed, I agree with Shields that in both "Goliath of Gath" and "Niobe" Wheatley goes beyond mere "biblical paraphrase a popular form of the time" (*Collected Works*, 258). However, in the case of her "Niobe" poem, it may be equally important to consider the extent to which her use of biblical paraphrase represents an extension of this popular form. In this regard, it may be useful to think of how she may have used biblical paraphrase to draw upon the allegorical associations to be had by highlighting the stories of such well-known biblical women as Eve, Mary, or Hagar. Such female figures were not typically the subjects of this popular eighteenth-century form. However, references to such figures are to be found with some regularity and predictability in various other literary forms. For example, in published religious writings from 1600 to 1790, one can find references to Hagar in discourses, sermons, and treatises addressing such issues of doctrine and canon as: God's Providence, Law and Grace (especially with regard to the Two Covenants of Old and New Testament Dispensations), denominationally and doctrinally mixed marriages, children's baptism, Psaltery primers, and even the inclusion of the apocrypha into the Anglican canon of scripture. Able to adapt and fuse the biographical form of puritan elegy to her own elegiac verses, the political form to her occasional poetry and her letters, biblical paraphrase to a heightened form of secular and sacred aesthetics not only predates and possibly informs nineteenth-century romanticism and transcendentalism, but also locates parallel black African envelopes in which to house her fused Afro-British American voices and messages.

Concurrently, Wheatley interrogates knowledge and power in order to complicate notions of race, class, and gender. She does so by rereading of histories of female empowerment and disempowerment through her revisioning of women's sacred history in the figure of Hagar. Indeed, this controversial biblical figure has generated much controversy among biblical and women studies scholars. Importantly, their work highlights the complex nature of women's relationships to one another, to patriarchal and matriarchal societal structures, to men, children, and history. For example, Phyllis Trible argues that "as one of the first females in scripture to experience use, abuse, and rejection, Hagar the Egyptian slave claims our attention. Knowledge of her has survived in bits and pieces only, from the oppressor's perspective at that, and so our task is precarious: to tell Hagar's story from the fragments that remain" (*Texts of Terror,* 9).

Savina Teubal suggests that the absence of any confirmable biblical accounting of the birth of Ishmael, which could have given a more balanced insight into the relationship between Hagar and Sarah, alongside a failure to sufficiently acknowledge the implications of these two women's surrogacy agreement as it related to matrilineal heritages of power and authority, have obscured some of the most dynamic elements of women's religious history (76).

Janet Gabler-Hover's *Dreaming Black/Writing White: The Hagar Myth in American Cultural History* is the only formal full-length study of Hagar from the perspective of literary analysis. Gabler-Hover provides critical insights into the difference between nineteenth-century white and black women writers' use of the Hagar myth. In particular, she notes that differences between black and white women writers' metaphorical use of Hagar's body result from their respectively distinct relationships to race, class, and gender. Further, she suggests that such differences provide evidence that both blacks and whites read Hagar as—if not directly then indirectly—a black woman. Gabler-Hover surmises that this conclusion is based at least in part on Hagar's Egyptian and slave heritage, but mostly on racialized stereotypes of black women's perceived freer sexuality.

A more important consideration may be what nineteenth-century women's symbolic investment in Hagar may suggest about Wheatley's own revisionary interpreting of this biblical figure of an African slave woman through "Niobe." Admittedly, Hagar was not available as an iconic image to the eighteenth-century white woman, at least not in the same way it was to the nineteenth-century women in Gabler-Hover's study. However, Wheatley's perspective as an enslaved African woman (like Hagar) may have permitted her another way of viewing and making similar symbolic use of this biblical myth. Gabler-Hover contends that nineteenth-century women used the Hagar myth to read and rewrite shifting societal values, and in terms that symbolically revealed intersecting poles of race, gender, and biblical symbolism. While we cannot know for certain, it is certainly plausible that Wheatley, as someone familiar with the Bible and the story of Hagar, might have been able to draw upon parallels between her life and this biblical character. Certainly, if black male writers of this period were able to draw on biblical characters in their narratives (for a variety of reasons) as Angelo Costanzo and other scholars have noted, then it is not so far-fetched that Wheatley, who was equally creative and intelligent, would have been able to make similar use of female characters.

Her "Goliath of Gath" poem provides ample evidence of her ability to integrate biblical myth into neoclassical epic form; that she did not similarly celebrate any female biblical characters, but rather chose to use a mythical secular goddess, and that she chose to critique negative rather than convey such essentially positive attributes of these female characters, offers a fertile site for analysis and recovery of perhaps what might be argued as the first attempt by a black woman author to render an imagined African female deity in her writing—albeit veiled. Surely, if Wheatley began her book of *Poems* by first imaging then invoking Maecenas as an African muse, and if she was well versed enough in Latin and Greek, and Roman mythology to poetically render "Niobe," she was clever enough to see the parallels between the secular and sacred worlds in which she lived and those she imagined in a mythical Thebes. Gabler-Hover contends that "the real question is not what happens when white women 'dream' Hagar but what happens when white women who are intensely invested in the disempowerment of 'real' black women dream a black, sexualized Hagar in their own narratives of white self-empowerment" (31). Analogously, Wheatley's "Niobe" perhaps enables us to consider what happens when an enslaved black woman who is intensely invested in the empowerment of real black women dreams a black goddess.

Importantly, part of Wheatley's recapture of Africa through her syncretic Senegalese poetics in the "Niobe" poem necessitates a return to a literal and literary *Genesis*—in order to reinsert the African women's voice that was more than once removed. Centuries before Teubal, Trible, or the nineteenth-century black and white women writers they study, Wheatley responded to the call of her Afro-Christian ancestors to speak in her poetry through the vehicle of a less traditionally sacred if equally spiritual form—the Ovidian neoclassical myths of *Metamorphoses*. And, it is through the reinsertion of the voices of Niobe and Hagar that we hear again the African woman's voice. It is significant that Wheatley's voiced expressions do not suggest a deific, omniscient position from above. Rather, her poetics listens for the spaces where these voices can in fact be heard—despite historical silencing through misinterpretation. In so doing, she makes clear the difference a *way* of hearing, or not hearing, speaking or not speaking, writing or not writing, makes. In this case, previously unheard voices come to the forefront through our listening for the unknown tongues, patterns of direction and indirection, and shifting registers of discord and harmony. Most significant is that "Niobe" invites Wheatley's African ways to aural and oral *palava* with her Afro-British American ways of knowing. Wheatley's own history plays an important role in her assumption, adaptation, and reappropriation of these multiple ways of knowing.

As early as age thirteen, according to Margaret Odell's biography, she demonstrates her knowledge both of the classic texts and rudiments of a proper woman's education and an understanding of Christianity well beyond her years and social circumstances. In "To the University of Cambridge in England," Wheatley admonishes the "sons of science / [and receivers of] the blissful News from messengers from heaven / [. . . to] suppress the deadly serpent in its egg" (ll.10–26). As self-appointed spokesperson for a society growing weary of the wastefulness of its prized youth and their diminishing reputations as young men unworthy of the privileges bestowed upon them, her poem is effectively "an exhortation"—in Muhktar Ali Isani's words—"to the boisterous students of Harvard to live a Christian life . . . put[ting] the luckier, yet less zealous Christians to shame" ("Gambia on My Soul," 65). Hence, in her advisory address to the white, wealthy, male students at this prestigious university, the young slave girl reminds them of their inherited privilege based on race, class, gender, and their equally important responsibility as Christians. Joanna Brooks poignantly argues, "Wheatley knew what the 'sons of science' were unwilling to acknowledge: that neither rational causes nor natural forces governed the events of this world" (*American Lazarus,* 5). Moreover, Wheatley's exhortation to her white brethren is meant to remind them that if they were bold enough and certainly smart enough to manipulate religion and science to justify slavery and the oppression of women, she—a mere "Ethiop" woman— would not through her silence be complicit in their actions against her and her African brothers and sisters. Instead, she exposes their feigned ignorance about one of the most blatant sins confronting their society—the removal of African people from their "dark abodes" to an even "gloomier" state of physical and spiritual enslavement.

The poet's charge to the young men to "see him, with hands outstretched upon the cross" (l.13) is meant to signify the great earthy and heavenly debts that are owed, for neither is without costs. Ironically, both the "sublimest skies" of spiritual salvation and the "transient sweetness" of the material wealth and comforts come as a result of the blood, sweat, and tears of others.[12] To see their "redeemer," who shed his "blood" upon the cross "with hands outstretched" to his enemies and friends, those who followed, denied, and crucified him should convict or prick the hearts of the poet's enslavers. More important, her admonition to "suppress the deadly serpent in its egg" (l.26) is meant to guide them toward salvation, as they begin to see others—including enslaved Africans—through the eyes of their redeemer. This veiled, but nonetheless powerful, antislavery protest through a reordering and recapturing of the true meaning of the spirit and the letter of the law of scripture is especially significant coming from an enslaved teenage African girl.[13] Similarly, in an often-quoted passage from "On Being Brought from Africa to America," the fifteen-year-old insists that while "some view our sable race with scornful eye / Their color is a diabolic die. / Remember, *Christians, Negros,* black as *Cain* / May be refin'd, and join the angelic train" (ll.5–8), Wheatley redefines the conceptual connections and cultural contexts of blackness and Christianity and resituates the historical misrepresentation of African peoples within Christian doctrine.

One of the most vivid illustrations of her role as African griotte defined as genealogist, historian, praise singer, and warrior may be seen in her longest poem, "Niobe." In this poem Wheatley translates Ovid's classic (Western) myth of pride and vengeance into an African praise song of motherhood and community. Simultaneously, she effects a historical indictment of the inhumanity of internal and external warring through her reimagining of mythological genealogy of the figures Niobe and Latona within African, American, and especially Afro-Christian contexts. As Holloway maintains, "Because belief in divinity and belief in the ancestors are both elements of traditional religion in Africa, the figurative presence of feminine deities (goddesses) in creative literatures by women indicates the creative relationship of this metaphor to the culture and gender of the author/artist" (*Moorings and Metaphors,* 165). While Holloway refers specifically to contemporary black American and African literature, I believe her critical views on the value of myth for revealing the recursive strategies of remembrance enhance our understanding of how an eighteenth-century black aesthetic operates in works such as "Niobe."

Further, in recovering her historical lineage through Niobe, Wheatley echoes the resounding cries of a "Hagar in the Wilderness." For Hagar, like the enslaved African Wheatley, comes to us without history and voiceless. Indeed, our first knowledge of Hagar (not unlike Wheatley) is that of one who is seemingly powerless from all perspectives. Egyptian handmaid and African slave, both Hagar and Wheatley are objects of patriarchal exchange and intragender oppression. Hagar is transferred from Pharaoh through Abram to Sarai. Wheatley is purchased by John Wheatley as a servant for his wife, Susanna. It will be rightly objected that Wheatley's experience with her tender mistress Susannah can hardly be compared to the cruelty Hagar experiences in her relationship with her mistress Sarai. The relationship between two women of unequal power—essentially rivals—is most certainly not the same as a surrogate mother/daughter relationship (albeit between a slave and her mistress). The point I am making here, though, is how Wheatley reflects on and then depicts multiple complementary and angularly related circumstances from literal experiences in the real world to mythic experiences in Niobe's world. Of equal significance is the way the poet extracts fragments from several different histories to imagine one history that tells many stories and serves many audiences.[14] Wheatley's ways—in the context of a Senegambian poetic—move beyond interpretations that suggest a one-on-one correspondence or merely parallel view of similar models of power relationships. Consequently, we need to be able to see such gendered and race-inflected models as expandable images—that is, as constituting parts of a larger single text. At the same time, such models can function interchangeably as the demands of the story change. As Bassard's poetics of recovery reveal, this African way of imagining enables us to see Wheatley's georacial unwriting "of the discourse of blackness/Africanity as a discourse of difference" (43). Such a way of imagining also enables Wheatley to rewrite this racially blackened discourse as well. Briefly, Wheatley's Senegambian poetics enable her to participate simultaneously in both an Africanist and Americanist discourse—without negating either. Crucially, as in the Senegalese women's *taasu*, Wheatley's "Niobe" is performed in the context of its expandability and portability to issues of particular concern to women, and in conjunction with matters that are central to others within the community.

Consequently, Wheatley's depiction of Niobe's distress is as much a way of talking about Wheatley's own distress over what happened to Africa's children as it is the impending doom facing America's black and white children—both the Ishmaels and the Isaacs. "Niobe" gave the black, devoutly spiritual poet yet another vehicle through which to convey her literary, cultural, political, and, most important, spiritual roles. It also permitted her to attempt to reconcile for herself (and others) what it meant to be both African and Christian. In so doing, she redefined and simultaneously complicated once sacredly held assumptions about what it meant to be both black and a slave. And she did so in ways that forever severed ties between the so-called Christian mission of saving Africans from their lives in darkness and spiritual enslavement on their continent to the light of spiritual purity and whiteness as enslaved bondsmen and women in the New World.

Quite brilliantly, Wheatley radically and symbolically repositions the enslaved African woman within the redemptive history and legacy of the fallen Eve, the outcast and enslaved Egyptian Hagar, and the venerated Mary. In this context it is possible to consider Eve, Hagar, and Mary as representative of symbolic female whiteness and blackness, with their concomitant and equally problematic class and gender assignments. Hence, Wheatley recaptures (and composes) deifying and reifying myths about blacks and women. Out of the religious texts of her Christian masters, the poet signifies on the biblically based raced and gendered narratives of oppressed peoples. While early black writers' relating of their struggles to that of Old Testament figures is well known, such associations are typically read within a context that assumes male-centered master narratives. In contrast, Wheatley, through Eve, Mary, and especially Hagar, reconsiders the religious history with regard to slavery by juxtaposing the symbology of daughters of Hagar alongside the sons of Cain and the sons and daughters of Ham.

Juxtaposing the harsh reality of her own experiences and America's impoverished, oppressed, and enslaved mothers and children alongside the American nation-building project, she exposes the means by which they are all kept in bondage. Not unlike the nation-building promises in the patriarchal covenants, the creation of a wealthy national body—through the American Revolution and slavery—would be fulfilled in the bodies of women and children. Wheatley was well aware that both the sacred and secular worlds exacted a similar level of violence on women. However, her own interpretation of Eve, Hagar, Sarai, and Mary through "Niobe" invests a certain measure of power and responsibility in women for their part in upholding patriarchal and national interests.

We can only speculate whether the image of Latona (as a woman, a mother denied) invoked the very memory of her own African mother pouring out water. Given Wheatley's knowledge of classical literature and myth, her attraction to the myth of the goddess Leto (Latona) is even more striking when one considers that Latona is the patron goddess of mothers. Leto's daughter Artemis (Phoebus) is depicted in images of classical Greek mythology as standing with bow, water jug, and bowl before her mother, who is seated. This mythic scenario in which the child stands before the seated mother with an offering bowl of water reverses a scene of Wheatley's literal memory. Yet, even as such a narrative unwrites one story, it rewrites another—that of the child's return to the mother as well as the child's fulfillment of the retribution for her mother's suffering. West African cultural traditions such as Mammywata (goddess of water) evoke similar themes of simultaneous barrenness and fertility. My intention is not to conflate either the vastness of West African goddess traditions into one monolithic myth, or to discount the continuum of traditions and reciprocal borrowing of African and Western traditions from antiquity to modern time. Rather, my intention is to further widen the spaces within which African conceptualizations and deifications of female principals can be represented. Karla Holloway has described this kind of metaphor—of summoning ghosts—in terms of African women writers' use of goddess traditions to engage splintered knowledge. In both Western and African traditions Wheatley offers Niobe and her abundant progeny as idealized yet analyzable symbols of the natural wealth and prosperity associated with motherhood.[15]

> Seven sprightly sons the royal bed adorn,
> Seven daughters, beauteous as the rising morn;
> As when Aurora fills the ravished sight,
> And decks the orient realms with rosy light,
> From their bright eyes the living splendors play,
> Nor can beholders bear the flashing ray. (ll.23–28)

Understanding that motherhood for displaced African women meant perpetual enslavement for their children and increased property values for their masters,[16] Wheatley's description of Niobe's children moves beyond their Ovidian use-value as producers of "sons- and daughters-in-law" (Ovid, *Metmorphoses* vi.183–84).[17] It is significant that this passage's transposition of the meaning of the relationship between children and their parents (in both Ovid's and Wheatley's time) undermines dominant ideological frames of reference for family by resituating family within an African context. Notably, Wheatley's remembering and reimagining of Niobe's children in all their splendid magnificence is also reminiscent of the way in which a young woman's beauty and fertility are emphasized in traditional African ceremonial wedding songs. Indeed, Niobe's children are more resplendent and glowing than Zeus himself, by Wheatley's embellishment of Niobe's account, suggested by the fact that Niobe's daughters, as well as her sons, number "seven," and therefore both Niobe's children, and metaphorically Africa's children, are lacking in nothing. Wheatley's description of them as perfect suggests that they, too, can potentially become gods, for it is quite clear that Niobe, an "empress with a goddess join'd" ("Niobe" l.74), sees herself as perfect in both heavenly and earthly realms.[18]

The supernatural luminosity with which Wheatley symbolically endows Niobe's divinely descended royal children is meant to expose the sociopolitical and economic systems which underlie the construction of naturalness. Wheatley's interrogation of the natural association of intelligence with brightness, through her incorporation of the terms that imply double meaning in the concept of brightness in her reinterpretation of Niobe's children, points to ways in which light (or white) people are thought to be brighter (smarter) than Africans. If, as Thomas Jefferson contends, "in the countenances [of Africans], [there is an] immoveable veil of black stars which covers all emotions" (*Notes*, 138), such is disputed in Wheatley's representations: in the "rosy light" of Niobe's (and Africa's) daughter's dawn, or the "sprightly" and animated faces of her sons, or by staring into the "bright eyes" that reveal a "play" of "living splendors" ("Niobe" ll.23–27). Like Wheatley's own mother, who in daily ritual obeisance "prostrated herself before the first golden beam that glanced across her native plains"[19] (Richmond, 12), Niobe is similarly overcome by the brilliance and splendor of her "blooming maid[s], and celestial boy[s]" ("Niobe" l.36).[20]

The play of colors in her imagery points to Wheatley's location at the crossroads as cultural interpreter. Implicit in Wheatley's revision of the dark and barren life of the slave child is an interrogation of both the spiritual and aesthetic devaluing of African children and, by extension, their African mothers. A similar type of alteration can be seen in Ogunyemi's twentieth-century deification of motherhood. Ogunyemi compares Chi[21] "to a woman who bears children and/or divides the largesse among them." She notes that "in Igbo comic wisdom, Chi is also conceptualized as dwelling in the sun," and "that, when one is at one's best, Chi is the sunshine within, almost turning one into a super being. To the child, the mother is the morning sun that shines on him/her specially; she is also the supreme being to be adored as a bountiful provider" (41). Both Wheatley's luminous evocation of children and Ogunyemi's radiant magnification of their mothers point to the centrality of motherhood and childhood in African culture. Wheatley authorizes, improvises, and mediates African and Western motherhood and in doing so imbeds a valuable legacy and marker of African experience(s) of motherhood in the eighteenth century both inside and outside slavery.

Although women's fertility is central to both African and Western women's cultures, Wheatley subverts dominant Western-based discourses that locate white women's symbolic and material value solely in procreation, while simultaneously ascribing a dubious and exploitative value to African women's progeny. Wheatley imagines autonomy and empowerment through a constructed African-derived concept of motherhood rather than an essentialized or natural one. Such a concept of motherhood relies upon women's spiritual wealth as manifested in and through their children, and more importantly, their ability to coexist in harmonious intragender relationships that ensure the survival of their communities as a whole. Hence, Wheatley's pronouncement that Niobe "had'st far the happier mother prov'd, / If this fair offspring had been less belov'd" ("Niobe" ll.31–32) can be interpreted as an indictment of Niobe's and Latona's virulent and myopic fixation on women's roles as supernatural propagators to the exclusion of their roles as maintainers of structures that sustain and continue life in all its forms. Both Latona's preoccupation with her royal lineage as "spouse and sister of the thund'ring *Jove*" (l.94) and Niobe's obsession with her "large progeny" (l.79) prevent either of them from combining and drawing upon their real rather than relative power.

What has been forgotten in slavery and colonization Wheatley attempts to remember: the political and social agency of African women as daughters, wives, and mothers. In her analysis of African (Igbo) gender systems, Ifi Amadiume emphasizes the value placed on women's equal participation in all matters of society. According to Amadiume, "Nnobi [African] women have always been articulate and not mere objects circulated among and acted upon by their men-folk. . . . Nnobi women made [and continue to make] political use of their roles as daughters . . . through the control of funerals of patrilineage members, wives and mothers . . . [and] fertility ceremonies during marriage and childbirth" (87). Clearly, Niobe and Latona (not unlike Wheatley's ancestors) lived in a world in which women had a similar power in society. Indeed, it is the abuse of such power to which Wheatley alludes. However, in demonstrating such abuse, she necessarily exposes the potential for a more positive wielding of the authority and privilege which these women possess. Indeed, the exploitation of power is not merely limited to Niobe and Latona, though theirs clearly represents the most extreme and irresponsible handling of power.

Certainly, Amadiume's observations point to the participation and centrality of African women in structures that both center and decenter women's social orders. In "Niobe," society is called into existence through the words of Manto. As I have noted earlier, Manto, like the Sankofa bird, had the gift of prophecy: "endu'd with mighty skill / The past to explore, the future to reveal" (Wheatley, "Niobe" ll.37–38). Thus, she must have foreseen what her "mandate" (40) would set in motion. Yet, her prophetic power compels her to instruct the women of Thebes to pay proper homage to Latona. Thus, it is the words—Manto's words—which are the spark that ignites the flame of bad blood. Indeed, the women of Thebes become mere pawns in what would end in a deadly game. "The Theban maids obey / And pious tribute to the goddess pay" (ll.47–48). Yet, if Manto—and the Theban society that listens to her—is representative of responsible actions in the execution of power, the same cannot be said of Niobe. As a queen of Thebes she should set the example for her people and pay tribute to Latona as a goddess. However, her power becomes a justification to deny proper respect to Latona. Instead, Niobe revels not only in the sovereign authority that she and her husband, Amphion, command, but also in her numerous issues. The history of the troubled relationship between Latona and Niobe is said to have been exacerbated by Niobe's taunting of the goddess, who has only two children, in comparison to Niobe's fourteen. To be sure, the story reveals that the pride she exhibits in her children proves to be her undoing.

Of equal importance to understanding the implications of abuses of power in "Niobe" is what Wheatley does not include. As Shields and other scholars have observed, the poet, who is quite thorough in all her details, deliberately omits Ovid's prelude to "Niobe." Thus, Wheatley signifies (through indirection) that which the Phrygian queen ignores: a history that might have saved her. Preceding the Niobe myth is a tale about Arachne, a young woman whose pride and arrogance in her skill at weaving result in her metamorphosis into a spider. Not only had the young woman failed to pay tribute, but she denied even the "suggestion of a teacher ever so great" (Ovid, vi. l.24) as the goddess Pallas. Instead, she engaged in a weaving contest with Pallas, which resulted in her tragic transformation. "Now Niobe, before her marriage, / . . . had known Arachne . . . as a girl / . . . And yet she did not / take warning by her countrywoman's fate to give / place to the gods and speak them reverently" (vi. l.148–51).

Thus, while Niobe might have heeded history, she was rather a victim of it. Ultimately, Latona, who as goddess wields the greatest power, succumbs to the same pride and abuse of authority as Niobe. Moreover, because her children are used as weapons to brandish her power and exact vengeance, Latona reproduces this corruption through her heirs. I have taken the time to consider the significance of power because, as I argue, it is a recurring image that sustains nearly every element of Wheatley's critique in "Niobe." Thus, the confrontation of power—through its assumption, use, and subsequent abuse—can be viewed in three ways. First, there is the power of the word—through Manto's ability to affect change in society. For Afro-British Americans like Wheatley, words represent both power and the abuse of it. In a historical moment when perceptions frame reality, the naming of a people as barbaric, inhumane, irrational, pagan, or chattel grants a society permission (provides a context or rationale) to enslave, brutalize, or otherwise marginalize such people. Thus, like Theban maidens, colonial Americans rush to pay homage to their own goddess "Freedom" (Wheatley, "To the Right Honourable William, Earl of Dartmouth" ll.8–11)—as the enslavement of others remains an unspoken history.

Second, there is the political power of the governing body—American aristocracy and British monarchy. Like Niobe's Thebes, colonial American authority resides primarily in its wealth—and ironically that wealth is upheld by the contracted (indentured) or free (slave) labor of the bodies. Like Niobe's children, such bodies are vulnerable to the attacks and violence their leaders bring upon them.

Third, there is divine power, which is manifested primarily but not only in the Christian Church. While it is potentially the most liberating power, it is also that which may be most easily and effectively abused. Indeed, the distortion and perversion of Christian values to serve political and economic demands of the developing American nation were very heavily critiqued by Afro-British American writers. In a society increasingly dependent on slave labor, religion proved a valuable tool for maintaining the status quo. Of course, it was equally utilized as a strong antislavery weapon. Ultimately, I am not arguing that "Niobe" can simply be read as an allegory with a one-to-one correspondence to Revolutionary American society—it cannot. However, I draw attention to some of the parallels as a means to grapple with what are complex threads of a dilemma facing the worlds inhabited by Afro-British America.

Hence, as we consider how power operates in both Wheatley's mythic and actual worlds, it is critical to acknowledge, as did the poet herself, that certain seemingly discrete elements of power are inextricable. Most evident is the way that divine power authorizes linguistic and political power. In order to more fully grasp the force of Wheatley's poetics—her African, British, American, and Afro-British American ways—it will be helpful to consider her particular approach to engaging the audience. Ernest Mason contends that "an aesthetic is fundamentally concerned with experience or with the act of experiencing or perceiving something . . . [with] black art in particular . . . understood as an elucidated experience" (2). Thus, examining Wheatley's strategy of elucidation is critical for our recovery of an eighteenth-century black aesthetic in "Niobe." More important, such recovery enables us to articulate more clearly how Wheatley's reconnection with African ways of knowing demonstrates one such aspect of this early black aesthetic. We can get a clearer picture, for example, of how Wheatley signals the dilemma of motherhood and gender in a slaveholding society by reflecting upon another text from Ovid's *Metamorphoses*—"Biblis":

> Biblis is a warning
> that girls should never love what is forbidden
> She loved her brother, and the way she loved him
> Was not the way sisters should love their brothers. (qtd. in Galinsky, 35)

Galinsky maintains that in passages such as this, Ovid's intention was to distance himself from the subject in order to depersonalize the relationship between the narrator and his narrative. In particular, Ovid wanted to "prevent the reader from recognizing in the mythological story [familiar] human experience" (Galinsky, 35). In this way, Ovid was able to insert his own authoritative narrative moral proscriptions concerning the dangers of excess and improper love, and, finally, through *Metamorphoses* to expose the complexities, potential, and enigmatic nature of humanity. Thus, Ovid's caveat concerning excess and incestuous love (in "Biblis") warrants attention not only because it is illustrative of his style (in *Metamorphoses*), which draws attention away from the myth by "drawing attention to himself" (Galinsky, 35), but also because in his warning to Biblis is echoed parallel sentiments in Wheatley's "Niobe." To wit: that a "love too vehement hastens to destroy / each blossoming maid, and each celestial boy" ("Niobe" ll.35–36).

Yet Wheatley's (equally calculated) strategy was intentionally designed to exact the opposite reactions from her readers. Namely, she renders a critical reading of Western contexts through West African lenses in her use of the direct mode of signifying. Wheatley reads Ovidian love in such a way that it makes a statement about literal and figurative experience of the African mother's right to love her children. As a result, she chastises her audience for its lack (rather than overabundance) of universal love and its participation in depriving a child of her mother's love. Wheatley wants her readers to see in the larger-than-life goddesses (Niobe and Latona) not merely the universal condition of motherhood, but the African mother and child in eighteenth-century society. She wants to draw her audience of mostly white, male, propertied citizens, who are already as distanced from their subjects as any audience could be, closer to these women, these mothers, these Africans. Further, she wants her white, male, propertied audience to recognize and reflect upon their own mothers, sisters, wives, and female slaves, in the tragic consequences of Niobe, Latona, and their children. The subject, the imagery, the word choice, and the deeply imbedded passion with which she reimagines both Niobe and Latona is purposefully employed to beckon her reader into her imagined community of independent and, therefore, free citizens, who must collectively fight tyranny and oppression in all its manifestations. She wants them to reflect upon the high black and white infant mortality rate and the poor free and slave children bartered and separated from their mothers due to society's devaluing of them as disposable objects ("throwaways"). Yet, if the consequences for poor whites are tragic, Wheatley insists upon directing their attention to the more markedly tragic consequences for the mothers of those deemed natural slaves, consigned to perpetual servitude.

Indeed, Wheatley's strong and stunning imagery in her description of Niobe's mythical children exposes both "the ravished sight" of "the holocaust of slave raiding and trading, [in which African children] were equated with economic challenge and servitude in the colonies," and the "flashing ray" of those African children who "had [once] represented wealth and the recycling of life" (Ashcraft-Eason, 76). Niobe's children are as much Africa's children as they are America's children, "beauteous," "bright," and "ravished." "Ravished" refers to the bartered and battered condition of eighteenth-century America's black and white poverty-stricken children, as well as the precarious condition of Revolutionary America's motherhood. Because of its supposed naturalness, motherhood is equally susceptible to the kind of blindness and distance that can lead to subjective understanding. "Ravished" is a term that even in the eighteenth century is as relevant to rape as it is to racism. To "ravage" is to take away, to snatch, to leave bare, and this is what happens in slavery, in rape, and in childbirth (*OED*). In considering what happens to a mother's body before, during, and after the childbearing process, the metamorphoses that occur in both the child and the mother speak metaphorically to the "ravishment" that occurred during the eighteenth-century rape of Africa,[22] colonization, and the subsequent birth of the North American nation, with the women and Africans discarded like afterbirth.

The purportedly natural process of nationalization that I have described here represents an integral part of national myths which belies the systems of power and knowledge that Wheatley's interrogation of naturalness from the perspective of motherhood and gender uncovers and historically reconstructs. At the same time that Wheatley affects a measure of sympathy for Niobe's distress, read metaphorically as America's (and Africa's) distress, she also interrogates Niobe's willingness to sacrifice some of her children for the sake of her position, her pride, and what she feels as her natural right of ascendancy to wealth and power over this "new-sprung deity" ("Niobe" 1.64). Thus, in Niobe's devaluing of Latona's parentage, we can see Wheatley's interrogation of national identity from the perspective of lineage and class. Symbolically, Titans, who are considered lesser gods assigned to the domain of earth, and Latona, whose past troubles have placed her in a precarious class position, are linked through Niobe's perspective in order to elevate her own lineage. Niobe's attitude is thus presented as a mirror image of eighteenth-century American men who, while fighting for their own freedom against the tyranny of the British, failed to consider the human rights of displaced African slaves and devalued white women. Wheatley's depiction of the devastating war between the "haughty" Niobe and

Latona underscores the dangerous presumptuousness of white, propertied males about Africans and women. Metaphorically, Niobe, who serves as both a symbol of African and white colonial motherhood, is a reminder of the shared oppression of colonial white and black women, whose freedom remains insufficiently addressed in the post-Revolutionary world. This kind of deliberate detachment from the equally valuable concerns of black people at the inception of the formation of the American nation produced a legacy of civil wars and "ills innum'rous" ("Niobe" l.2), against which we can still hear the "woeful" cries of "Niobe[s] in distress for [their] children slain by Apollo."

In Niobe's voice, one can also hear the voices of Wheatley's African ancestors and African American descendants. Alicia Ostriker's articulation of "alternative portrait[s] of female pleasure" (165) is germane to an exploration of Wheatley's remembering of "Niobe." Specifically, in "Niobe," Wheatley creates a metaphorical African woman who, not unlike herself, is "composed of [her] parents, extended in her children, vitalized by the powers of spiritual ancestress, determined to identify with and redeem the defeated" (178). Wheatley's critique of class in her interrogation of Latona's "indignant" ("Niobe" l.80) reaction to Niobe's attempts to subvert her superior position, and the subsequent excessive anger that triggers Latona's wrathful destruction of Niobe's children, comments ironically upon Revolutionary America's simultaneous assumption of national identity at the expense of personal and particular identities and liberty.

As Wheatley makes clear, while Niobe, Latona, and indeed America failed to imagine the freedom of others in their own conceptions of national identity, they did so with the full expectations that their own rights would be upheld. One notes the self-righteous tone with which Latona's children express their intent to defend their mother's honor. Apollo and Phoebe pledge "to punish pride, and scourge the *rebel* mind" ("Niobe" l.104; my emphasis). Ovid's phrase "a long complaint is but delay of punishment" (Ovid, vi. 1.215) is equally harsh but much less moralistic. I emphasize *rebel* here to underscore Wheatley's use of Revolutionary rhetoric to evoke images of courageous Revolutionary American soldiers battling tyrannical British ones for their freedom. At the same time, *rebel* signifies on the scores of rebellious slaves whipped daily by their masters for insubordination—asserting their rights to freedom.

Wheatley points throughout "Niobe" to the irony of such a double standard of freedom, and the implications such arrogant and self-righteous attitudes may suggest for Christianity. For example, Latona's authority to exact vengeance on Niobe is based on her kinship to the deity "thund'ring *Jove*" ("Niobe" 1.94). Ironically, Niobe cries out to the same god for retribution of Apollo's murder of her seven sons: "Why sleeps the vengeance of immortal *Jove?*" (1.168). Here, Wheatley interrogates the self-righteous arrogance of white American citizens who use Christianity to uphold slavery, while simultaneously invoking images of the very people they enslave—Africans and women—to exact sympathy for their own freedom from British tyranny. As Erkkila argues, the polemic of the American Revolution was couched "in the language of two primary social tropes: the family and slavery, with America figuratively represented as the natural right of the son or daughter to revolt against a tyrannical parent and the natural right of a slave to revolt against a master" (225).

Yet, if the slave had a natural right to revolt against his or her master, such is disputed by the actions of the slaveholding colonists who daily invoked their rights to scourge their slaves for such rebellion. As Erkkila suggests of both Abigail Adams and Phillis Wheatley, women and slaves used similar rhetorical strategies to voice their respective struggles for enfranchisement and freedom. The most important gift of the American Revolution "was not real or political rights, but the knowledge, the moral ground, and perhaps most of all the language and metaphors with which to 'foment' further rebellion against the constituted orders of white masculine authority in the United States" (239). While Erkkila's assertions are historically valid, women like Wheatley understood that it would take more than moral ground to free them. Slaves knew that standing on such moral ground had yet to result in their freedom. In eighteenth-century Revolutionary America, an African woman like Wheatley always had to be consciously aware of not only her African self, but also her gendered self. Thus, Wheatley's "Niobe" renders visible the historical oppression and alienation of both the African slave mother and the poor white woman that is often veiled within the masculinist rhetoric of revolution. Johanna Miller highlights the plight of the white, female, indentured servant: "If a woman serving a term of indenture became pregnant, not only did she lose her child to the legal system, but her term was extended by one year as a punishment . . . such a system had the potential to hold women prisoner almost indefinitely if they became pregnant by their masters, willingly or unwillingly" (202). As an African and as a woman—consigned to what white propertied male society deemed her *rightful* place—Wheatley was doubly silenced; therefore, her poetry countered such censoring through a simultaneously direct and indirect (or doubled) type of signification. One example of Wheatley's attempt to unbind her own poetic tongue can be seen in the way she makes use of signification as a tool that highlights presence through absence. Thus, signifying facilitates the construction of particular history Wheatley wants to bring forward.

I want to return now to an earlier discussion in this chapter about Wheatley's use of African time as a way to consider the poet's engagement of historical landscapes through yet another Akan myth—the Bird of the Wayside. You may recall from the introduction that the Bird of the Wayside is the narrator in the prologue of Aidoo's play *The Dilemma of a Ghost*. "Significantly, the Bird of the Wayside, a literal translation from the Akan, referring to the unseen eye of public opinion . . . also serves as a dramatic device to engage the audience with the subject . . . and to invite it to make up its mind about the transpiring events" (Elder, 159). Wheatley's "Niobe" functions much like this "dramatic device" as the poem creates a space for her audience to trouble static views of history—African and European—by inviting them into a conversation between the mythical women characters. Much like the conversation between the two village women in Aidoo's *Dilemma*, Latona and Niobe engage in a kind of verbal warfare throughout "Niobe" that echoes the devastating action occurring in the tragic narrative scenes that depict the massacre of Niobe's children. Oddly, in many ways, the physical combat is but a backdrop—at best, exemplum—to the catastrophic dilemmas their conversations reveal. In truth, the words that pass between Niobe and Latona can hardly be considered conversations as neither woman actually listens or speaks to the other. In the spirit of Sankofa, it is the messages, lessons, and information to be passed on that are most important. For in such words are survival mechanisms and codes for reconnecting with one's community and one's self. Equally important, then, are the words that pass among the members of the Theban community.

Particularly revealing, both for what it highlights and what it obscures, is Latona's response to Niobe's call for a dialogue about their respective lineages. Essentially, what emerges from the verbal warfare between the two women is a more completely reconstructed, if problematic, history of both. Latona reminds her children of Niobe's history:

> Niobe sprung from Tantalus inspires
> Each Theban bosom with rebellious fires;
> No reason her imperious temper quells,
> But all her father in her tongue rebels. ("Niobe" ll.95–98)

A comparison between Latona's and Niobe's narrative exposes the dilemma of history as yet another vehicle for silencing and misnaming—especially for African-descended people like Wheatley. We first come to know Niobe from Wheatley's description of her motherly grief and distress, a "queen, all *beautiful in woe*" (ll.9–10; my emphasis). Next, we learn of Niobe's lineage and from a perspective very different than that of Niobe's. In Latona's version (above), Tantalus is a "rebellious," hot-tempered father whose equally unreasonable daughter inherits her father's "imperious temper" and his "tongue." This view of Niobe's history provides a striking contrast to the Phrygian queen's description of her father as: "*Tantalus* divine / He most distinguish'd by *Dodonean Jove* / To approach the tables of the gods above" (ll.14–16). Indeed, Niobe's royal lineage is further enhanced by her "grandsire *Atlas* / . . . / and her other grandsire / . . . *Jove*" (ll.15–21).

The context in which Latona describes Tantalus is a negative one. Her purpose is to discredit Niobe's status as equal to her own. Latona means to characterize Niobe as being from ignoble parentage to remind her own children (Apollo and Phoebe) of their high parentage and their high birth, as well as their responsibility to defend their nobility. While Latona is correct in emphasizing Tantalus's bad temper, her motives are suspect. While Niobe is correct in her celebration of her father's high position at "the tables of the gods," she provides a rather incomplete history. A more complete history follows:

> Tantalus . . . son of Zeus . . . is best known for the punishment he suffers in Hades. . . . he stands in the midst of a lake, but when he bends to drink, it dries up; a fruit-laden bough flies up when he reaches for it; and an overhanging stone threatens to crush him. . . . The punishments were inflicted for various crimes. . . . [He] betrayed [the gods'] secrets and gave ambrosia to his friends . . . offering a banquet to the gods . . . he served his dismembered son Pelops. (*Benet's Reader's Encyclopedia*, 1006)

Thus, Tantalus's history is symbolic of perpetual desire and deferral. He was consigned to an eternity of desiring the very thing that was within his reach, yet he could never obtain. Clearly, "*Tantalus* divine" ("Niobe" l.14) had fallen. Yet, because the variant myths of Tantalus suggest a range of identities from villain to Promethean-like hero, even when the facts are more fully apprehended, only a kernel of truth remains. Far more important is what both Niobe and Latona (from Ovid to Wheatley) make of the history that remains. For Latona, Tantalus's history—after his fall—is far more valuable for what it allows her to deduce about Niobe. First, that like her father, Niobe is both unworthy and far too "haughty" to be considered equally among goddesses such as Latona. Indeed, Latona may be said to be signifying that Niobe, like Tantalus, is doomed to want what she cannot have—true status as a goddess.

Whereas Niobe describes herself as both an "empress with a goddess join'd" ("Niobe" 1.74), it is Latona, after all, who is the goddess and therefore worthy of the tribute Niobe refuses to pay. While Niobe's beauty, royalty, and large progeny, as well as her marriage to King Amphion, provide evidence of her rightful place, Latona demonstrates that Niobe's history suggests otherwise. Notably, she "inspires" rebellion and lacks control over her emotions, to such an extent as to make it impossible to reason with her. The cause of this teeming and abundant anger—which is second in its excessiveness only to her procreative powers—seems explainable only in terms of her bloodline. "All her father in her tongue rebels" ("Niobe" 1.98). This statement is doubly inflected as it suggests that Tantalus's history is that of an overreaching mortal whose punishment is an eternity looking at that which he cannot have. In addition to Latona's anger at being shunned by Niobe, her words reveal she is far more threatened by what Niobe inspires, a rebellion of Theban society. Ultimately, it is Niobe's "tongue" that most offends Latona—Niobe's words carry great power. Recall that at Niobe's command the "*Theban* dames . . . / [No] longer off'rings to *Latona* pay" (ll.83–87).

Beyond unveiling the power of history to name and unname others based on different ways of creatively interpreting facts, absences locate additional spaces of reconnection with Wheatley's African ways of knowing. The first noticeable absence is Niobe's mother. It might be argued that if, as I suggest, Wheatley's intent (at least in part) is to highlight the shared oppression of women, then the absence of both Niobe's and Latona's mothers points to the devaluing of women's history—in the missing maternal line of ancestors. More likely, Wheatley doesn't include the name of Latona's mother because it is simply unavailable. Ovid comes as close as contemporary scholars do to naming Niobe's mother. In his version, Niobe's "mother . . . is a sister of the / Pleiades" (Ovid, vi. ll.174–75). Far more perplexing, and perhaps ironic, is Wheatley's decision not to include even the limited information available. Her choice not to include the reference to the Pleiades is especially puzzling given the possibilities it offers for the young griotte's praise song to her ancestors.

Perhaps it is in such a space of absence as this that we find Wheatley's own mother—hiding in plain sight. Clearly, the poet's reference to the Pleiades would have allowed an additional signification of brightness, ascent, and perfection. The seven sisters of the Pleiades were known for such beauty that they attracted, had affairs with, and bore children for gods ranking as high as Zeus. Certainly, such an illustrious female line of ascendancy would have further exalted the stature of Niobe's "Seven daughters, beauteous as the rising morn" (1.24). Indeed, Wheatley's embellishment of Ovid's "seven daughters" from whom Niobe expected to "soon have sons- . . . in-law" (Ovid, vi. ll.183–84) does just that, as it resurrects the Seven Sisters of the Pleiades in the seven daughters of Niobe. In this view of the seven daughters as recovery of Niobe's own matrilineal line, we are able to revisit the use-value of daughters to make good marriages—a focus I earlier argued is overshadowed by their internal and inherent radiance. Revisiting Niobe's seven daughters as resurrections of the Pleiades, as a recovery of Niobe's (and Wheatley's) mother, we are reminded that six of the sisters (and in some myths all seven) married well. Specifically, they each married gods, and did prove valuable producers of wealth. Indeed, if one of the Pleiades is Niobe's mother, then she (Niobe's mother) produced a daughter who in effect reproduced the Pleiades. Yet, even as we sift through multiple layers of signification to locate and recover Niobe's (and Wheatley's) mother through her daughters, we do so just in time to observe their demise. As in the African dilemma tale "[t]he end is not quite . . . an end. The adventure is finished but it is the audience that gives the conclusion. The end is an enigma to resolve" (Bascom, 2).

Thus, Wheatley offers war as a dilemma for both Theban and colonial American society to ponder. Namely, though both black and white women were at risk, the false consciousness of nationalistic claims of equality for all through American independence produced a historical divide between the Niobes and the Latonas. Rather than working together to resist and abolish their common oppression(s), both white and black women became accomplices in their own respective destruction(s).[23] Though Wheatley emphasizes "Apollo's slaying" of Niobe's children as the primary and most violent manifestation of oppression against mothers and children, she also draws attention, by apostrophe, to Latona's mandate to "wrap [Niobe's children] in the shades of death!" (1.90).

As illustrated metaphorically by "Niobe," and supported literally by "To the Right Honourable William, Earl of Dartmouth," Wheatley inserts herself into the space of a newly independent American nation

as the rightful heir to citizenship. In contrast to the self-indulgent goddesses Niobe and Latona, Wheatley offers "Freedom" as a "*Goddess* long
desir'd" ("Right Honourable William, Earl of Dartmouth" l.11), not only
for an "enslav[e]d" "*America*," but also for its enslaved "*Africans*" (ll.15–
25). In what Shields describes as "a rare autobiographical portrait"
(*Collected Works,* 235) Wheatley likens her physical enslavement to the
"enslave[ment] [of] the land" ("Right Honourable William, Earl of Dartmouth," 19), with her poignant depiction of the "excruciating" manner
in which she was "snatchd from *Afric's* fancy'd happy seat" (l.25). Her
poetry and her life point to the way in which the history of both whites
and blacks can represent an attempt to escape from the oppression
of tyranny and slavery. Wheatley refused to write and imagine herself
from the position of a permanently enslaved and disenfranchised African. Rather, she wrote from the position of an American with the same
rights and privileges as any other citizen. In her elegy "On the Death
of General Wooster," Wheatley identifies with both her African and her
American self as she "maintains that . . . an American military and political victory over Britain" should necessarily mean freedom for Africans
(Shields, *Collected Works,* 238). "But how, presumptuous shall *we* hope to
find / Divine acceptance with th' Almighty mind / While yet (O deed
Ungenerous!) *they* disgrace / And hold in bondage Afric's blameless
race?" ("Death of General Wooster" ll.26–30; my emphasis). Wheatley
radically saw her struggle for freedom from slavery (and less directly
patriarchy) as synonymous with that of white America's struggle for independence from Britain.

Wheatley's poetry refigures and resituates Africans at the crossroads
between slavery and independence in the American Revolutionary landscape. Her works reveal through their reinterpretation and improvisa-
tion complementary spaces of freedom and independence. Seen thus,
an eighteenth-century Afro-British American aesthetic emerges and with
it a model for an interrogation not only of its temporal, but also of
the spatial boundaries of freedom and enslavement. Clearly, Wheatley's
revisionary designations of freedom and independence as that which
ignored the enslaved, indentured, and nominally free existence of the
peoples it claimed to represent demands a more radical contemporary
interrogation.

Wheatley imagined herself as a natural and equal member of the
soon-to-be independent community of free Americans. For, although
Wheatley may legally have been a slave, much of her work points to her
affinity for liberty. "Niobe" in particular suggests a conception of herself

as a part of the newly independent American nation. Shields contends that "so complete was her absorption in the struggle for freedom [both in this world and the next], that [it] governed her conception of poetry" (*Collected Works*, 230). Dissatisfied with a "world which allow[ed] slavery to remain legitimate," Wheatley "buil[t] in her poems another, acceptable world" (xxix).

Thus, in "Niobe" Wheatley envisions a world in which African women, like her, inhabit the space of the independent American citizens rather than the enslaved objects. Moreover, Wheatley recuperates the lineage of "the [beautiful] Phrygian queen" (Emily Watts, 10) as that of potent gods, rather than that of Ovid's usurping, undeserving, and overreaching mortals. Niobe is, after all, "the wealthy heir to Tantalus divine" ("Niobe" 1.14), son of Zeus, the ruler of the gods. Of equal importance, especially to an eighteenth-century British audience, is the image of slavery and freedom that the term *Phrygian* invokes. Wheatley was certainly aware of the import of the term's well-known iconic value, especially during this historical moment. In particular, "during the eighteenth-century, the Phrygian cap evolved into a symbol of freedom, held aloft a Liberty pole during the American Revolution" (*OED*).

Further, the fact that "Phrygian" and "queen" are linked in this poem suggests Wheatley's awareness of the complex and yet common association of the dual imagery that women and enslaved Africans suggest for the white American males who would no longer be enslaved under British tyranny. Erkkila's analysis of the poet's manipulation of gendered and racial associations of the Revolutionary period invites us to direct critical attention to the unmistakable links between the figure of "Niobe" and "'Britannia Mutilated' . . . [in which] Britain appears as a naked female figure, enchained, amputated, and deprived of her former power by aggressive colonial policies of king and Parliament" (226). In fact, the black slave poet's coupling of the seemingly unrelated terms—"Phrygian" and "queen"—point to the paradox of the parallel injustices endured by both the white American citizen and the enslaved African. It is the latter term that Wheatley means to emphasize—as her use of "Phrygian" signifies on its double meaning. It serves as both an image of liberty denied by the British and liberty attained by America. However, Wheatley is all too aware of the "Phrygian" cap of freedom that continues to elude the enslaved African woman. To her credit Wheatley fully understands the implications of her use of such inconsistent terms of reference—both in the mythic tale of Niobe and the real history of the British colonies—the enslaved black and the nominally free white woman. Tragically, sovereign ascension is inextricably and perpetually contingent on the maintenance and upholding of the legacy of slavery by both king and queen.

As for the Phrygian cap which symbolized both British subjection and American entitlement, for the enslaved black woman it represented an identifiable marking (or branding) and constant reminder of her immutable difference. For, even if she attained freedom, and in so doing the Phrygian cap, it would always be worn as a symbolic reminder of her former status as a slave and her current status as at the bottom of the chain of being. Moreover, unlike the emancipated Roman slaves whose freedom this cap signified, the formerly enslaved African's descendants remained slaves as a condition of their birth to a slave mother. There is little doubt that Wheatley's poetic preoccupation with slavery and freedom —as demonstrated in her linking of the images of woman and liberty— clearly identifies the Revolutionary strain in her poetry.

Notably, in "To a Gentleman of the Navy" Wheatley laments the "Phrygian hero" Paris's "set[ting] the world in arms" over Helen's "resistless charms" (ll.10–15). Far more interesting, and related to the poet's rendering of "Niobe" is the conversation—the call and response that ensues during "The Answer [By the Gentleman of the Navy]" and "Phillis's Reply to the Answer." One cannot miss the classical Greek allusions to Phoebus and Apollo echoed in "The Answer," "Niobe," and throughout many of her other works. For example, given Wheatley's knowledge of Greek, Latin, and the neoclassical tradition, as signified by this brilliant and original translation of Ovid's texts, her choice of subjects is deliberately complex in order to draw critical white propertied males' attention to undervalued, dehumanized, eighteenth-century black humanity— certainly a new twist on traditional eighteenth-century poetic forms of indirection and Afro-poetic signification.

It is literally Wheatley's objection, as much as it is metaphorically Niobe's, that "Coeus' offspring is obeyed / while to [her] goddesship no tribute's paid" (ll.67–68). Clearly, the Revolutionary voice of the slave poet Wheatley is as much a "rebel against an established order" (Emily Watts, 38), as the mythical heroine Niobe. As Ostriker notes, "Niobe could rail despairingly against the gods in a way that Wheatley, who is elsewhere demurely Christian and patriotic, could not" (214). Hence, Wheatley's poem is about "women and power" (214), and the "natural" right of all mothers to maintain and sustain their progeny, despite dominant Western assumptions of ownership. More importantly, "Niobe" is a remembering of African and American subjectivity in terms which are restated by African voices in an attempt to neutralize the devastating effects of slavery and racism. Wheatley's historical encoding of African worldviews and her synthesizing of African and Western ways of knowing in both the form and content of her poetry point to ways in which early Afro-British American writers struggle for self-definition and determination in the literal and figurative landscapes of the world they inhabit, rather than the worlds that attempt to capture them.

Wheatley's creation of such a setting through her arrangement of color and light to emphasize physical beauty and fertility echoes the biblical renderings of Eve and Hagar. Like Wheatley's biblical foremothers, the mythical women she captures in "Niobe" express a similar lament at the suffering as well as their pride in God's gift, their progeny. As dangerously heretical as Wheatley's analogy between perceived "pagan" goddesses and the mother of the Lord, Jesus Christ, seems, her use of "Niobe" to expose the horrific consequences of an ethnic other, nearly her mirror image, as it applies to social conditions, is a far more dangerous proposition. Thus, images such as Niobe must be far more cautiously presented, as they might dangerously threaten to empower, if only metaphysically and spiritually, African women, and indict white Christian patriarchal and matriarchal power. Thus, "Niobe" becomes a bridge through which the devoutly Christian poet can simultaneously invoke and recuperate the fallen and bruised African woman. Unlike her white and black literary descendants, with the exception of the nineteenth-century author Pauline Hopkins who wrote about Hagar, Wheatley projects the black woman's desire for freedom, respect, and power onto a racially ambiguous figure—Niobe, the Phrygian queen. In so doing, she captures "Niobe" as a vessel through which she can regain a legacy of empowerment. Wheatley—through "Niobe"—traces a reconnected line of descendants through Eve and Hagar to the venerated Mary. The movement from illegitimate outcast to authorized and sanctioned citizen is enabled by means of a symbolic passing though multivalent gendered states.

What I am suggesting here is what is unique about Wheatley's subtle rendering of the Hagar myth is the way in which she uses the neoclassical and secular to get at this idea of the "fallen" and certainly outcast and exiled woman. Thus, the pious Christian slave–poet figures Niobe as representative of both African and European womanhood in order to render scathing critiques of race, class, and gender. In particular, she signifies upon the divisiveness that separates actual white and black women in America—through the figures of Latona and Niobe.

Latona and Niobe signify both black and white women who are similarly oppressed on the basis of gender and whose children are similarly
vulnerable. Wheatley underscores such risks of superficial pride and
assumed superiority based on relative power, in her depiction of the
consequences that arise in the parallel lives of mythological goddesses.
Latona, as a representative of the history of exile, in her story that
precedes the Niobe myth, of the homeless, landless mother wandering
in the wilderness without water or food, while the wicked and pride-
ful "Niobe" wallows sinfully in her abundant fertility, echoes the Virgin
Mary, who wanders looking for a place to give birth to her son Jesus.
Further, early black writers like Wheatley—using popular scriptural
allusions and Revolutionary language—reverse the gender symbology of
the "fall" of mankind. However, between Eve and Mary there remains
Hagar to be recovered and it is in the neoclassical myth that Wheatley recovers through repetition the exiled mother who is parched and
ejected perhaps from humanity, but not from God.

Wheatley's revelatory arrangement and paradoxical juxtaposition
of the "distress" experienced through the dark and barren life of a
mother and child alongside Niobe's celebration of such brightness highlights the "fall from grace" which results in the spiritual devolution of
the position of motherhood. Certainly, the differently cast versions of
banishment which are equally oppressive to Eve, Hagar, and Mary are
worth considering. Eve, not unlike the enslaved African woman, bears
the responsibility, through childbirth, of the enslavement and "fall" of
her posterity. The legal mandate that the child shall follow the condition of the mother cannot only be seen to be useful in a socioeconomic
and political structure of a society that depends upon the institution
of slavery for its prosperity and growth, but such a mandate can also
be seen to advance the biblical *Patriarchal Narratives* which promulgate
the edification of the Christian God's Kingdom through the legacy of
the patriarchs, such as Abraham. Hagar's perceived helplessness and
oppressed situation as a slave who was at the mercy of a mistress and a
master, and who is punished for what little bit of "haughtiness" or pride
she is bold enough to demonstrate in her ability to procreate, are linked
(through "Niobe") to Eve's own sins of pride.

Cain, the son of Eve—the woman who was the instigator of the
action which leads to the banishment of mankind from the Garden of
Eden—who kills his brother Abel, is linked to the history of enslaved
Africans.[24] Enslaved Africans, who like Cain are "tillers of the ground,"
"fugitives and vagabonds," are said to bear the mark of Cain, manifested

in their "blackness" which is a sign of their sin and one of several significant biblical justifications for their enslavement—in perpetuity. Similarly,
Ishmael, the "son of the bondwoman" Hagar, the "wild man; [whose]
hand [would] be against every man; and every man's hand against him"
(Genesis 16:12–13), had also been represented as the historical marker
of illegitimacy, and therefore questionable inheritance, at the same time
that he is the "lad" out of whom God "made a nation" because "he was
[Abraham's] seed" (Genesis 21:13) and because God responded to the
cries of Hagar. Even the most revered of all, Mary, the mother of Jesus,
not only experiences homelessness during her most crucial hours, but
she also risks, if only fleetingly, societal rebuke for what is initially perceived as a sin of sexual indiscretion. "Espoused to Joseph" meaning not
yet married, she is "with child." And, despite the fact that her pregnancy
occurs "before they came together" (Matthew 1:18) or perhaps because
of this circumstance, Joseph doubts her chastity. "Being a just man, and
not willing to make her a publick example, was minded to put her away
privily" (Matthew 1:19). Mary experiences additional suffering as a new
mother, as she, her husband, and her child must "flee into Egypt" to save
her young child's life. As in the narratives of Hagar and Eve, the Lord
intervenes and fulfills promises and covenants made to the patriarchs.[25]

Once again these images of motherhood (and parallel barrenness)
ring strikingly familiar for an eighteenth-century woman well aware of
both the significance and dangers of childbirth. Though of course at
the time Wheatley wrote "Niobe," she was not yet a mother or a wife, but
a young girl, her elegies to women and children are testimony to her
consciousness of this type of woman's suffering. Later in life she would
lose one child in infancy and die in childbirth with another. Alongside
Wheatley's linking of the enslaved eighteenth-century African within a
Hagarian circle of spiritual and physical "distress" associated with motherhood is the young poet's celebration of God's divine intervention as
significantly signaled in the following passage:

What! shall a Titanness be deified,
To whom the spacious earth a couch denied?
Nor heaven, nor earth, nor sea received your queen,
Til pitying Delos took the wand'rer in.
Round me what a large progeny is spread?
No frowns of fortune has my soul to dread.
What if indignant she decrease my train?
More than Latona's number will remain. (ll.75–82)

In this passage Niobe's indictment and harsh mockery of Latona must be reckoned with and balanced against Wheatley's equally revelatory pointing to the self-righteousness with which Latona orders and receives the pledge of her two children, Apollo and Phoebe, "to punish pride, and scourge the rebel mind" (1.104). Latona aims to murder all of Niobe's children and she intends to use her children as the instruments of murder. Thus, both women become implicated in the horrific slaughter. Equally important to look at is the way Wheatley's imagery remains focused on parental anguish or "distress." Niobe's mythical children, like Eve's and Hagar's, occupy unstable positions on earth—despite God's favor in heaven.

Such is echoed in the lives of the sacred mothers of Christianity and Islam respectively, Sarai[26] and Hagar. It is interesting to note that in the biblical narrative of Hagar and Sarai both women have been at some level, at one time or another, "sacrificed" for Abraham. First, in Genesis 12, Abram asks Sarai to pose as his sister so that the Egyptian kings will not kill him—a situation that, as biblical scholars have argued, puts Sarai in a precarious position. She is taken to be a single woman and brought into the harem of the Egyptian king. Before God's intervention, Sarai, not unlike Hagar, becomes bondservant or "slave" to the dominant male authority. Notably, the exception is that Hagar (as scholars have pointed out) endures a further level of oppression and subjection as bondservant to the woman Sarai. This increased level of violence enacted upon one woman by another is brought forth in "Niobe." As I noted earlier, Niobe's reminder to the other Theban women of the unfortunate circumstances under which Latona gave birth to her twins draws attention to their class differences.

In the Ovidian version of Latona's displacement, to which Niobe refers, the relationship between slavery, women's oppression, and religion is more vividly punctuated. "Stirred by / the later [Niobe's fate], they tell / . . . [of one] whom the queen of heaven once shut / out from all the world / . . . [who] / brought forth her [divine] twin babes / . . . weary / of her long struggle, / [and] faint by reason of /sun's heat and parched with thirst; / [her] hungry children had drained her breast dry of / milk" (Ovid, vi. ll.315–43). This history of a mother with breasts milked dry, parched with heat who is denied even a cool drink of water, a mother who is denied even a place to rest her tired body, a mother who is cursed and abused, echoes the historical oppression and alienation of both the African slave mother and the economically and socially oppressed white woman.

In Niobe's voice one can also hear the voices of Wheatley's African ancestors and African American descendants. Consequently, when Wheatley reaches outside of the mythological realm of neoclassical Ovidian myth, the political rhetoric of the Revolution, and the sacred writings of the Word, she reaches inside to unlock her own pain and distress. In this revelation Wheatley highlights the presence of that which appears invisible—an awareness of the absence of the African child's father and mother as equally heart-wrenching.

Wheatley was not unaware that while white Revolutionary fathers were highly and heroically visible, white and black mothers and daughters and black fathers and sons were rendered invisible. In the same way that Wheatley unearths women's historical oppression through her reference to Latona's history, the young African woman Christian poet's repetition of the *distress* of the "fallen woman—Eve," the "outcast Egyptian bondswoman—Hagar," and "the Virgin Birth of the Christian Savior Jesus, through Mary"—she indirectly signifies on the displacement of African fathers with one Western and Christian Father, who is problematically constructed as a god in support of a white patriarchal structure, which sanctions those fathers who embrace some sons and deny others, even as he sacrifices his own son, Jesus Christ, for all of Ishmael and Isaac's sons and Eve, Hagar, and Mary's daughters. Wheatley re-members African and American subjectivity in terms that redefine and celebrate a more "authentic" women's Afro-Christian spiritual self. In so doing, she poses critical questions that remain to be answered as we explore the complex relationship between religion, slavery, gender, and race.[27]

THREE

Kaleidoscopic Re-memory
in Equiano's *Interesting Narrative*

Shifting the Lens to Replace the Landscapes

Whether the love of one's country be real or imaginary, or a lesson of reason, or an instinct of nature, I still look back with pleasure on the first scenes of my life, though that life has been for the most part mingled with sorrow.

—Olaudah Equiano, *The Interesting Narrative*

Notable black American travelers, from poet Phyllis [*sic*] Wheatley onwards, went to Europe and had their perceptions of America and racial domination shifted as a result of their experiences there. This had important consequences for their understanding of racial identities.

—Paul Gilroy, *The Black Atlantic*

The first epigraph above reminds us of the paradoxes with which Equiano grapples in his attempt both to remember and recover his African Igbo identity as he simultaneously constructs an Afro-British American identity—mourning/mooring both cultural identities, neither of which can be realistically or wholly adaptive to the worlds which he inhabits. Equiano remains faithfully an African Igbo and an Afro-British American. Consequently, any exploration of the African lenses through which his narrative can be read must consider the extent to which—whether Equiano is found to be an Igbo by birth or by choice, for whatever reasons—his text can be said to be representative of an Afro-British American or African-descended identity searching for its African origins, real or imagined.[1]

Fortunately, given the scholarly focus in the last twenty years of Africana literary and cultural studies on the impact of foundational African structures as paradigmatic strategies, scholars now have some of the tools necessary to interrogate early black texts such as Equiano's within African frameworks and contexts.[2] Thus, the *Interesting Narrative* replaces insidious exotic myths with scrupulous indigenous particulars, thereby reckoning with the history of unpropitious sophisms about African people.[3] Specifically, Equiano's use of his life story to both reclaim an "authentic" Igbo heritage and recount a narrative of "progress" in the New World punctuates the dilemma of eighteenth-century aesthetics of blackness and Africanness in which black identity and its narration are embroiled. In so doing, Equiano's narrative defines an eighteenth-century black aesthetic that is both submerged in and emerges from the "dilemma of a ghost."

Such an aesthetic demands a reconsideration of how—rather than whether—fractured histories can be mended. First, one must confront the quandary of a limited worldview that proposes only one "Western" or African way of being and knowing. Such myopic cultural visions typically result in African structures of knowledge being overlooked or devalued and non-African cultures being given precedence. My interpretation of early African American literature demands attention to coeval African and Western cultures and histories from which such literature is constructed. Second, and conversely, one must engage theoretical impasses which assume a whole or "authentic" Africa as grounds upon which to reverse or reimagine the earliest Afro-British American literature within a context of what is being mourned/moored. Challenging the implications of unproblematized and overstated claims of Africanisms and catastrophism, one must necessarily interrogate the misplacement and displacement of African people and cultures. Certainly, Africa as a term must continually be (re)defined and reflected on in diverse critical and political terms. Further, such analysis requires an interrogation of "Western civilization," which has been aptly described by Edward Said as "ideological fiction."[4]

Abiola Irele's reasoning, although in regard to contemporary African discourse, is particularly relevant here.

> If nationalism in Africa and the Third World aspires in each domain of its expression toward a reintegration of the communal past within the collective awareness, it has perforce to acknowledge an epochal break with the past provoked by the colonial, Western incursion. The historical consciousness implicit in nationalism thus involves in this case an acute sense of discontinuities in the history that the colonized themselves have undertaken to refashion. (*The African Imagination,* 75)

In fact, such texts locate subjects that confirm black existence—real and imagined. They make possible constructive and critical irruptions at the very core of perceived knowledge about Africa. It is for this reason that an integrative approach to reading eighteenth-century Afro-British American identity demands fully embracing rather than suspending the dilemma of conjointly employing European, American, African American, and African ontologies and epistemologies.

It is critical, of course, to understand that such mended histories always bear scars or incisions that not only provide paths for reentry and recovery, but also, importantly, locate the site of initial rupture. In this way, an invocation of ancestors can function as a form of mediation for dissonant black and African identities. Eighteenth-century Afro-British American texts like Equiano underscore recurrent African and Western themes that remain pivotal to literature. As a displaced African in the New World, Equiano judiciously bears witness to this European knowledge and invention of Africa and dares to reimagine himself—Gustavus Vassa—as Olaudah Equiano, the African.

This chapter's second epigraph reminds us that for "travelers" such as Phillis Wheatley and Olaudah Equiano, the experience of Senegambia and Benin (Africa) preceded the experience of England (Europe). Significantly, these displaced Africans and their texts managed to survive by reconnecting with and rearticulating their fragmented African ontologies and epistemologies alongside Western ways of knowing. Just as Wheatley heroically appropriates African lineage and American identity in her revisioning of the neoclassical "Niobe" myth, Olaudah Equiano boldly asserts his right to reconnection and re-memory with his native Igboland through his skillful manipulation of Enlightenment and nationalistic discourses.

Equiano's move is equally heroic, as he signifies upon the historical efficacy of imagined, but nonetheless real, national and natural loyalties. Highlighting the indeterminacy of national and natural origins—through his reference to "real or imaginary"—the author acknowledges both his "intermingling" of fact with fiction, and his textual privileging of African vistas alongside Western ones. If, as biographer James Walvin suggests, "Equiano's autobiography was written as a contribution not merely to the rising tide of British abolitionism, but as a story which spoke for millions of other African slaves who had no voice" (*An African's Life*, xv), then *The Interesting Narrative* is multifunctional in its representation of a life in progress, not a static representation of a former state of slavery or the penultimate moment of freedom.

Consider, for example, Equiano's conversions from African noble-
man to enslaved African, from English subject to Christian missionary,
from antislavery writer and abolitionist to African, American, and Afro-
British American ancestor. Representative of the extent to which early
African, British, and American landscapes engage one another in the
cultural and geographic registering of the Black Atlantic journey from
Africa to America to Afro-British America, the narrative's depiction of
continually floating and hybridized identities permits an exploration
of the inter- and intratextual layers of dialogue used by eighteenth-
century black Americans. Highlighting the circular journey from the
African homeland to the African Diaspora, *The Interesting Narrative* participates in what Gilroy calls a "redemptive return to an African homeland" through Equiano's literal and imaginary "motion across the spaces
between Europe, America, Africa, and the Caribbean" (*The Black Atlantic*, 4). For example, at the same time that Equiano reflects introspectively upon "the first scenes of [his own] life," he also projects "the
manners and customs of a people among whom [he] first drew breath"
(*Interesting Narrative*, 43) and disrupts dominant visions of "almost every
event" in between (236).

Neither willing nor able to sacrifice one way of being or part of
himself for another, Equiano builds upon familiar cultural resonances
present within his physical world while he simultaneously recreates and
constructs the distant, indistinct, unfamiliar, or unreachable spaces
within his African and Western worlds. Central to this act of simultaneous recognition and imagination is the invocation of ancestors as a
means of reconciling the seemingly irreconcilable selves that inhabit
interconnected literal and figurative worlds. In Houston Baker's terms,
"[T]he African who successfully negotiates his way through the dread
exchange of bondage to the type of expressive posture characteriz[ed]
in *The Life*'s conclusion is surely a man who has repossessed himself and,
thus achieved the ability to reunite a severed African humanity" (38).

Although Baker locates African recovery squarely within economic
exchange rather than identity interchange, the discursive fields of commerce and cultures remain, nevertheless, interrelated. Rather than a
psychoanalytic misrecognition that occurs when one mistakenly reads
the reflection in the mirror as somehow more "real" than the (sometimes unrepresentable) self, Equiano recognizes the way in which master
texts, and the master's texts, have misread his multiple selves. Through
an act of doubled reading and self-speaking in his narrative—through
a thematic placement and strategic engagement of his multiple and

hybrid identities—he corrects those misinformed readings. Significantly, his corrections—or narrative interventions—are heavily inflected with cultural resonances and fragments that suggest the presence of African worldviews at work in his consciousness. And, more importantly, these fragments demonstrate the interchange and exchanges between African and Western ways of knowing and expressing the self. Adapting the psychical material present in the worldview he inhabits—rather than being inhabited by its worldviews—Equiano imagines or recreates links between the African and Afro-Western in ways that reaffirm a continuum of active cultural consciousness which informed African agency and autonomy.

Hence, in contrast to existing and pervasive myths of uncivilized and heathen Africanness, Equiano constructs an epistemology of eighteenth-century otherness in *The Interesting Narrative* that allows him to speak from within and outside the margins while taking up the multiplicity of discourses necessary to improve political, spiritual, and economic conditions for his African and Western brethren. Importantly, *The Interesting Narrative,* which is simultaneously spiritual autobiography, slave narrative, and protest narrative, challenges the enormity of slavery in its most oppressive, virulent, and various forms. Holding up a looking glass to the divisiveness and greed underlying both African and New World slavery as well as the Christian hypocrisy, incorrigible brutality, and the moral and physical abuses based on color and gender prejudices underlying New World slavery, the author spoke both for and from the perspective of other('s) voices.

In his article "Disguised Voice in the *Interesting Narrative of Olaudah Equiano, or Gustavus, The African,*" Wilfred Samuels asserts the cultural and literary significance of Equiano's "creation of a self whose muted voice veils covert intentions" (65), while simultaneously refashioning himself into the "epitom[e] of the African man [heroic and ideal]" (67). Consequently, Equiano's multiple visions and vistas have everything to do with "his efforts to build subjectivity in a world of reification. Equiano reclaims his voice by masking and disguising it" (69). Alongside the societal mirror, Equiano offers a looking-glass image of a self remade, a self that not only comprehends and reflects a critical awareness of oppression and its debilitating effects upon the human body and soul but also seeks simultaneously to find ways to live, adjust to, and shape changes in a society that assigns little or no value to his existence.

Demonstrating the transformative potential of traversing intra- and intercultural landscapes while simultaneously revisioning historical, cultural, geographic, and political boundaries, *The Interesting Narrative* highlights the significance of diverse views which, like a kaleidoscope, utilize shards to "produce changing reflected patterns when shaken" (*OED*, 483). Equiano's kaleidoscopic narrative vision manipulates varying remnants of shards, mirrors, and lenses to refocus concentrated or narrow readings of African life patterns. In so doing, such manipulations suggest the wide scope of Equiano's interpretive lenses. Further, his multiple floating and hybridized identities not only make it possible for him to narrate and interpret the life of an African in the New World from African, European, and American trajectories. They also illustrate the author's ability to integrate Western and African ways of knowing in a quest for self-discovery and re-creation that does not disengage him from his indigenously derived African culture.[5]

As Angelo Costanzo notes, "unlike most of the later autobiographers, the eighteenth-century [black] narrators" had a closer connection to Africa, which revealed a particularly "African view of spiritual life." Their works often conveyed a "confident sense of themselves as individuals . . . with a belief in their ability to play commanding roles in Society's spiritual and secular affairs . . . providing portraits of men who never [lost] faith in themselves or God" (25). Illustrative of this close connection is Equiano's presentation of African landscapes that underlie his incorporation of multiple visions of African cultures alongside Western landscapes while offering his own multiple selves as a metaphor (or trope) for these landscapes. In this way, Equiano analyzes and participates in the foundational groundings of Western and African logic and philosophies of history, politics, aesthetics, race, culture, slavery, religion, and spirituality.

The Interesting Narrative unfolds the multitextured dialects of slavery and racism within the context of its implicit rhetoric of inter- and intracultural marriage. Viewed through both a concentrated, unilineal directed lens that focuses in one or two primary directions, Equiano's narrative reads and exposes the dichotomous relationships between slavery and the trajectory of the path to metaphysical and physical freedom. In the movement from freedom and slavery in Africa to slavery, freedom, and racial enslavement and oppression in the New World, Equiano complicates the superficial notions of the concept of freedom through his developing and changing kaleidoscope that imagines communities across geographical and historical landscapes of literatures and cultures throughout the African Diaspora.

Carol Fabricant's concept of "landscape as vision and place," as outlined in the introduction to her 1995 edition of *Swift's Landscape,* is particularly useful to an understanding of *The Interesting Narrative* as "an exploration of [the author's] interconnected physical, textual, and ideological 'landscapes'" (xi). In fact, the life of eighteenth-century Afro-British American author Equiano is not unlike that of his Irish-English contemporary Jonathan Swift. Like Swift's life, Equiano's might easily be characterized by his complex and multiple cultural sites which "exemplify . . . his dual position, both as a man 'determined' by history and as one '*free*' to create his own history" (xi; my emphasis). What this suggests is that the question "What is 'African' in African American literature?" emerges in Equiano's narrative through his consideration of an imagined Africa. Significantly, this invention is accomplished through three African ways of knowing that underlie Equiano's vision and his relationship to the selves and the societies he inhabits: the concept of *chi,* its related Igbo concept of duality, and the complementary discursive mode of *palava.*

In "'Chi' in Igbo Cosmology," Chinua Achebe notes that "without an understanding of chi one cannot begin to make sense of the Igbo worldview." "*Chi,*" he explains, brings together "two clearly distinct meanings of the word *chi* in Igbo. The first is often translated as god, guardian angel, personal spirit, soul, spirit double. . . . The second meaning is day, or daylight, but is most commonly used for those transitional periods between day and night or night and day" (67). In their 1989 article "The Invisible *Chi* in Equiano's *Interesting Narrative,*" Paul Edwards and Rosalind Shaw argue that the "central position given to God's providence [in Equiano's framing of *The Interesting Narrative*] had its roots in the Igbo conception of *chi* . . . sometimes described as a 'personal god' responsible for the individual's destiny" (146). Pointing to the integral relationship between *chi* and the notion of duality, Achebe explains that "in a general way we may visualize a person's *chi* as his other identity in spiritland—his spirit being complementing his terrestrial human being; for nothing can stand alone, there must always be another thing standing beside it" (67). As a result, "nothing is totally anything in Igbo thinking; everything is a question of measure and degree" (60). The concept of "Wherever Something Stands, Something Else Will Stand Beside It" supports this resistance to totalizing structures or absolutes articulated in *chi,* as well as the concomitant and fruitful *palava* it enables. As I noted earlier, the concept of *palava* refers to a productive mode of discourse that involves troubling or quarreling a problem or issue while working toward a viable consensus. Thus, this form of argumentation not only provides a structure for understanding the notion of duality, but is also fundamental to a more fully and more culturally contextualized rendering of Equiano's *Interesting Narrative,* which enables the reader to imagine the achievement of meaningful dialogue that always leads back to Africa.

This chapter argues that, faced with the dilemma of self-naming and unnaming for personal and political reasons, Equiano performs three key narrative actions through a reconceptualization of place, memory, and insistence. First, he returns Africa to its proper place. Second, he attempts to recollect and reorder those fragments of Africa that have been disconnected. Third, and finally, he maintains repeated quests toward a more valid culturally based self-identification through his refusal to yield to definitions of the self imposed by others outside and inside of his cultural spaces. There are several compelling dilemmas of the narrative that invite a recuperation and revisiting of the African origins of Equiano's Western selves: naming, travel, religion, and literacy.

A brief analysis of a few key passages highlights Equiano's somewhat complex use of naming as a vehicle for revivifying and recovering African identity. First, in a passage that describes Igbo traditions of circumcision and naming, seemingly as a mechanism through which Jewish-Igbo comparative culture can be endorsed, Equiano signifies on his relative identity. Specifically, beyond a very important and conventional element in the genre of slave narration and spiritual autobiography—that of parallel identification of Africans with Old Testament Israelites—Equiano's thoughtful deliberation on Igbo naming provides the reader with very specific information about offerings and ceremonies that accompany this ritual, with the most accurate details about the significance of his own name.

> We practiced circumcision like the Jews, and made offerings on that occasion in the same manner as they did. Like them also, our children were named for some event, some circumstance, or fancied foreboding at the time of their birth. I was named *Olaudah,* which, in our language, signifies vicissitude, or fortune also, one favoured, and having a loud voice and well-spoken. (41)

This passage can best be understood by considering its placement in the narrative. Strategically, it is located between several other passages that offer meaningful ruminations on the value of naming in general and the value of the person named *Olaudah* in particular. One of the earliest assertions of name "calling" occurs on the title page. There Equiano demonstrates his conviction in the ultimate power of naming with a Christian invocation to "the Lord Jehovah" who possesses supreme authority to bestow "Salvation" to those who would "call upon his name" (Carretta, title page).[6] Accordingly, Christian salvation is dependent on God's existence as well as the energy that is released through the act of naming—understood as the power of the divinity that is spoken into existence.

Although the use of a scriptural epigraph is commonplace in the literature of this period, and is especially appropriate within the context of spiritual autobiography, the verse might also be said to serve as a cross-cultural marker which anticipates the Igbo narrator's claims to a type of culturally specific preeminence enacted through the potency of African naming or *nommo*.[7] Although Equiano exploits the potential of this naming force in all its manifestations—Western and African—it is within the context of an Igbo universe that he derives his greatest authority. For it is within this African ontological framework that Equiano is able to experience God as not only actively present in his actual world, but it is also within the context of an Igbo worldview that *Olaudah* is manifested as both instrument of and integral to God's creative process—god in human form. Moreover, Equiano's ancestors function as necessary intermediaries in this spiritual and physical regeneration. For, "without the participation of the ancestors *nommo* cannot be completed, since the dead are the agents who continue to energize the living. They assure us that the discourse of life will not be chaotic, and we take this, in whatever society we live, as a permanent expression of rebirth" (Asante, 111). In Equiano's terms "those spirits, which are not transmigrated, such as our dear friends or relations, they believe always attend them and guard them from the bad spirits or their foes" (*Interesting Narrative,* 40). It is perhaps as much for "those spirits" (or ancestors) as for his European antislavery audience and his enslaved "countrymen" that Equiano retains, and thereby affirms, the full import of African naming as complementary and necessary to his quickening and regenerating African identity—beginning with his own.

Accordingly, after differentiating between the "sufferings" of a "European" and "that of most of [his] countrymen," Equiano declares, "I regard myself as a *particular favourite of Heaven,* and acknowledge the mercies of Providence in every occurrence of my life" (31). Three things become quite clear in this distinguishing between the typical lived experiences—the "lot" in life—of the European and the African. First, he does not "consider [himself] a European." Second, he fully acknowledges that he has not experienced suffering to the extent that other Africans have. Moreover, he credits his comparatively privileged position on earth to God's providence. Indeed, such "mercies" might be said to function as signs of his position of *favor* or election within Christianity. Third, he assigns an equally important place to the meaning of his African name—*Olaudah*—as that which preordains his similarly connoted status as *one favored*.

Equiano offers further evidence of privileged status when he "speak[s] from [his] own knowledge" about those circumstances under which "the greatest offerings are made. . . . [When] those children whom our wise men foretell will be fortunate are then presented to different people. I remember many used to come to see me, and I was carried about to others for that purpose" (41). More than a mere validation of African humanity in European terms, or an attempt to move to a European center from African margins, what Equiano contributes is a model of organizing and understanding African identity with dual contexts. Certainly, there is little doubt that the narrative's primary audience was a white British powerful one that was invested with the tools by which to end or ameliorate the slave trade. However, Equiano's presentation of images that privilege his African culture suggests the degree of personal awareness that framed eighteenth-century black views of identity. This is yet another perspective from which to glean knowledge of African and Afro-British identity constructions.

Noticeably, Equiano's reference to the fact that Igbo people "never polluted the name of the object of [their] adoration; on the contrary it was always mentioned with the greatest reverence" (41) suggests dual meanings. Mockingly, while a Christian Afro-British-American Equiano cites "swearing" as yet another example of the moral inferiority of "more civilized people," he also conjectures about his own position as not only *favored* by a Christian God, but also one who might be equally deserving of a kind of *reverence* "more civilized people" reserve only for God. He questions both the Christian application of charity and the European's capacity for imaginative and rational reasoning (45). Specifically, he refers to whites as "limiting the goodness of God, [by] supposing he forbore to stamp understanding on certainly his own image, because 'carved in ebony'" (45). At the level of nation or community, Equiano unnames European values, by indirectly arguing that as God's image is "carved in ebony," Igbo people—not unlike Jews—were foreordained or chosen.

Moreover, Equiano asserts both African and European ways of knowing as they inform his understanding of humankind's relationship to the divine. Within the context of European ways of knowing, he summons repeated occurrences such as those stated above to draw attention to what had by this time become a powerful tool in antislavery rhetoric—the assertion of an antislavery argument within the context of Great Awakening egalitarianism. Specifically, if the "message that all people (including according to Whitefield, slaves) had the possibility of winning salvation meant that all people were equal before God" (Reich, 219), then such heavenly equality could be extended to earthly equality.

Not content with yielding to impositions imposed by European others, Equiano insists upon extending such natural/supernatural interconnectedness outside the boundaries of Western Christian contexts. Indeed, Equiano's identification of the inextricable relationship between ethereal and corporeal worlds is even more pronounced in the Igbo concept of "chi," which, as I noted earlier, refers to "god, guardian angel, personal spirit, soul, spirit double." Igbo duality is neither epistemologically analogous to Christian egalitarianism, nor is it based in an understanding of qualitative gestures which connote "balance." Rather, "from the point of view of duality [Equiano's] narrative (written against slavery and for posterity) provides a point of agreement between Equiano and his *chi*" (Kalu, "Readers Notes," 1). Thus, *The Interesting Narrative* can be read as a textual commemoration of a world in which the *favored* Olaudah exists alongside the archangel Michael, the Jewish patriarch (and Lord Jehovah's descendant) Jacob, and the Swedish freedom fighter and liberator Gustavus. However, as the passage below suggests, *standing beside* this celebratory view of the narrative is also an understanding of Equiano's text as cultural condemnation of the very same world that not only requires, but also orders the reality and contexts with which these coexistent identities are located.

> While I was on board this ship, my captain and master named me *Gustavus Vassa.* I at that time began to understand him a little, and refused to be called so, and told him as well as I could that I would be called Jacob; but he said I should not, and still called me Gustavus: and when I refused to answer to my new name, which at first I did, it gained me many a cuff; so at length I submitted, and was obliged to bear the present name, by which I have been known ever since. (64)

Given the author's previous ambivalence regarding the earlier name changes—for certainly one would have expected him to resist the first name change—it is not unreasonable to consider the significance of the name *Jacob*.

One consideration for his puzzling nonreaction—or at the very least rather casual reference to—his earlier (Michael) name change might be explained by the conditions under which it occurs. Namely, in a passage laden with "distress" about everything from his laborious work, his lack of companionship, and his horror at encountering unfamiliar images, objects, sounds, and wonders, the changing of his name by his master seems almost trivial. Of the name transfer from Michael to Jacob, Equiano simply remarks, "In this place I was called Jacob; but on board the African Snow I was called Michael" (63). Certainly, one might also argue that the representation of relative insignificance is in reality the author's echoing of earlier Igbo/Hebrew cultural parallels.[8]

Equally important is the narrator's repeated resituation of such parallels within the context of earlier claims about the special meaning which Igbo names possess, and the ways in which such names and their meanings typically refer to an especially propitious circumstance, which in this case would be a rather ironic assertion, given there is no apparent "circumstance," "occurrence," or "happening" that justifies this rather perverse act of naming. It should not be overlooked that Equiano's reference to the degree of punishment he was willing to endure to maintain his Jacob identity—he "at length submitted"—is a strong indicator of the seriousness and gravity of the power of naming, in the mind of the African narrator to call into existence. For we know that the adult narrator writing back about his early experiences has a full knowledge and understanding of the significance of all his names (Olaudah, Michael, Jacob, and Vassa).

In fact, the care with which Equiano describes the way in which he is compelled to "bear the present name, *by which [he] has been known ever since*" (Equiano, 64; my emphasis) suggests—contrary to his assertion above—that he never fully "submitted." Further, this passage seems to suggest that Equiano continues to resist, by reordering the terms under which he will accept Vassa—as the title *Olaudah Equiano or Gustavus Vassa the African. Written by Himself* suggests. Vincent Carretta refers to the author's self-conscious use of both names as a deliberate manipulation of his "dual identity . . . [as represented by] the frontispiece [which] presents an indisputably African body in European dress" (xvii). Further, Carretta argues that "to call him consistently by either one name or the other is to oversimplify his identity" (xvii).[9] Indeed, the anti-slavery abolitionist context within which an authentic ("indisputably") African is represented as so displaced by the diabolical institution of slavery that he is robbed of even his birth name—so carefully bestowed upon by his native Igboland—is a brilliant rhetorical turn. Moreover, to assume that after decades of using the name, and after having established himself as a man of letters, of some worth and respectability in his society, through the one name, Vassa, that either an Afro-British American or Igbo person would suddenly discard such discursive power or word force is to misunderstand Vassa/Equiano in both his Western and African texts.

Undoubtedly, *Gustavus Vassa* has a different meaning for a leader of prominence in the antislavery movement—one who has published, pronounced the indignity of the enslavement of his brethren, and fought relentlessly for the amelioration and end of the slave trade; one who might be said to embody the characteristics of a freedom fighter—than it does for an enslaved and disposed African viewed as no better than an animal or inanimate object to be ordered at will and for whom the very act of naming that once represented a cherished cultural ceremonial ritual has perversely come to represent further proof of the brutish and degenerate state of mortality into which Equiano had been thrust. Carretta notes that "slaves were often given ironically inappropriate names of powerful historical figures like Caesar and Pompey to emphasize their subjugation to the masters' will" (252). Further, he suggests that "Equiano probably expected his readers to recognize the parallel between the Swedish freedom fighter and the modern leader of his people's struggle against the slave trade, as well as the irony of his initial resistance to his new name" (252). In this context, Equiano's refusal to respond to *Vassa* is symbolic of a further objection to misnaming of his true identity or character.

While it might also be argued that to use *Equiano* is "against the author's own *practice*" (Carretta, *Olaudah Equiano: The Interesing Narrative,* xvii; my emphasis), to fail to critically consider the magnitude of *Olaudah Equiano the African* outside of colonialist and antislavery discourse is to undervalue African epistemological and ontological bases from which such meanings are derived. Further, to interpret what was once a symbol of cultural perversion and as superseding or supplanting the original object of reverence, as manifested in the name *Olaudah Equiano,* is to oversimplify the power, preeminence, and, yes, the reality of African cultural identification. As with his Christian conversion, when Equiano states "now the African would be converted," he recollects this instance of naming to assert his use of *Vassa* as reinscription of his condemnation of cultural domination, and, more importantly, as reordering of the terms under which *Vassa* will be embraced or accepted, rather than that to which he will when compelled—under the threat of violence—submit. The Igbo narrator will now be called Vassa, even as he insists on the preeminence of Olaudah.

Appreciably, Equiano's voyage of self-edification and ethnic retrieval began long before the publication and writing of the first edition of his narrative in 1789. Indeed, the fabric of his literal and literary journey is fashioned from events that occurred during his passage from and through African and Western states of freedom and enslavement. For example, Equiano passes from the physical and geographical place of freedom in Essaka—one of the most remote provinces of one of the most remote kingdoms, Benin, located in one of the most remote parts of the continent of Africa "hitherto . . . unexplored by any traveler" (32)—to equally remote emotional states of enslavement as manifested by his utter desolation, grief, and despair at familial and kin separation. Seemingly imponderable, the narrator recounts with compelling precision the wraithlike repercussions of his pre–Middle Passage experience in Africa. In this particularly revealing and intimate passage, the author exposes—through deliberate indirection—the way in which shards of his African being—indeed soul—have been severed.

> But, alas! ere long . . . In a moment [the robbers] seized us both . . . without . . . time to cry out, or make resistance, they stopped our mouths, tied our hands, and ran off with us . . . overpowered by fatigue and grief . . . we were soon deprived of even the smallest comfort of weeping together. The next day . . . my sister and I were then separated, while we lay clasped in each other's arms. (47–48)

In stark contrast to Equiano's earlier description of the careful manner in which children in his village are reared and protected—his own upbringing and thwarting of an earlier kidnapping attempt as exemplum—he puts forward the preceding cataclysmic saga with swiftness. Indeed, the rapidity with which Africans are stolen away from their nations, each other, and even their own selves or identities is amplified in Equiano's tone and rhythm. With two simple yet powerful words: "But, alas!" Equiano voices his personal grief at the instant of his capture, the impending danger that will overtake him and his sister, and the ghastly fate that continues to loom over entire African nations.

Significantly, in an act of identification and authentication of his Igbo self he emphasizes, through amplification, the consequences of lost time—between the "moment [they were] seized" and the time it took to "cry out or make resistance"; the ravages of temporal time that "ere long" would not only rob them of their freedom, but also, and "soon . . . [indeed] the next day" would rob them of "one another"; and, most importantly, the recovery of historical time which remembers and replaces Igbo worldview and history. What this way of viewing time suggests is that catastrophism is not the inevitable consequence of the tragic reality of the physical, permanent, and inherited slavery of Africans in the New World. To take a case in point, Equiano insists that "*time* could not erase" the memory of his African identity, for not only had his culture been "implanted . . . with great care," but it had "made [such] an impression on [his] mind" that his "experience[s] served only to *rivet and record* " his cultural memory (46; my emphasis).

Given the narrator's quest toward meaningful dialogue that reflects Igbo consciousness and identity, a European view of *things* cannot be allowed to stand *alone*. Consequently, Equiano's integration of balance, continuity, and complementarity into a narrative of rupture and disjunction is significantly informed by the Igbo concept of duality—a dominant factor in the shifting narrative tones. Alongside travel journal entries that catalog the "manners and customs of [Equiano's] countrymen" (43) are records—accountings—of the measures taken to disrupt these African traditions and modes of living.

Apart from the trauma caused by forced removal from one's village, kingdom, nation, family, and kin, Equiano's depiction of the horrific scene of capture and initial enslavement betrays the more devastating loss—of his identity. With that comes the shattering or splintering of any recognizable means of recovery. Indeed, this monumental forfeiture is one that would oppress and possess the narrator's "real" and "represented" life.[10] Despite such mental and physical self-alienation, dispossession, and displacement, Equiano refuses to wholly surrender, even as he admittedly and necessarily assimilates into his captors' New World (*The African Imagination*, 47). As scholar Abiola Irele deduces, this "sense of loss" (47) in Equiano's narrative can be read "as a rhetorical gesture against the state of dispossession . . . which . . . attests to an abiding sense of origins and marks a gesture of self-affirmation as African subject" (48). Ultimately, in describing the physical upheaval of being bound, immobilized, and silenced, the narrator inconspicuously reminds his audience of what can neither be silenced nor bound—his memory, his intellect, and his insistent recollecting of his cultural remains. Which is as much to say, that while he effects a narrative reenactment of the physical state of bondage, he simultaneously recovers a mental state of freedom—ultimately evidenced in his ability to recall and reflect upon this experience.

Interestingly, initial devastating losses such as those of village, country, kingdom, nation, family and kin, and especially culture (African origins) are synchronously recuperated and surrendered by means of—Equiano's necessary, but arguable—European/New World literal and rhetorical assimilation. Understandably, because they "came to be produced . . . as a mode of self-validation," texts such as Equiano necessarily privileged—or gave the pretence of adhering to—"Western frame[s] of reference" in order to retain a voice with which to "express the African experience or present an African perspective on the world" (Irele, 49). However, African writers like Equiano were clearly aware of the existence of both African and Western ways of knowing and, where possible, attempted to mine and exploit both modes in an effort to (re)locate themselves. Driven by both a desire and a need to represent himself as human and worthy of the freedom attributed to his white English and American brethren, Equiano has striven in his narrative to address the need for veracity in the interpretation and portrayal of his authentic African and European worlds. By "authentic" I refer not only to the writer's actual lived experiences, which provide evidence of a truer literal existence—with the concomitant implications and repercussions—but also to the narrator's need to conceive and establish a plausible, verifiable, locatable, and culturally specific African identity.

As Elizabeth Alexander[11] argues, "[T]he American way with regard to the actual lived experience of African Americans has been to write a counter-narrative, where needed, that erased bodily information as we knew it and substituted a counter-text which has, in many bases, become a version of national memory." Put another way, "so 'black' is always a metaphor and 'black' is always real" (201). In this respect, Equiano is certainly not unlike other eighteenth-century writers who found it necessary to keep their writing in line with such established conventions of this historical period as the concept of the Noble African Savage.[12] However, for Equiano, there is far more at stake than mere convention or demonstration of one's humanity through literary prowess. As an African Englishman, his expert/insider knowledge of both cultures will always be challenged, and therefore demands a thoughtful engagement with existing and competing expressions and perceptions of whiteness and blackness. In the passage that follows, Equiano manipulates conventional "knowledge" about African and European progress toward the achievement of civilization. This interpretive strategy allows him to enter into a critically provocative analysis of the progressive stages of dispossession, indoctrination, education, and assimilation in the continually changing systems of classification within the transatlantic slave trade.

> From the time I left my own nation, I always found somebody that understood me till I came to the sea coast. The languages of different nations did not totally differ, nor were they so copious as those of the Europeans, particularly the English . . . and while . . . journeying thus through Africa . . . I [saw] brought to the house where I was . . . my dear sister. (51)

At the earliest stages of physical disengagement or displacement he places emphasis on the fact that he remained in contact and connected to others who at the very least "understood" him. Although it is clear that he is referring to linguistic understanding, it should not be overlooked that the author also wishes to call attention to the importance of shared systems of cultural knowledge by his use of the term "understood." Equiano's physical movement prior to reaching the "sea coast"—though quite a distance from the remote kingdom of Benin and even remoter province of Essaka—not only permitted him to communicate effectively with those of other "nations," but this communication between those of different African languages[13] also enabled a comparative intra- and intercultural dialogue or reflection on the nature of community, kinship, and culture, and its relationship to language.

It is certainly worth considering what the adult, fully assimilated Afro-Briton might have been trying to suggest about the complex nature of national identity, especially given his personal experiences as an enslaved and free person both inside and outside of Africa. Although "nation" has typically been used to identify those who share language, history, and geography, the term has also—especially in the eighteenth century and within the context of the transatlantic slave trade—been used to classify or categorize a specific class or kind of "human being, or race of persons" *(OED,* s.v. "Nation"). Equiano's attention to the copious nature of European languages in general and the English language in particular underscores the dual function of language as that which both constructs and deconstructs the community, nation, and individual. His pointed reference to how "readily and *copiously*" profanity or "swearing" "find[s]

[its] way into the tongues of more "civilized" people (41; my emphasis), exposes the extent to which language marks culture, and points to language as a potentially destructive means by which a nation of people tear each other down through "reproach and abuse" (41). Further, Equiano's attention to the richness of expression in the English "languages" (51) is revealed to be less than useful as it is too numerous to be understood by its people. Overabundance and excess in language, community, and nation are linked in the narrator's reference to the "*copious* perspirations" (59; my emphasis) on board the putrid, overcrowded slave ship.

What is more, Equiano's discourse on the function of language as cultural creator and mediator from an African's perspective is especially striking given that the context within which eighteenth-century preoccupations with cataloguing and classifications occur are usually the province of white men. More important, though, is the narrator's attempt to probe the limits of the consequences of his life experiences and the implications of such experiences for what Equiano had already come to realize as increasingly unrepresentable and splintered African and "Western" worldviews.[14]

Thus, the narrator corroborates the testimonies of Africa's objectified subjects and the New World's subjected objects—peoples of the African Diaspora both enslaved and free. Further, Equiano records the continued existence of black literature and highlights its deliberately persistent assignation with aesthetics that both evince and belie a "catch-22" or "no-win" situation for those who were considered enslaved nonhuman beings within the development of human landscapes of cultural, biological, and national identifications.[15]

Structurally epic, through its elaboration of themes of national significance and its presentation of significant characters who embody heroic[16] traits, and noble in its attempt to adhere to both connotative and denotative standards of valuation, the early black spiritual autobiography, slave and travel narrative, demanded fidelity of character and representative characterizations. Not surprisingly, such literature was dependent upon black writers' ability to fuse—from intrepid exploitations and recuperations of dominant illuminations—complementary and necessarily intertwined African and Western self-perceptions. At the same time such literature was expected to operate within a realm of faction[17] that could fully comprehend and respond to the paradox of multiple and competing visions of Africa. What I am suggesting by my use of this term faction is that Equiano understands the extent to which travel narration and antislavery and proslavery texts incorporated elements of fact and fiction in both their observations and subsequent reflections of eighteenth-century African cultures. In order to counter negative effects of such literature, Equiano's narrative attempted a delicate rebalancing of truthful interpretation of his personal remembrances and his recollection of others' recordings of Igbo culture. As a result, Equiano's narrative evinces a primary concern with truthful reflection, as truthfully represented "outsider" observations could not always be counted on to accurately represent African cultural knowledge. Somewhere between where human memory did not fail and written and oral accounts did not misrepresent was knowledge of Africa and its people that was situated within the realm of undeclared or tacit faction. The Igbo were very real people who were often "situated" within the context of a fictionalized black world. At the same time, fictionalized black characters were painted on to an already existing "real" African landscape. Equiano understood the delicate maneuvering it would take to balance this representational dilemma.

If the contemporary reader found it difficult to reconcile elements of fact and fiction in the metaphorical and symbolic inferences present in the works of such eighteenth-century satirists as Jonathan Swift, Alexander Pope, or even Daniel Defoe, he or she would find it nearly impossible to locate (with any measure of certainty) an acceptable level of veracity in those texts which sought to express and examine African life and from perspectives that acknowledge its complex contexts within which African people existed.[18] This is true in great part because of the tacit fiction present in travel literature of the period and the cultural fictions that emerged as a result of skewed readings of such "ethnographic" narratives that counted as "truth"—a fact of which Equiano himself was all too aware. Consequently, Equiano's colonialist discourse not only bemoans the disconnections between emblematic and literal blackness, his narrative simultaneously links the symbolic imagery of Africanness with real pictures of Africa and Africans.

Thus, in the creation of his narrative, he necessarily appropriated fictive readings in order to replace cultural and historical gaps created by fiction and reclaim a more "authentic" or truthful Igbo reality. A clear example of such a response was Equiano's description of Africa as—at once—a kingdom in which "the manners and government of a people who have little commerce with other countries are generally very simple," and one in which "the history of what passes in one family or village may serve as a specimen of a nation" (32). Equiano's unflinching signification of a continent that is both culturally, geographically, and economically vast in its diversity and richness and yet somehow knowable and readable is testament to the complex nature of identity—especially eighteenth-century black African cultural identification. Emily Dickinson's caveat "Tell all the Truth but Tell it slant—Success in Circuit lies" is worth remembering.

For these reasons—the identification of culture, history, geography, and economy with the context of collective and personal authenticity—I use the terms "replace" and "remember" to suggest the necessary thought and action processes by which particular attention is paid to restoring that which is of value and has somehow either been omitted, discarded, or otherwise misplaced. Such terms signify both the vital restoration and the measure of compensation that occupies *The Interesting Narrative*. More carefully considered, I use these terms to draw attention to the deliberateness of Equiano's narration, its persistent imagery, its recurring metaphors, and, most important, histories that repeatedly assert (even demand) that the value of African peoples be restored, even as the value of African people to restore and rewrite themselves within "foreign" contexts and "subdomestic" contexts remains questioned.

In so doing, Equiano's narrative demonstrates a constant refusal to yield to images of a distorted continent and cultural cataloguing for the purposes of maintaining and supporting slavery. What Equiano's travel narrative might suggest, then, with regard to the need to represent a particular cultural reality is a supplanting of dominant representations of Africanness or white visions and envisionings of the supposed inferior nature of blackness. For instance, he attempts to restore the former place of Igbo people—and by extension all African-descended people— by emphasizing locations, areas, functions, and roles which present more accurate pictures of their existence (inside and outside of slavery). As a result, Equiano's narrative contributes to definitions of truer, more authentic black humanity.

When one reflects on Equiano's presumably successful and nearly "seamless" cultural transformations as represented by the numerous narrative selves depicted, one comes to realize that the certainty and consistency of interactions between early black and white colonial societies provide a backdrop for African representativeness. Pre- and post–Middle Passage myths, metaphors, and personal episodes are etched into the reader's memory for the purposes of cultural recall and reestablishment of the stratum of parlance lost during enslaved Africans' literal and figurative Atlantic crossings. Nonetheless, he is clear that his intent is to "excite" empathy for his enslaved brethren and an understanding of the productive nature of the dismantling of the pernicious institution of slavery.

Equiano understands that full physical and metaphysical atonement for loss will not occur directly; moreover, he knows that a reparative narration or piecing together of his-stories will never compensate for the loss of his African reader's history. Clearly, such an attempt at cultural replacement will not be enough to convince his non-African audience to abandon the wealth and economic standing that the institution of slavery has enabled. He can only hope that his narrative will contribute to a dismantling of slavery and play a role in the reassembling of bits and shards of their (Africans') stolen legacy. What is important to understand is that Equiano's attempt to reconcile his Igboness with his Englishness stands as an eighteenth-century metaphor for global cultural reconciliation at some level. Therefore, his life stands as a model—paradigm or position—from which it is possible to envision the (New) world in which neither Africans nor their diverse traditions and ways of knowing are enslaved.

Again, such an imagining requires a simultaneous tearing apart and sewing together of the manifold cultural seams—such that a widening of the pattern will permit a more accurate rendering of African space here throughout the Black Atlantic. Equiano embraces this dilemma of brokenness by engaging in *palava*[19] with those who inherit dysfunctional relationships based on severed humanity. He converses with his own life story through a series of images that demand audience reflection and participation from multiple perspectives. The white audience must engage in metaphysical "blackness" that goes beyond putting oneself into another's shoes, or projecting one's alter ego into an "other."[20] The audience is asked both to engage in and distance itself from an African or Igbo worldview. Thus, Equiano's narration emphasizes the complications involved in fulfilling the demand of eighteenth-century travel narrative to bring the familiar home.

Importantly, his direct challenge to the institution of African enslavement is manifested not only in his skillful manipulation of the content, but also in his use of genre or form to redefine such concepts as "home" and "familiar."[21] Fundamental to Equiano's identification of the intersecting lines of representation and reality is his method of summoning forbearers for a convergence of literal and figurative worlds that matter equally. Therefore, Equiano ushers his African ancestors into the New World through repetition of yet another site of self-knowledge and naming. In the tale below he echoes his earlier insistence upon the proper

meaning and value of his personal and collective identity through his
remembering of the significance of snakes to the people of his village.

> We have serpents of different kinds, some of which are esteemed omi-
> nous when they appear in our houses, and these we never molest. . . .
> I was desired by some of our wise men to touch these, that I might
> be interested in the good omens for which I did, for they were quite
> harmless, and would tamely suffer themselves to be handled; and then
> they were put into a large open earthen pan, and set on one side of
> the highway. Some of our snakes, however, were poisonous: one of
> them crossed the road one day when I was standing on it, and passed
> between my feet, without offering to touch me, to the great surprise
> of many who saw it; and these incidents were accounted by the wise
> men, and likewise my mother and the rest of the people, as remark-
> able omens in my favor. (43)

Confronting the dilemma of a narrow understanding of African and
Western ways of knowing, the passage above allows an acknowledgment
of the "universal" symbolism[22] of the snake (often read Western European). At the same time, what might be seen as Equiano's tale of personal and communal reconciliation privileges the very culturally specific
Igbo origins. Moreover, such a view of snakes permits the *Olaudah the
African* to engage in a meaningful discourse on and revaluation of cultural and personal self-identity.

Thus, through his relating one of several encounters with snakes,
Equiano both invites and obscures any simple interpretation or meaning
in the prophetic foreshadowing that occurs in the antiphony between
the young Equiano and the Igbo wise men, as they negotiate their relative concepts "ominous" and "harmless" as represented in snake imagery.
This is a reminder that a person's *chi* has ultimate vetoing power and if
either the individual or his *chi* does not agree on his destiny, bad fortune
may occur where good fortune was assumed. Equiano said "yes" to good
fortune, but his *chi* did not agree. As Kalu argues, "[F]rom the point of
view of duality his narrative (written against slavery and for posterity)
provides a point of agreement between Equiano and his *chi*" ("Reader
Notes," 1). For although both snakes fail to do bodily harm and are, in
fact, symbols of good fortune, in the chapter that follows we learn of
Equiano's abduction into slavery. Lurking, then, in the unforeseen shad-
ows of both the "ominous" and "harmless" snakes were African, British,
and American "snakes" waiting to mishandle him. While Equiano does

not directly refer to any person as a snake, his three narrative references to snakes provide a balanced view of snakes as both indicators of good and bad fortune. Costanzo contends that Equiano "shows that evil snakes exist who are the whites—mainly the Europeans—who have entered Africa to corrupt and pollute, resulting in the fall and enslavement of the noble savage" (*Surprizing Narrative,* 56). Equiano's parable-like intervention into his narrative not only stands as a sign of the double-sided nature of men and the varying levels and types of slavery in Africa—African and Western—but also provides a prophetic foreshadowing of the life of one who is "favored" among all types of snakes.[23]

In this context, it is possible to read Equiano's acknowledgment of his life as a slave as far less dehumanizing than those of his brethren as a continuation of the promises of his African community of elders and wise men. In a praise song to those prescient wise men who "carried [him] about . . . for the purpose" of announcing his preordained fortune," Equiano reconfirms his advantaged position as one who is everywhere *favored* and *fortunate,* by unveiling his ability to both avoid bad fortune and attract good fortune. Not surprisingly, the "good *omens*" that the suggested "*touch*" confirms has been sanctioned by his *chi.* This is made evident by the fact that the "poisonous" snakes" that pass between [his] feet, without offering to *touch* him" mark incidents which signify "*remarkable omens* [in his] favor." I have italicized the above words to emphasize Equiano's signifying by means of amplification in order to explore the diverse and heightened implications of touch. For example, the first touch shows the action of the boy whose touching of two snakes portends good omens, whereas the second touch—the failure or refusal of the snake to touch the boy—forecasts a remarkable omen.

For, as the prophecy suggests, he manages to touch the hearts of good men, who like the "harmless" snakes do not mishandle him, as well as maneuver and navigate safely through the paths of those men who would abuse him. Equiano illustrates that the good and evil nature of humankind, the varying effects of slavery and the degree to which it affects the human soul, can be seen in Africa as well as in Europe. Though the "peculiar" institution of slavery in the land of the "red faced" or white men—for example in Europe, the West Indies, and America—is, by degrees, more horrific than on his native continent, Equiano does not represent a picture of Africa as a prelapsarian, Edenic, pastoral experience. As evidenced by his intense contemplation and multiple celebrations of naming, Equiano's comparisons and contrasts of his Christian and pre–Christian landscapes are not as artless as that. Rather than a simplistic morality tale of the necessary balanced nature of good and evil, the parable of the snakes—in an Igbo context—offers an opportunity for reflection on the multiple African contexts within which snake imagery can be interpreted. In fact, depending upon the use of words, tone, and form, the narrative performance can extend well beyond the boundaries of traditional African storytelling, to include griot functions such as historian and earlier praise singer. What this suggests then, is that in the telling of a narrative of his Essaka village Equiano relocates the origins of his predestined and providential self to its proper place in Africa. At the end of the day, he records African history, celebrates African spirituality (vis-à-vis) his recourse to myth or storytelling, which I will discuss briefly below, and reclaims an African identity.

When I say that Equiano celebrates African spirituality, I am referring to the Igbo view of the relationship between this spirit world and the earthly world, and one of the most important intermediaries or channels between the two realms: the ancestors. It is here that Equiano's narrative can be seen to extend the boundaries of Afro-Western signifying; rather than mere differentiated and discernable repetition—either in words or in concept—the Igbo narrator literarily invokes the presence of his ancestors through his depiction of the snake. In Igbo cosmology, snakes represent one of the paths through which ancestors enter the living corporeal world. Juxtaposing "the doctrine of eternity" with the "transmigration of souls" (40) as different but related aspects of Igbo and Christian religion, Equiano points to the uniqueness of Igbo spirituality. Alongside his rendering of an Igboland with plentiful resources, with talented, virtuous, intelligent, and pragmatic people, he offers a society that deals with the same types of "disputes" and "crimes"—such as adultery, jealousy, and internal battles—as any other society.

Indeed, the ex-slave narrator suggests there is a "strong analogy . . . in the manners and customs of [his] countrymen, and those of the Jews . . . particularly . . . in [their] pastoral state" (43). Clearly, Equiano manipulates the "widespread belief among both supporters and opponents of slavery" (Vincent Carretta qtd. in Equiano, 246) about the shared lineage of Africans and Jews to assert, among other things, the shared "pastoral" and "uncivilized" states of the origins of all societies. His positing of Africans as simultaneously "analogous" to and yet distinct from Europeans is a resituation (from an African perspective) of the ancestral history of the "polished and haughty Europeans" (45). At the same time, *The Interesting Narrative* also points to Western slavery's exacerbation of existing quarrels and its exploitation of existing systems of slavery in

Africa. We are reminded of violations and intrusions into Igbo existing culture and society, as Equiano recalls for his audience that it is during his pre–Middle Passage journey in Africa where he first experiences the oppression of Western slavery and a yearning for freedom. Equiano and his sister are physically "overpowered by fatigue and grief" at their initial capture. Later, after they are emotionally "deprived of even the smallest comfort of weeping together," Equiano "embrac[es] every opportunity to inquire the way [back] to [his] own home" (47–48). "I therefore determined to seize the first opportunity of making my escape . . . for I was quite oppressed and weighed down by grief after my mother and friends; and my love of liberty . . . [which] was strengthened by the mortifying experience of not daring to eat with the free-born children" (49). Equiano longs to be free (physically), but he longs as well for a return to a life which places him materially (and here I refer to his lack of material goods owing to his social status as slave) in his deserved position as the son of a chief or an elder.[24]

Beyond his focus on African ways of knowing, Equiano also signifies on such universal concerns as the Judeo-Christian myth of creation, pseudoscientific schemes in which human beings are hierarchically ordered, and an antislavery agenda. What is most important about this multicultural and multilevel rendering of narratives is the way in which they point almost "universally" (read cross-culturally) to the liminal relationship between humanity and inhumanity. Equiano's narrative intervention at the sites of language, naming, and interpretation of self and identity remain grounded in a philosophy that refuses to negate African presence. Africa, whether "real or imagined," remains the foresight/site from which the literal and textual Equiano emerges and that to which he persistently returns, and with the full understanding that such a resituating of self connotes neither a static nor monolithic African nor European.

Essential to replacing African people and culture within a tolerably legitimate taxonomy, *The Interesting Narrative* provides truths that counter negative descriptions of blacks in travel literature. Countering the belief that blacks are more like beasts than humans and therefore without the necessary capacity for reason and especially incapable of reflection and analysis, Equiano uses the fundamental practice of naming to demonstrate the mental prowess and intellect: he not only names himself, but he also interprets the significance of all his names (British and African). Further, he is careful to name others (objects, ships, peoples, places) and analyze their significance. His use of naming replaces and therefore renames Africans and humans as enslaved African people rather than African "slaves." Indeed, Equiano appears to be almost obsessed with naming. He catalogues the names of trees, wise men, towns, ships, geographical locations, people, places, animals, inanimate objects, and of course his own names as thoroughly as any travelogue would and more expansively than others—especially with regard to his interpretations. The effort to locate, identify, describe, and analyze through naming is significant not only because it describes foundational generic (travel narrative) concerns, but also because Equiano's persistent insistence on naming also identifies him as one capable of and authorized to name. Representing himself as one who can and will name, he invokes his position as a knowledgeable subject engaged in a form of creation and replacement.[25]

Ironically, Equiano provides cultural reeducation through ability to manipulate and achieve conventional standards which required travel narrators to name, define, and describe others through written observation and reflection.[26] Certainly, he understood that the value ascribed to viewing others, as well as the socioeconomic implications of such new "knowledge" to one's society, were both motivating factors in the popularity and dissemination of travel narratives. Indeed, it was not difficult to realize that through their ability to authenticate and interpret stories of nonwhite others white narrators had exercised their God-given authority to name those black and African others over whom they exercised dominion. As a result, these narratives contributed to a substantial body of knowledge that existed about enslaved and free blacks as subhuman others—authenticating notions of Africa as a barbaric and pagan continent. Such narrative naming was also used to confirm the childlike innocence of people whose self-governing was equally problematic. Represented as noble but hopelessly incapable savages or naturals, Africans, as evidenced by travel narration, became known as quintessentially untutored people, who if they were cast as incapable of evil, were equally incapable of understanding and controlling evil in their societies.

More important, such new knowledge contributed to the creation, implantation, and mooring of African and African-descended peoples on the continent of Africa as well as throughout Europe and the newly colonized worlds to a history of inferiority and baseness. Such "histories" at best substantiated claims made by the transatlantic slave trade proponents who claimed that the institution of slavery, rather than oppressing and debasing Africana people, actually saved or improved conditions for people who, because of the inherent "inferiority" and "baseness," actually needed such an institution. At worst, many (nominal and genuine) Christian enslavers claimed slavery as a divinely sanctioned recompense for African barbarity, and a path toward civilizing and cultivating an entire continent.

Although African slavery is no less a blight on his soul than New World slavery, we recall that years later Equiano "still looks back with pleasure on the first scenes [of his] life, though [it] has been for the most part mingled with sorrow" (46). Equally important, he remembers with care the things that were carefully implanted in him as a young boy—most prominently the significance of his Igbo name. In this respect, the parable about the ominous snakes who fail to harm him functions equally well to uphold the venerated African tradition of naming. "I was named *Olaudah,* which in our language, signifies vicissitude, or fortunate also; one favoured, and having a loud voice and well spoken" (41). As Samuels so convincingly argues, "[R]esounding in the walls of this ideological foundation [of Essaka folkways, mores, and beliefs] is the constant reinforcement of his given role provided by his name: OLAUDAH EQUIANO . . . its meaning rivets and records his unique identity" (*Making Crooked Paths Straight,* 8).

While an audience of British or American abolitionists and slaveholders could hardly miss the political significance of an imbedded antislavery narrative—implicit in his indirect reference to the barbarity of the "snakes" who daily engage in the enterprise of slavery—as well as an underlying parallel between Christian providence and Igbo *chi,* such an audience might not recognize Equiano's simultaneous signification of African-centered authority in invocation, through snake imagery, of African ancestors.

The simultaneously harmonious and cacophonous registering of Africanness and Westernness highlights significant tensions between conflicting but nonetheless cooperative worldviews. *The Interesting Narrative*'s calculated ambiguity subverts any simplified reading of the act of black signifying. The underlying textual patterns which inform Equiano's African consciousness, and which enable him to bring a community of elders and ancestors into his Afro-Western text, must be interpreted through a systematic unraveling of the multiple layers of meaning imbedded in Equiano's deliberate encoding of religious and spiritual practices from his West African Igbo culture. Encoded cultural interventions such as Equiano's snake parable are illustrative of the ways in which early black writers identified African traces and markers. Rather than revealing merely blatant Africanisms, Equiano's autobiography demonstrates the extent to which some black writers critically confront their deep sense of physical and metaphysical loss by attempting to recover or reimagine Africa through an invocation of the ancestors. If, as Malidoma Some suggests, the ancestors "represent one of the pathways between the knowledge of this world and the next" (9), and if one of the forms ancestors take in their transition from the living to the spirit world is that of a snake (Heusch, 48), then Equiano's snake parable might be meant to provide an imaginary realm through which his Igbo ancestors can enter the literal (New) world and the figurative (narrative) world. Integrating his Igbo world into an Afro-British American narrative, Equiano embodies an intertextual tradition with spiritual and natural forces that interdimensionally link African worldviews with African American literature.

Further, Equiano's integration and registration of both Western and African traditions of "snake" lore are additional significations of his own multiple and competing selves. For, we can be certain that the Western Christianized Equiano is aware of the biblically based literary allusions that his snake imagery—vis-à-vis the Genesis narrative—evokes in the imagination of his readers. *The Interesting Narrative* demonstrates Equiano's consciousness of the contradictions between his Igbo worldview, which regarded the venerated snake as a good omen, and his Afro-British (and Afro-American) worldview(s), which associated the snake with the downfall of humankind. Evidence of the origins of the serpent and its troubled relationship with mankind can be evidenced in scriptural sources. "And the serpent . . . and the great dragon was cast out, that old serpent, called the Devil, and Satan, which deceiveth the whole world: he was cast out into the earth, and his angels were cast out with him" (Revelation 12:9). "And when the dragon saw that he was cast to the earth he persecuted the woman, which brought forth the man child" (Revelation 12:13).

Consequently, there can be seen a critique of the pervasiveness of one-dimensional Western thinking which acknowledges one source of evil (or mankind's destruction) to the exclusion of other, equally pernicious sources of evil such as slavery and the oppression of women and children. Equiano's recasting of the myth of epic degeneration exposes a flawed reliance on the premise that it is original sin—rather than regenerative sin—which disrupts the perfect Edenic world and remains statically and forever the cause of mankind's depravity and evil. Ironically, because Equiano does not fail to mention that these snakes "crept into . . . [his] *mother's* night-house, where I [he] *always* lay with her" (43; my emphasis), he indirectly posits a reversal of this static disruption of the Edenic world through his resituation and revisioning of symbolic enmity between the woman and the snake. Not unlike Wheatley's repositioning of African motherhood in "Niobe" through her allusion to the biblical Hagar, Eve, and Mary, Equiano, too, utilizes such imagery to effect an Africanized Christian aesthetic based in radically exegetical re-memory which reorders and exposes the dilemma of race and gender within the context of North American slavery. However, whereas Equiano does so through direct reference to indigenously derived African knowledge (in which he is well versed), Wheatley (who has limited knowledge of Africa) depends upon the neoclassical traditions to build an imaginary bridge to Africa. Thus, Equiano moves reciprocally from African to European myths and back. Notably, the Fall of Man is reversed as the "man" child sleeps and both he and the woman (mother) emerge victoriously from their encounter—with the man-child, woman, and snake intact. Viewed through the lens of *palava* and Igbo duality, power is distributed equally among the three of them, as the snake, the woman, and the boy all sleep peacefully.

Equiano's revisioning and revisiting of dominant political and spiritual discourses through subdominant lenses is illustrative of his complication and deployment of African-centered gendered critiques of racial oppression. Hence, what we see in this male author's sanctioning of an African woman's centrality—through an insertion of his mother into the narrative's critique of the Western myth of origins—is the emergence of an African woman's voice as a significant antislavery tool. Equiano's narrative thus reveals the interrelated struggles of African men, women, and children—as it is the human "snakes" that enslave and oppress all African people (respective of gender) who disrupt the sense of the "beautiful" and "sublime" that the delicate balance of the Edenic world and its representative humanity is meant to symbolize. Indeed, the tranquility of Equiano's mother's "night house" sharply contrasts the chaotic brutality of the bed he later shares with his master and sister in slavery. He understands that his mother's struggle will be with the unrecoverable loss of two of her beloved children, Equiano and his sister, to a race-based—rather than gender-based—system of domination and oppression. In this context he painfully acknowledges the African mother's deep sense of loss that comes as a result of the oppressive structures of domination that are fueled by the need for black bodies—male and female—and the attendant removal or disfiguring of black humanity upon which the institution of slavery feeds.

Equiano's lamentation—during what might be called a second Middle Passage to slavery in the West Indies—vividly captures the freedom refrain Wheatley invokes: "I called upon God's thunder, and his avenging power, to direct the stroke of death to me, rather than permit me to become a slave, and to be sold from lord to lord" (Equiano, 98). Notably, Equiano reenacts a *palava* between God, revenge, and death over the disposition of an African. To be sure, biblical references enter into the dialogue. Images of the People of Israel and Egyptian slavery as well as Job, Jonah, Joseph, and other biblical figures are consciously invoked by the narrator.[27] However, as Equiano directs our attention to his "former slavery" (98), we are invited into a dialogue about the very nature of slavery itself. Certainly, an eighteenth-century audience would have recognized this antislavery subtext.

However, what Equiano offers here is more than a critique of the trade—a focus on the evils of the trade as an institution rather than slavery itself—as was the eighteenth-century narrative convention.[28] Rather, his attention to the excess of emotions, the "paroxysm of [Equiano's] grief" (98), directs us toward his mental state. And in so doing, we are thus able to see how his consideration of slavery disrupts his African ways of knowing and processing such seemingly commonplace issues as death, revenge, and God. Equally revealing is the way in which multiple images of duality that can be seen at work in Equiano's *Interesting Narrative* highlight underlying African (and especially Igbo) structures of identification. Notably, Equiano's hyperconsciousness of the complex relationship between identity formation and simultaneous naming[29] (in Western and African contexts) suggests an ontological engagement with the duality discourse. In particular, his narrative exposes through dual framings the paradoxical relationship between self and identity in eighteenth-century Afro-British America: harmful and harmless snakes,[30] united and separated and sister and brother, honorable Englishman and noble savage African, literally enslaved and nominal free, successful merchant and unsuccessful merchandise. Clearly, such dilemmas constitute aesthetic elements to be theorized in terms of African ways of knowing. For Equiano, the construction of an African self does not, as many scholars have suggested, necessitate an undoing of his Western selves. Indeed, what *palava* permits is a more critical dialogue about the African self he extends through his narrative.

Beyond Equiano's problematization of dominant constructions of gender, consider *The Interesting Narrative*'s complication of the notion of intertextuality, as both an internal and external structure, in his strategic placement of the *Talking Book* sequence.

> I had often seen my master and Dick employed in reading; and I had
> a great deal of curiosity to talk to the books, as I thought they did; and
> so to learn how all things had a beginning: for that purpose I have
> often taken up a book, and have talked to it, and then put it to my
> ears, when alone, in hopes it would answer me; and I have been very
> much concerned when I found here it remained silent. (68)

Henry Louis Gates has suggested that in signifying, Equiano's shifting
tenses "represent the very movement . . . from African to Anglo-African,
from slave to potential freedman, from an absence to a presence, and
indeed from an object to a subject" (*Signifying Monkey,* 157). However,
an examination of the shifting tenses does not adequately address the
African slave narrator's consciousness of his preexisting condition of
humanity. Recall that he has already been named and sanctioned by his
Igbo ancestors. Wilfred Samuels points dramatically to the source and
structure of this African authority, asserting that:

> Prior to his deracination from his African motherland, Equiano's total
> orientation is centered around his recognizing and comprehending
> the forest of salient primordial signs, symbols, belief, and practices
> of his Essakan culture and community that are in place to ensure
> both their continuation and his legacy and role as rightful heir and
> participant . . . theoretically, his age group provides an ideological
> field—a vehicle of being-in-the-world for him. (*Making Crooked Paths
> Straight,* 7)

Hence, Equiano's engagement with dominant discourses is far more
complicated than a naive assumption of white literacy as a means of
self-identification. Equiano "often takes up a book" to read his master's
subjectivity rather than his own, and, in being better able to understand
the "beginning" of his master's "things," he might be able to settle contradictions between his own understanding of Christianity and slavery
in the context of European ways of knowing. *The Interesting Narrative*
clearly outlines Equiano's path to Christian conversion and sanctifica-
tion. His link from nature to God comes not in the automatic "delight"
(a physical manifestation of the sensation of the Holy Spirit) as it does
for other Great Awakening converts. Rather, it is the master's tongue,
the act of interpreting through speech the written word that finally converts him. One hundred and twenty-three pages later we find that the
"Ethiopian [is now] willing to be saved by Jesus Christ" (190). Equiano's
deep understanding of Christian doctrine surpasses the emotionalism of

the masses indoctrinated with evangelical enthusiasm. Equiano understands the deeper and scripturally based meaning of the foundation of Christian salvation, the command that "faith comes by *hearing*" (Romans 10:17; my emphasis).

Clearly, then, what *palava* enables is an understanding that it is not merely Equiano's desire to make his *book talk,* and thereby to invoke an oral presence within a literary text through his use of signifying. Rather, while the symbolic inscribing of African humanity in this way is significant, of equal importance is the way in which his narrative underscores from an Igbo perspective the coexisting books—oral and written, *one book standing beside another*—imbedded within and without African, British, and Afro-British American covers. These talking, testifying, signifying books are fragments but nonetheless critical building blocks of an eighteenth-century black aesthetic that reconstitutes the parameters of what we have come to term the *Black Aesthetic.* These *books* speak to coexisting oppression and oppressors within colonial Afro-British America. Such aesthetic fragments invite careful inquiry about the nature of nation, slavery, freedom, and identity in a colonial British context, and open conversation with new speakers for and about the Afro-British American experience, even as the aesthetic shards refuse to lose Africa along the way. As a result, such *palava* makes possible an unbinding of the parameters of symbolic interpretive analysis and perceptions of eighteenth-century black texts. Thus, the structure of *palava* both dislocates linguistic disparity and denaturalizes colonial American historicity.[31]

Further driven by a foundational and African-derived ontology that privileges duality and indeterminacy but values tradition and ritual, Equiano is continually amazed by the incongruous nature of Western cultures. While he seems "pleased" that "these white people did not sell one another, as [his countrymen] did" (68), Equiano questions their failure to sacrifice or make offerings, and their practice of eating with unwashed hands. Here, as throughout his narrative, Equiano expresses his astonishment at what he perceives as white women's lack of modesty in comparison to Igbo women, and initially finds the "slenderness of [white] women" "not to his liking" (68). What we find in these examples above is that, based on what his young white companion (and slaveholder only a few years older than Equiano) Dick tells him, Equiano appears pleased by what he knows of the Christian God. On the one hand, his critique of white people's ways is based on African spiritual traditions, while, on the other, his "cleanliness based" critique of morality (women, etc.) is also grounded in his fusion of the scriptures and Christian doctrine with his African ways of knowing.

The Bible speaks extensively of the white man's slavery of his people and others. This is why he includes the "Talking Book" in this section. However, the book is not only silent to him, but Equiano is remarkably silent on the issues in the *Book* (or the *Bible*) that show the history of the white man as problematic or at least contradictory to the will of the white man's God.

As can be seen, early black writers like Equiano expose contradictions imbedded within conflicting worldviews that constitute the ontology and epistemology of Judeo-Christian texts and contexts. In the act of transposing the Western "ur-text" into the register of the African "ur-trope," Equiano is clear in his demonstration that he has the ability to reason—the demonstration of his ability to read or write. According to Gates, "the trope of the Talking Book . . . first occurred in a 1770 slave narrative and then [was] revised in other slave narratives published in 1785, 1787, 1789, and 1815. . . . Making the white written text speak with a black voice is the initial mode of inscription of the metaphor of the double voiced" (130–31). But if the "ur-trope" establishes black intertextuality, black writers' concerns with authenticity, and the literal and literary inscription of blacks into "being," the trope of the Talking Book also early established black writers' challenges to Enlightenment and humane letters. The seeming failure of the Bible to "echo" the voice of the black man (Gates, 136) is contradicted by Equiano's exposure of the white act of misreading blackness. Countering white people's literal reading of black (African) people as a sign of insufferable subhumanity, the Bible is used by Equiano to support claims of humanity for all people. As such, the scriptural associations of figurative *blackness* and *whiteness* signify upon spiritual rather than physical characteristics, as they were properly and originally intended.[32] Hence, Equiano's multiple and multidimensional ways of knowing "seeing" culture and people as texts of discovery and recovery "reads" back in the written word what was seemingly absent—black humanity.

Equiano dismantles and deconstructs the Bible as "ur-trope" of white literacy by exposing the "life" or the "seen," the present and even the spoken as more effective, vital, dynamic, viable, and abounding than the Bible itself. Equiano understands that the book can only narrate or relate life experiences—it is humanity which interprets and in doing so gives meaning (and life) to the Book. Thus, in many ways, his juxtaposition of and engagement with the "ur-trope" can be seen as a critique of Western society. The life of the Anglo "ur-text" informs Equiano's intratextual and multipurpose reading as he unravels the threads of the Anglo "ur-text," the Bible, by signifying on the behavior of the whites.

Equiano writes back, resituating the story of his African and Afro-British American spiritual and cultural conversion by means of a kaleidoscopic memory that is informed by Afro-Western textures which authorize him to depict synchronous themes of Western, African, and Afro-Western life.

Although Gates suggests that Equiano presents the trope of the Talking Book "in a self-contained paragraph, which does not refer directly either to the paragraph that precedes it or to the one that follows" (155), I would argue that Equiano's juxtaposition of seemingly commonplace objects in a slave's life—a watch, a portrait, and a muzzled slave woman—is strategic. More important, Equiano registers yet another reading of this trope within an Igbo concept of duality—*Where one Talking Book stands another stands beside It.* Standing beside the soon to be converted Christian Equiano's yearning for a book (the Bible) that talks is the recently enslaved African's equally gripping desire for "companions" with which "to speak," his yearning to continue "conversing with [his] countrymen" (92), and his fear of talking inanimate objects (like the noisy watch he fears will "tell" his master of any wrongdoing). In the passage below, Equiano speaks intratextually to his own African memory text as he rereads the historical moment of his early capture in Africa.

> Generally, when the grown people in the neighborhood were gone far in the fields to labour, the children assembled together in some of the neighbors' premises to play; and commonly some of us used to get up a tree to *look out* for any assailant, or kidnapper, that might come upon us; for they sometimes took those opportunities of our parents' absence, to attack and carry off as many as they could seize. One day, as I was watching at the top of a tree in our yard, I saw one of those people come into the yard of our neighbour but one, to kidnap . . . I gave the alarm of the rogue . . . till some of the grown people came and secured him. But, alas! ere long it was my fate to be thus attacked, and to be carried off, when . . . only I and my dear sister were left to mind the house, two men and a woman got over our walls and, and in a moment seized us both; and, without giving us time to cry out, or make resistance, they stopped our mouths, tied our hands, and ran off with us. (47)

In this reading the narrator's recollection of his watch not only juxtaposes the successful watch of Equiano alongside the failed watch of others, it also reinvokes the significance and relationship of time with freedom. Literally a lost "moment" is time enough for their captors to muzzle them, in much the same way the "unfortunate creature" is muzzled. The time for "crying out" is literally lost, not because of the failure of the watch that symbolizes recorded time, but due to the failure of the watch on the lookout for the difference between slavery and freedom. His anguish and fear at losing his freedom and his sister's is repeated in the image of the slave woman whose "mouth [was locked] so fast that she could scarcely speak" (63). Equiano, like the "poor creature," is "tied fast" and his "sister's mouth" is "also stopped" (47). Yet, note that unlike the slave woman in the New World who is also tied so tightly that she "could not eat nor drink," he and his sister refuse "victuals" out of their anguish at being deprived of their freedom. Equiano, as the Talking Book, testifies, based on personal experiences, about the horrors of slavery from one side of the Atlantic to the other. As he highlights the extreme cruelty of New World slavery, he signifies on the common spiritual and metaphysical cruelties of both African and Western slavery, emphasizing the feeling of desertion, of being separated from one's kin, the loss of freedom, and the loss of control over one's own body and one's own speech.

As Equiano mourns the physical and metaphysical loss through narrative remembering, he recaptures his right of ownership to his memory and the right to remember cultural and personal history. Ironically, despite a narrative voice which evokes the very real terror and fear of capture and enslavement, Equiano's memory and personal history as an Igbo has been questioned by scholars, who argue that Equiano constructs an Igbo memory and identity out of antislavery texts and travel journals. Certainly, he admittedly fully appropriates antislavery texts of the period. Indeed, the first edition of his *Interesting Narrative* was published some five years after the death of Anthony Benezet and one year after the 1788 publication and twenty-seven years after Benezet's 1762 edition of *Some Historical Account of Guinea, Its Situation, Produce and the General Disposition of Its Inhabitants.* Equiano's claims have been supported by West African Igbos who recall that period. Ambrose, a "native medicine man" of Isseke, confirms that kidnapping of young children in this area was a primary concern: "Children [were] never moved from one spot to another without the protective presence and guard of a strong man. It was customary to keep children constantly under the protection of stout, strong men to protect them from those who stole human beings and sold them for money" (Acholonu, 48).

Rather than see Equiano as borrowing facts for a conceived African history, we can see the author as authorizing certain white texts (such as Benezet's) to speak about African people. Consequently, Equiano's narrative is generously sprinkled with important truths and statements about Igbo people in particular and all Africans in general. Don Oha-dike suggests that "the absence of professional historians and story-tellers may well explain the confusion that characterized the early [written] history [such as Equiano's] of the Igbo people" (4). Given the devastating risk involved in the loss of history, and its concomitant cultural genocide, it is worthwhile to consider not only, as many schol-ars argue, the contributions of Equiano's narrative to that history of loss, but also his use of existing factual and historical evidence about Igbo culture and society to reconstruct and put in place a written record of Igbo history from an Igbo perspective—perhaps the earliest of its kind.

Within the parameters of a dually constructed faith-based aesthetic—grounded in Igbo and Afro-British American ways of comprehending the profound depths of his spiritual and material self—Equiano maps out a place for himself in the Western world while resisting its oppres-sive states. Realizing the impossibility of returning to Africa, Equiano worked toward improving conditions for Africans on both sides of the Atlantic. Just as Equiano reimagines gender, race, and religion in his rereading of the relationship between the woman, child, and the snake, he rereads the truths of his African homeland against (and alongside) the falsehoods of his New World detractors. The *Interesting Narrative* will stand—for his eighteenth-century audience and posterity—*beside* the cultural fictions which the majority of his European audiences have accepted as the truth of Africa and African people. In her essay "Racism, Imperialism, and the Traveler's Gaze in Eighteenth-Century England," Margaret Hunt provides an excellent historical and cultural analysis of such fictions as she traces the shift from the popularity of religious tracts in the seventeenth century to a continually increasing popularity in travel literature throughout the eighteenth century. She states that "while the seventeenth century was the first century to see widespread literacy among urban middling groups, non-elite reading tastes inclined strongly to devotional books," with at least "one third" to "one-half or more" of their "book collections" devoted to "religious books" and only a "sprinkling" to "travel and exploration" (333). However, by the turn of the eighteenth century, not only was there a "rapid rise in [the] popular-ity of secular forms of writing, with the travel books prominent among them," but "the eighteenth-century literate public['s] enjoy[ment]" of them was "especially associated with and increasingly addressed to, the interest of the trading, commercial, or middling classes" (335). Of particular interest to "literate middling classes [throughout] England well before the last quarter of the eighteenth century" were "books on travel" that "bore on British colonies or on parts of the world" as yet "unclaimed" by Europeans" (337).

Moreover, "central" to "this type" of literature was the "ceaseless need it seem[ed] to inspire in the traveler to reconfirm received stereotypes about the people he or she encounter[ed]" (339). Not surprisingly, "visitors to Africa inevitably remarked upon the nakedness and heathenish character of Africans" (340). Costanzo also confirms that this "literate white audience composed mainly of middle-class religious persons" seems to have been substantially influenced by travel literature (17). Over time, most whites, without ever having been to Africa, held preconceived notions of the continent from the travel literature, which remained a viable source of the affirmation of the inferiority of blacks, and, by extension, justification for their enslavement and cruel treatment. Travel accounts by people such as William Bosman, who claimed "*Negroes* are all without exception, Crafty, Villainous and Fraudulent" ("Letter IX," 117), and John Harris, author of *Collection of Voyages,* a prominent eighteenth-century travel journal, laid the foundation for race prejudice and justification of slavery that spread like a cancer in the white European consciousness. Eighteenth-century travel literature's account of Africa was not different from the range of "scientific," pro-slavery, antislavery, and even religious works, which provided unsettling myths regarding Africans to the same audience that read Equiano's *Narrative.*

On the one hand, Equiano's narrative faced audiences whose opinions regarding this "sable" race were as moderate as those expressed in William Blake's "Songs of Innocence and Experience" and Thomas Day's "The Dying Negro," and as extreme as those expressed in the "scientific" notions of Linnaeus's *Systema Naturae* (1735) and Buffon's *Histoire Naturelle* (1749)—both of which support varying themes of "biologically" based racial hierarchies. Even favorably disposed audiences began to view blacks as immoral, lascivious heathens, whose Christianization and freedom from forced bondage would make them docile and, therefore, "acceptable" servants. Yet, perhaps one of the most pernicious of all these influences upon eighteenth-century "enlightened" audiences remains its religious works. As I suggested earlier, works which long before the eighteenth century had already planted the seeds of black inferiority and white superiority in the fertile minds of not only the white, literate, middle-class audiences had also affected the minds of poor illiterate whites and blacks as well. Suspended thus between nobility and savagery, moored to an alien class of citizenry, and mourning a deplorable, but requisite, distance from one's native community, eighteenth-century Afro-British Americans like Equiano confronted these comparably objectionable options head-on—first, by fashioning, and then by transforming, a marginalized space of recovery into a liminal and functional space of knowledge reproduction and redistribution between the two competing societies of "nobility" and "savagery."

In light of such existing knowledge, Equiano understood that the African, real or imagined, represented a figurative space symbolic of what was wrong with the (European and African) world, the very "thing" that ought either to be managed or purged. What is more, with the institution of slavery represented in many instances as a corrective to African cultures, *The Interesting Narrative* attempted to render anew the African's caste and color—with, ironically, some very established narrative techniques. Against the late eighteenth-century parade of travelogues, Equiano understood his text as replacing fiction with faction, imagining, structuring, and putting together a more palatable and African history.[33] Loosening fixed conditions and characteristics imposed on Africans by white histories—informed in great part by contemporary travel literature—Equiano's narrative recollects and reexamines the risks and rewards of existing truths about Africans.[34]

In this context, it is useful to consider Equiano's narrative in terms of what Elizabeth Alexander[35] has called "presentational space"—to extend to Equiano's narrative a notion of space as that in which the eighteenth-century Igbo can replace and remember who he is through aesthetic rearrangement and visualization of an African (black, Igbo) imagination. And, in so doing, we are told to read his narrative as physical and imagined "presentational space" that not only reflects a "black interior," but also imagines, creates, and protects the "life" it narrates. In her description of "presentational spaces," Alexander refers to this type of phenomenon as "the creation [of] a pragmatic space in which the black body is not only visible but also safe" (9). Like many eighteenth-century writers, Equiano embraces and passes through aesthetic dilemmas that imagine—in various fractured forms—a "black" visibility and that simultaneously validate and negate the existence of real and imagined African presences. As a result, a focus on the ways in which *The Interesting Narrative* signals a return to—and bringing together of—dispersed

African experiences and locations serves to highlight the value of those narrative transactions and translations to enable a cultural recuperation of manifold and complementary African character traits. Such transactions demand first and foremost the narrator's attention to the devastating effects and risks of totalitarianism and repressed ideologies that are incompatible with such psychical predispositions. However, Equiano's narrative must also (at the same time) reflect an imaginary "white" and "black" exterior world through which the conditions under which enslaved blacks lives might be abolished at best, and at worst their conditions ameliorated.

Equiano's *Interesting Narrative* could only improve conditions of enslaved and nominally free blacks and poor whites by appealing to the hearts and minds of the middle-class whites. As such, this narrative was written in order to motivate powerful whites to join in the antislavery movement. Of its motivations, Equiano's announces, "the [narrative's] chief design [was] to excite in [their] August assemblies a sense of compassion for the miseries which the Slave trade had entailed on [his] unfortunate countrymen" (7) with the hope that the production of this document might "become an instrument towards the relief of his suffering countrymen" (7). Yet, his very skillful manipulation of multiple layers of meaning reveals intentions far beyond that of the antislavery movement. In fact, Samuels suggests that Equiano is not to be taken at face value, but rather that he "is overtly genuflecting but covertly . . . slashing away at his oppressors" (qtd. in Orban, 662). Orban asserts Equiano is establishing "a distinction in the narrative between two different kinds of Europe" (ibid.). I agree with both Samuels and Orban, and would add that the distinctions they make with regard to the slave narrator's masked intentions reflect Equiano's speaking to a multiplicity of discourses necessary to effect change in his efforts to negotiate between several worlds. Hence, I suggest—against Orban's claim—that "those at whose feet Vassa lays his narrative with the greatest deference and respect are" most definitely "the same as those he is condemning and rebuking" (ibid.). Brilliantly, however, Equiano's narrative stands as evidence that both deference and condemnation are earned, not inherited, on the basis of one's race.

As an Igbo, with a conscious awareness of the concept of *chi* and the notion of duality—"Wherever Something Stands, Something Else Will Stand Beside It"—any such lack of distinction or any negation of the particularity of Europeans (white men) would be a complete distortion of his African ontology. As a Christian, prejudicial rebuke or sanction would be antithetical to such a scriptural caveat as "There is neither Jew nor Greek, there is neither bond nor free, there is neither male nor female: for ye are all one in Christ Jesus" (Galatians 3:28) and would amount to a distortion of the word, for which "God shall take away his part out of the book of life" (Revelation 22:19). As a rational and intelligent man of the eighteenth century, such totalizing essentializing of white Europeans would amount to the same type of stereotyping that had plagued his own black brethren, a fact Equiano is fully aware of. In fact, Equiano is careful to document a progression, throughout the narrative, of his knowledge of the white man based upon personal, first-hand experiences rather than upon an isolated experience or hearsay or race prejudice. This is evident from Equiano's first experience with the "white men with horrible looks, red faces, and loose hair," who, at first glance, he was certain would eat him (55). This experience is probably not unlike the white man's early encounters with the Africans, whose apprehension is only part of the author's intent here. The adult narrator is self-reflexively looking back on his early prejudices against whites, in order to illustrate (by example) the ways in which cultural prejudices are typically based on ignorance. In particular, African inferiority and European superiority was originally based on such ill-informed assumptions.

Equiano's subtle use of this understated style of indirection should not be overlooked, as it sets the pattern for the narrative's multilevel discourses that, while appearing to pass lightly over seemingly minute incidents, actually reflect a critique of larger issues. This narrative device questions not only his audiences' "ways of knowing," but also forces them to evaluate the basis upon which they have acquired certain assumptions about blacks. Moreover, he offers his audience a cogent example of how one ought to proceed when confronted with this type of fear. He first "inquires" "amongst the chained men" of some men of his "own nation" and, more importantly, his own status—of the intentions of these white men. When he is told he is in no grave danger as these men only intend to carry him to their country to work for them (56), he is a "little revived" (56), but still continues to observe the actions of these men in an attempt to learn more. It is not until Equiano becomes what he calls "almost an Englishman," through his extended exposure— "between three and four years"—to English culture and customs, that he relinquishes such fears, which he attributes to his "ignorance [which] wore away as [he] began to know them" (77). Equiano relies solely neither on his limited experience with the white men nor on the opinions of others, but weighs each "way of knowing" equally and carefully. Yet it cannot be overlooked that in this period of his life, "every circumstance [which he] met with only served to render [his] state more painfule and [reinforce his] opinion of the cruelty of the whites" (58). Clearly these men belong to the category of those whom "he is condemning and rebuking." And although these types of men appear repeatedly through-out *The Interesting Narrative,* they no more provide the only example of white European men than their kind and benevolent brethren, upon whom Equiano confers "deference and respect."

That Equiano encounters, in his quest for freedom and self-recreation, masters and friends whom he uses to depict varying degrees of benevolence is a testament to Equiano's ability to address the multiple narratives of slavery, those of both the slave masters and the enslaved. For example, though Captain Doran proves a kind master, he is quick to remind Equiano of "his power over [him]" (94). On the other hand, that "Mr. Robert King, a Quaker" is immediately distinguished as "the very best master in the whole island" (99) has more to do with his hon-est interactions with Equiano than his apparently humane treatment of his other slaves. Once again, the author's understatement allows the audience to consider not merely truisms concerning "kind and benevo-lent" slave masters who do not wrongly use or abuse their slaves, but also the audience is asked to scrutinize what "true" benevolence might mean for a slave. Mr. King, who lets Equiano know that "the reason he ha[s] bought him [is because] of his good character," gives Equiano a tool of empowerment "which [he] afterwards f[i]nd[s] of infinite service" (99). This notion of benevolence is not only a far more complex one than *The Interesting Narrative*'s audience has probably examined before, but it conflates an antiracist agenda into an antislavery text or narrative—a daring move for this type of text and for these times.

Additionally, Equiano's presentation of African landscapes that underlie his multiple visions of African cultures, through the lenses of different types of slavery, undercuts many critics' assertions that Equi-ano presents an idyllic African life that suggests a prelapsarian, Edenic African paradise to expose, in stark contrast, Europe as the "true" coun-try of "savages." Equiano's comparisons between "primitive" and "civi-lized" are not merely superficial inversions of conventional paradigms of civilization and progress. That said, while this is clearly the type of appositional reasoning that Equiano's *The Interesting Narrative* is trying to (de)construct and indict, one cannot overlook the pronounced dis-similarities between European and African society. However, Equiano intentionally uses such distinctions to engage enlightenment philosophies which argue that the "progression" of civilized society represents a devolution rather than evolution, in order to problematize the role of slavery and other types of oppression in the "progress" of both African and European civilizations. As a merchant bondsman, Equiano is in a unique position to have firsthand knowledge as an insider and outsider of both societies. While still a slave in Africa, he is rendered an Igbo outsider by virtue of having been removed from his own people. In Europe and the New World, Equiano is an African outsider living inside an alienated (though assimilated) Western culture. As a result, he sees Africa from different vistas. As such he is privy to each country's beauties, as well as its blemishes.

What such a way of viewing Africa suggests, then, is that it is Equiano, the Igbo, as much as it is Gustavus Vassa the Christianized Englishman, who constitute (and therefore are inscribed into) the fabric of his Western, African, and Afro-Western lives. Equiano's narrative points to the ways in which early African American writers translate limitations into possibilities and impingements into opportunities for imaginative and creative integration of alternative worldviews. By reconfiguring literary spaces into literal and figurative junctions, his dialogues lead back to a constructed and "imagined," but nonetheless real Africa.

Ultimately, such discourse—especially within the frame of Igbo duality—connotes the significance of naming as a mechanism for replacing fragments of African identity and cultural consciousness misplaced during the Middle Passage. Equiano figuratively and metaphorically reinscribes cultural memory, identity, and African humanity in his snake myth. Significantly, as a child he was "named for" the "circumstance" of his noble African birth, and preordained as a result of the "fancied foreboding" of his eventual capture and enslavement. Further, his life story evidenced the burdensome physical and metaphysical changes as a result of his enslaved undervalued condition and subject position as African in a non-African world However, what resonates most profoundly is the "loud voice" of the "well spoken" Olaudah that reconciles his Western sentiments, circumstances, and determinations to a newly regenerated picture of African values, cultures, and identity.

FOUR

Reading "Others"
in Eighteenth-Century
Afro-British American Literature

The Promise and the Dilemma of New Ways of Reading

> While the "African" part of "African American" gives us a place in this world as much as "American" does, it also teasingly asks us to find it, in a haystack as big as a continent.
>
> —Robert Stepto, *From Behind the Veil*

> Non-aboriginal Americans born in the Americas were called Creoles during the eighteenth century. Thus all African or Creole Black authors . . . publishing in North America before . . . 1783 were Afro-British writers, though several . . . accepted . . . the new status of being African Americans.
>
> —Vincent Carretta, *Unchained Voices*

This chapter revisits the dilemma of the unanswerability of the question of what is African in African American literature by looking at the ways in which the writers briefly explored in this chapter are both atypically typical, representative, and yet not representative of writers' development of an eighteenth-century black aesthetic. Hence, in this chapter I shall consider the implications of the use of various elements of Afro-British American ways of knowing I have outlined in the preceding chapters, through brief readings of the works of Lucy Terry, James Albert Gronniosaw, John Marrant, and Venture Smith. It is my hope that this epilogue of sorts will offer some conclusions about the promise and dilemma of a culturally specific reinterpretation of Africa that recovers a nonstatic and dynamic African cultural and critical presence, even as it opens more questions to be explored through theorizing the ghostly dilemmas of eighteenth-century black aesthetics.

Admittedly, the question "What is 'African' in African American Literature?" deserves a legitimate attempt at a response. However, the quotations above suggest that it can also be a rhetorical question that invites us to consider national, racial, and cultural premises upon which African American—and indeed American—literature is identified. From Countee Cullen's 1925 "Heritage" poem which asks, ironically, "What is African to me?" to Langston Hughes's 1949 "Theme for English B," which ponders race in texuality,[1] issues of African culture and identity loom large in the history of African American literature. As early as 1897, W. E. B. DuBois contemplates, and complicates, the relationship between African Americans and their competing American and African selves. In "The Conservation of Races" DuBois asks, "What, after all, am I? . . . American . . . Negro . . . both?" He answers: "We are Americans, by birth . . . citizenship . . . political ideals . . . language . . . [and] religion. Beyond that, we are members of a vast historic race [asleep] from the very dawn of creation [and] but half awakening in . . . its African fatherland," contributing to "America, its only American music, fairytales, pathos, humor"—its American identity! (182–83).

With regard to this simultaneously American and African identity, Stepto[2] isolates the practical *dilemma* of African-centered recovery of indigenously derived African ways of knowing implied in the question: "What is 'African' in African American literature?" Extricating eighteenth-century black literature from the *ghosts* that would bind it solely to sociohistorically British and/or American origins depends upon a self-reflexive interrogation of the pervasiveness of the dislocation and relocation of African cultural and historical memory. Yet, the importance of "employ[ing] in 'African' a term that could stand in parity to 'American'" and that could stand equally as a marker "for a generation of people [who have] insist[ed] that the sign of their racialness, their blackness, should be a whole word, a 'real' word—'African'" (*From Behind the Veil*, xii) has meaning far beyond a sociolinguistic framework. Indeed, naming is claiming. The power of naming can be clearly seen in the underlying philosophy governing Vincent Carretta's[3] restatement and relocation of the Western origins of African writers. Significantly, the movement from naming to claiming—they "were *called* Creoles . . . thus [they *are*] all African or Creole Black[s]"—is represented within the span of one sentence. Further, while this naming and claiming of an identity for authors who admittedly "do not easily fit into a coherent group united by any organizing principle other than their African heritage" (1) assumes a critical awareness of the powerful process by which "Africa is carved up by imperialist European powers" (1), it does not account for the totalizing processes by which a continent of indigenous and diversely self-identified ethnic groups was first named, then claimed in the aggregate as Africans.

Historian Sylvia Wynter notes that "there were, of course, no 'Africans' then. Indeed it is only within the 'mode of subjective understanding' of liberal humanism that 'Africans' could have existed" ("1492: A New World View," 33). Sources of the origin of the word *Africa* vary, from a country on the southern coast of the Mediterranean, roughly the equivalent to the modern Tunisia, to "south wind" or "land of Carthage" (from *Afer* or *Africus*), to the Arabic word *afar* meaning "dust," to the Hebrew word *ephra* meaning "fruitfulness," which is thought to refer to the hinterland beyond Carthage.

Frameworks which resist reliance on origins or essences also discursively remove Africa from the center, and they do so precisely at historical moments when it is most advantageous for people of the African Diaspora to resituate and recenter themselves within literal and figurative African sites. Consequently, the location of early African authors within an imagined, but nonetheless real, African community is represented as an essentialist distortion or exception to an otherwise logical and more acceptable and liberal Eurocentric framework.[4] Within this type of framework it is the European Diaspora, not the African Diaspora, that is expanded. Moreover, the Western world is resituated in relationship to an a priori and paternalistic relationship with the cultures and peoples of the African Diaspora. As a result, an unproblematized reading, such as Carretta's, of black writers' acceptance of the institution of slavery fails to read nondominant modes of resistance. Such unproblematized readings also myopically (and somewhat ahistorically) assume that *demonstrated* nonacceptance (even for free blacks) is always a viable and practical alternative for eighteenth-century writers. The conflation of blacks' *tolerance* and *survival* of an impossible (and often inescapable) social condition with that of blacks' *acceptance* of Western cultural practice of black oppression is akin to *Black Atlantic* readings of eighteenth-century culture such as those advanced by Paul Gilroy,[5] which problematically support literal applications of DuBoisean double consciousness to a reading of eighteenth-century black literature. In the same way that writers of African descent resisted the institution of slavery even while they engaged in *palava* with its practitioners, Africans throughout the Diaspora resisted negatively connotative and denotative *blackness* and positively connotative and denotative *whiteness* even as they embraced its possibilities and limitations. As Echeruo argues, "What is at stake is not the possibility of living as an African (or a black) in the modern European (or white) world, but in supposing that both identities are equivalent in ontological terms. For it would not occur to any European advocate of modernity to phrase the European conditions in similarly quixotic terms" ("An African Diaspora: The Ontological Project," 6).

Thus far, I have read the work of Equiano and Wheatley within theoretical frameworks that accept rather than except their African heritage. Here, I want to further consider and explore what such strategic replacements of Africa within African American literature suggest for less prominently known writers Lucy Terry, James Gronniosaw, Venture Smith, John Marrant, and Briton Hammon by considering some of the ways in which their work and their lives evince a more conflicted relationship with both African and Western origins. Consequently, I revise and restate the question, "What is 'African' in African American Literature?" by reading these seemingly ambivalent Afro-Western texts through hybridized African and Western contexts. I contend that while issues such as the division of literary labor and reliance on Western aesthetics and sociopolitical aims, as well as lack of verifiable written historical documentation, make it difficult to locate cultural consciousness or encoded worldviews from both sides of the Atlantic, integrative African-centered approaches should not be abandoned. Admittedly, there are significant challenges with regard to reading early black writers' attempts at inscribing their personal, racial, and gendered selves into the master narratives of the New World. However, our response to such challenges requires critical and systematic analysis of the aesthetic and philosophical diversity present in early African American cultures, as well as a more extensive integration of indigenously derived Africanstructures into existing frameworks. For example, a more complex understanding of African-centered dynamics of conversion and naming might enable a resituation of Christian conversion, invocation of noble lineage, and other barely audible voicings of subjectivity within an African context.

Before turning to the writing of the first-named African American poet, Lucy Terry, I will briefly examine the complex counternarrative that is her life. Like Wheatley and Equiano, Terry was born in Africa and brought to America as a child. Her talent as a great orator and storyteller is legendary among whites and blacks from Massachusetts to Vermont, especially in the Deerfield community. Moreover, some of the facts of her life suggest that she was something of an activist who insisted upon equal treatment with regard to education, property, and civil and human rights. She is said to have waged, though lost, a battle with college trustees to gain admittance to Williams College for her son. Often outnumbered, but never outsmarted, Terry is said to have argued convincingly and strategically against powerful opponents from the local Norwich town government to the Supreme Court. Unfortunately, there are currently no existing official written records that substantiate such claims of courageous activism. Much of what is known about her life has been passed down orally, and later recorded by historians George Sheldon, Rodney Field, and David Proper. Of the three, Proper's work is the most recent and appears to be the most accurate. The verifiable facts of her personal life are the dates of her death, August 21, 1821; marriage, May 17, 1756; baptism, June 15, 1725; her church membership, August 19, 1744; and the birth dates and baptisms of her six children. The absence of a ship's manifest or a bill of sale—to Ebenezer Wells, any other master prior to Terry's arrival in Deerfield, or to her husband, Abijah Prince—render any definitive statement about her age, national origin, or slave status conjectural. Although verifiable proof of her successful "petition . . . for redress of grievances" against the Noyes families exists, the most well-known political incidents in Terry's life, such as her brilliant argument before the trustees of Williams College to gain admittance for her son, cannot be substantiated. Neither is there written evidence of Terry's eloquent Supreme Court argument against her prominent white neighbor, Colonel Eli Bronson's encroachment on her family's land. Proper offers, "as with the tradition connecting Lucy Terry to Williams College, there is probably some truth behind this anecdote, although it defies documentation despite its plausibility" (34).

Ironically, though Terry's claims to the African American poetic, West African griotte, and Deerfield historical traditions are validated by means of oral transmission, similar evidence which should support her naming within a tradition of politics and activism is regrettably nonexistent due to the lack of written documentation. Given Terry's relationship to the communities she and her husband, Abijah Prince, lived in, and the supposed lack of historical evidence of central events in her life, in what sense then can she be definitively claimed and named as "African griot and Deerfield historian and storyteller"? I suggest that the validation of Terry's cultural life and the exclusion of her dynamic political life are connected.

Deirdre Mullane notes that Terry's "poem recalls the popular captivity narrative genre of the colonial period, in which the writer recounts his or her experience among the Indians" (Mullane, 24).[6] I agree, and would further argue for a reading of "The Bars Fight" as poetic variation on the traditional late eighteenth-century captivity narrative which subverts dominant anti-Indian sentiments and ideologies in New England communities like Deerfield.[7] In so doing, it provides a complement to the gaps in Terry's unsubstantiated history of political activism. The *Something Else standing beside* the comforting domesticated narrative of colorful local character expressed in the entertaining black woman telling homespun stories for the pleasure of the local folk is a more discomfiting counternarrative of a politically savvy, intelligent, African woman who would not be denied equal protection and rights to citizenship. To be sure, the sociopolitical counternarrative of eighteenth-century black resistance recuperates remnants of African women's centrality to the home and hearth as well as the literal and figurative battlefield. Moreover, such a counternarrative of empowerment resituates African orality within the history of early African American literacy, and claims Terry alongside Equiano as yet another Talking Book.

A brief reading of "The Bars Fight" in light of aspects of it that signify upon the heroic history of Deerfield citizens subverts the anti–Native American sentiments it was thought to uphold. In other words, an otherwise seemingly ambivalent poem, "The Bars Fight" actually subverts dominant paradigms even as it appears to celebrate them. Lucy Terry Prince's "The Bars Fight" was composed about an encounter between Deerfield citizens and Indians in 1746. It has been cited as evidence both of the "last Indian attack on Deerfield" (Proper, 16) and of "the first poetry by any black American" (4). As with the captivity narratives of Hammon and Marrant, her thirty-three-line doggerel[8] radically and simultaneously documents African, Native, and European American history. There is as much to learn from Terry's repetition of key words and phrases as there is from her indexing of the names of people of Deerfield. In the poem's historical registering of events, we learn that in the summer of 1746 Native Americans lay in wait to ambush, take away, and kill as many of their neighboring white Deerfield citizens as they could catch. The poet's cataloging of "some very valiant men . . . whose names she [does] not leave out"[9] (ll.4–7) partly explains why this black poet's verse was preserved and transmitted orally for more than a century before it was printed in 1855. It must have given the men, women, and children of Deerfield—including Terry, who was said to have been quite fond of singing this verse—a great deal of pride to celebrate through song the memories of their neighbors, friends, and relatives.[10]

Also, preserved within the artist's memory were cultural markers that trigger her association of the horrors of the Middle Passage with the horrors of the capture and murder of Deerfield settlers by its native population. One must wonder from what physical and metaphysical vantage points the poet speaks her representation of the latter (Deerfield) slaughter through remembering of the former (Middle Passage and slavery). After all, Terry was presumably kidnapped from Africa as an infant and whatever minimal cultural memories of Africa she may have brought with her to New England (excepting those transmitted by older Africans she may have met) would have been so deeply embedded within her subconscious that it would require an act of metaphysical excavation, or extreme trauma, to recover such artifactual fragments of her consciousness. However, her memory of the circumstances of the Middle Passage and the reprehensible conditions and violent depredations committed against that community of forced immigrants with whom the infant Terry and her mother or caregiver lived is very likely to have been brought to the surface at a later scene of similar terror. Hence, as the artist paints with broad strokes words that reinforce the Deerfield settlers' lamentable (and sadly preventable) adversity, the African praise singer composes a sorrow song (a bittersweet refrain) that simultaneously masks and unmasks her understanding of a collective black anguish and mourning of tremendous loss of African lives during the Middle Passage and enslavement in the New World. Unlike traditional captivity narratives of the late eighteenth century which often portray white settlers as helpless victims at the mercy of savage beasts and a providential God, "The Bars Fight" depicts both sides valiantly. While a myopic reading of "The Bars Fight" might suggest that the Indians are presented as quite brutal, Terry's poem clearly depicts both Native Americans and white settlers as actively engaged in a justifiable act of warfare, spurred by internal conflicts and differences over the encroachment of white settlers onto the rights and property of the indigenous native population of Deerfield. The poem's title gives the reader a clue as to the equal footing on which the poet places whites and Indians. The poet's use of "fight" rather than "attack" or "massacre" resituates Native and Anglo-American conflict outside dominant ideological conceptions, which assume that a defense of property and human rights by indigenous America is less honorable than those of immigrant settlers who seek to colonize and dislocate them. The title of the poem sets the tone for our reading of the last Deerfield Native/Anglo conflict as one final battle in a war as honorable to the indigenous American as it is to its European and African immigrants.[11]

Finally, both the poem and the counternarrative of Lucy Terry Prince's life reveal the relationship to orality that both the poet and her community share. This relationship can be most clearly seen by the oral preservation of her poem for more than a century, and the strength given to oral evidence by early Deerfield historian Robert Sheldon with regard to the equal measure of validation he accords the anecdotal and the written documentation in his recording of history. Indeed, "The Bars Fight" might have remained more unsubstantiated anecdotal evidence of a historical event had it not been for the significance of this singular event and the form—song—in which it was composed and transmitted. One can only imagine the pride with which Deerfield sang of "Samuel Allen [who] like a hero foute" (1.1) or the morbid humor with which they may have imagined Eunice Allen's hysterical flight with "petticoats [that] stopt her" (1.18). One can also imagine the tears with which the death of young Sim(e)on Amsden, age nine, and the presence of the kidnapped young Samuel, age eight, are mourned. The repetition of the words which denote overlapping and differently registered keys of a central motif of death—slay, kill, grief, and slaughter—are used to highlight the interconnectedness between men, women, and children. Indeed, the poem's narrative progresses from the slaying of valiant men to the outright killing of old and young men alike, to the grief for a slain boy, and the escape of one man from the "dreadful slaughter" (1.15) that claimed five men, one child, and "left . . . for dead" one woman. The slave narrator of Terry's poem watches and records from a safe distance her master's and the master narrative. Ultimately, it is through the unsubstantiated, the gaps—for example, the escape of nine-year-old Caleb—that so much more of what is left of the "bitters and the sweets" of both narratives is revealed. In this way, we self-reflexively resist reproducing a type of invisibility by reducing the significance of a single life, text, culture, or cultural experience to myopic and unilineally constructed standards of authentication.

However, as promising as Terry's work seems in terms of theorizing competing dilemmas of race, class, and gender in the context of an eighteenth-century black woman's historical spoken (and transcribed) words, I am reminded that genre expectations for poetry are decidedly different from those of narrative. While each genre intersects and parallels with regard to issues of form and content, importantly each genre also functions and operates within unique frameworks that enable a particular way of relating to its unique subject matter. Nonetheless, reliance on the limitations of form imposed by genre expectations, like the dichotomization and polarization of the sacred and secular, the personal and political, the raced and gendered, is exactly what the unorthodoxy of the early African in New World literature vividly exposes. I do not mean to suggest that *unmediated* contextual hybridity is either possible or desirable at this—or any other—historical moment. Rather, I offer such genre blending as a type of *palava* which enables the representation of the un(der)representable within multiple and simultaneous contexts and constructions of Africa. Going beyond the critique of the representation of a single, solitary self, to a community where, in Equiano's terms, "one will stand for many," we should be wary of critical stances which assume that unmediated progress is attainable through syntheses or hybridizations of identities; such assumptions often equate to melting pot theories of differently constructed sameness. It is incumbent upon scholars, then, to be self-reflexively aware of the extent to which constructs and conceptualizations of simultaneity, such as those I have presented in this study's attempt to engage with the *dilemma of a ghost,* remain grounded in a duality discourse. Indeed, what is most clearly identifiable as African within the narratives of Hammon, Marrant, Gronniosaw, and Smith are the open-ended possibilities for multiple and diverse formulations and articulations of multiple selves, societies, and continuums of simultaneously moving and changing cultures that name and claim Africa and Africanness. Hence, what I initially saw as a dilemma to reading these early narratives—limited as they were by amanuensis–editor relationship, assimilation of dominant sacred and secular themes, structures, untraceable ethnic markers or signifiers, outside initial identification in the title or a minuscule sprinkling in the body of the narrative—I have come to realize as the real promise.

In the same way that Lucy Terry's extratextual life tells us much about interpreting her poem, John Marrant's journal and sermons inform our reading of his narrative. Reading his multiple texts in light of distinct aspects of African American spirituality and the relationship of its people to the Divine is central. Significant to this understanding is a close look at the way in which he amends one of John Watts's hymns as well as a closer look at the itinerant preaching and multiethnic communities that both celebrate and denigrate him. Here, we must consider, as we do with many elements of Terry's life, the way in which the political has as much to do with class as it has to do with race. Also worth considering are the ways in which he is drawn toward or away from imagined sites of home. *A Narrative of the Lord's Wonderful Dealings with John Marrant* (1785) mediates conventional form and ideology even as it disrupts and upholds the paradigms of otherness they contain. Although it is clear, as scholars have noted, that his black body is meant to heighten the savageness of Native Americans through an associative principle, Marrant's narrative doubles the associative principle, and in so doing negates the full effect of its representational power as a foil to the more civilized and homogenous nation. His narrative thus reverses the trope of master/servant. In order to read the way in which the reversal occurs, we must shift from a reading of race to that of spirituality. This involves performing an exegetical maneuver to reread and reimagine master/servant simultaneously inside and outside the paradigms of race.

Phillip Gould's reading of this reversal is a useful entry point. His insightful analysis rests on a rereading of Marrant's negotiation of "the language of divine deliverance," his "capitali[zation] on the ambiguities of liberty," and Marrant's "fulfill[ment] . . . of the expectations of evangelical Methodism and the anti-authoritarian theme residing just below the narrative surface" ("Free Carpenter," 670). Further, Gould suggests that Marrant's "likening [of] himself to a king, and the Cherokee king to a 'child' . . . stages yet another successful negotiation of masters" (670). This is because it restages redemption within a chain of signifiers that resituate symbolic and linguistic meaning in the word *child*. The term "child" used in a Christian sense—especially with regard to rebirth and regeneration—suggests that the king's becoming like a child provides him entry though regeneration into a Christian community (and family) of saints.[12] This aspect of conversion could not have been missed within the context of a conversion narrative.

Indeed, placed within an intertextual moment that links Marrant's captivity narrative to Gronniosaw's and Equiano's is his reference to the little child that indeed does "lead" the family back to Marrant—his sister. Like Gronniosaw's sister Logwy, Marrant's younger (unnamed) sister is his only advocate in his Christian journey. Literally and spiritually she is the only one who sees him. While both Logwy and Marrant's sister remain in their respective cultural communities (Bornou and black colonial America), their roles as mediators and facilitators are interpreted somewhat differently. Logwy ushers Gronniosaw into the Christian world through her unconditional support and encouragement; Marrant's sister receives him upon his return as a fully converted Christian—from the wilderness experience. Marrant's sister's words, her acceptance of the link (symbolized in her brother) between their community and the white Christian world, underscores Marrant's physical and metaphysical reentry into the African community. Simultaneously a bridge to Christianity and a signifier of communal constancy and stability, his sister's warm reception and acceptance of Marrant is a sign of God's favor, upon his return from the wilderness—as a member both of the Christian family and of their own.

Thus, the subversion of white colonial power occurs in the black narrator's direct signification of the Christian interpretation and meaning of secularly imposed hierarchical structures. It is the biblical text which questions colonial whites' rights to ascendancy based on race, class, and even position within the family hierarchy (Christian and "scientific") as the human family is read alongside the spiritual family in which the white child is first. Marrant relates his narrative "to Aldridge in a way that capitalizes [not only] on the ambiguities of liberty" (670), but his method of narration also takes advantage of his audience's preconceived notions about children, as well as blacks and others as childlike and therefore innately depraved—as spiritually devoid "naturals." Moreover, Marrant expands his boundaries as a black convert and interprets the Anglo "ur-text" rather than merely restating or relating the Native American's conversion. In a radical act of cultural and spiritual redemption, he reorders the Christian chain of being. Marrant's narrative act is radical because theoretically, at least, in his new schema, conversion places blacks, Indians, and whites into the same family. Consequently, former masters relinquish their possessions, which not only include property like "golden ornaments [and] chains and bracelets" (*A Narrative of the Lord's Wonderful Dealings with John Marrant*, 120),[13] but their slaves as well as their claims to power over Africans and Indians. These early black narrators further extend their rhetorical and symbolic engagement with the "paradox of liberty and slavery" by simultaneously confronting the dilemma of race and liberty. Clearly, narrators like Marrant mourned/moored liberty in contexts that directly addressed their experiences of nominal or tenuous freedom, thus invoking an aesthetic and rhetorical image of eighteenth-century black liberty and slavery as different from white liberty and slavery.

This unconventional approach to conversion is achieved through Marrant's speaking in multiple tongues. His view that all who were equal before God should be ensured an equal opportunity at redemption is demonstrated more fully in his 1790 *Journal,* which he wrote, published, and sold. Joanna Brooks highlights the significance of this text for a more complex understanding of the "Lord's wonderful dealings with John Marrant":

> What fascinates about the *Journal* is Marrant's specificity of purpose. Few itinerants assumed roles as covenant theologians, historians, or political activists in the town where they preached. Eighteenth-century Huntingdonian or Methodist missionary writings rarely engage with local "peoples" in an intimacy. But Marrant came to Nova Scotia seeking his own people—Black Loyalists from America, including members of his own family . . . [he] believed himself divinely appointed to serve his "brethren," the Blacks of Birchtown, as a prophet. (Brooks, "John Marrant's *Journal*," 33)

Not only does Marrant's journal document a successful and driven mission to convert the blacks of "Birchtown," but it chronicles an equally successful itinerant ministry among whites, Indians, Irish, and Scottish immigrants, and Armenians as well. His encyclopedic entries of his conversion, meetings, conflicts, encounters with bears, floods, and being lost more than once in the hostile woods of Nova Scotia, among "free thinkers" as well as various other incidents, illustrate the extent to which Marrant's narrative had been limited by a literary division of labor (as related by Aldridge), and the extent to which he was able to negotiate such limitations.

Just prior to the talking-book sequence and shortly after the "wonderful affect" (Marrant, 118) of his prayer in the tongue of his Indian captors, and the subsequent conversion of the executioner, Marrant begins to sing "two verses of Dr. Watts hymns" (119), the last two lines of which he alters. In a hymn about God's presence as light in darkness, Marrant establishes a more personal relationship with the Divine by changing "He is my soul's bright morning star / and he my rising sun" to "*Thou art* my soul's bright morning star / and *thou* my rising sun" (Marrant, *Narrative,* 119). Such intimacy reveals Marrant's deeper awareness of the theological implications of culture and literacy. For it is at the moment of his great success in speaking in different cultural tongues—Native American—that he expresses humility at the inability of his "feeble tongue" to translate his "unspeakable joy" in unknown spiritual tongues. These acts of worldly and otherworldly interpretation in oral and aural registers suggest a preeminence of the Word in all its forms. Both Wheatley and Equiano share Marrant's consummate linguistic artistry. Wheatley masterfully manipulates simultaneously parallel and diverging imagery of darkness through lightness, visibility through invisibility, vulnerability through power, and the feminine through the masculine, in her recasting of the neoclassical "Niobe" myth. Equiano's antiphonal narrative structuring is used to depict the complex nature of cultural and spiritual conversion through intertwining and imbedded African and Western cultural images. Clearly, these early black writers share the gift of different and unknown tongues, and more importantly, the gift of spiritual and secular interpretation of these tongues.

My position is counter to Gates's argument that "Marrant's gift of tongues backfired, and he was sentenced to die once more for being a witch" (*Signifying Monkey*, 143), and that in Marrant's "inversion of the trope of the talking book . . . it is only the black man who can make the text speak" (143–44). Alongside the secular and this worldly talking book which the black man reads and translates is the otherworldly sacred text—the Word—which contains power in oral or written registers. For it is not man or woman, white, black, Native American, or otherwise who can "make" the book speak. The itinerant preacher understands that while he is the medium through which the Word—God, the Divine—speaks, his powers of translation are limited to an earthly realm, and even then only through God's revelation, as in "the Lord impressed a strong desire upon my mind to turn into their language" (118). Marrant's refrain "God was with me" and his direct address to that deity using "thou" and "thy" affirms his relationship to the talking book within him—that is, God. This reinterpretation of the talking book is echoed throughout Marrant's *Journal* and most vividly illustrated in the concluding lines: "These are ever learning, but never able to come to knowledge of the truth; let such as these tremble whilst they read these lines, and no longer reject the spirit of God against their own souls. Now, may God bless them in reading of these words, so that God may be glorified in their conversion" (78). The timbre and tone of these words are intended to invoke an otherworldly spiritual, for as a preacher, the power of the Word is transmitted orally. "So then faith cometh by hearing, and hearing by the word of God" (Romans 10:17).

While the implications of an eighteenth-century black aesthetic for the final three narrators in this chapter constitute by far a more comprehensive project than this chapter will contain, I will point briefly to several trajectories for future scholarship. Gronniosaw's *Narrative of the Most Remarkable Particulars in the Life of James Albert Ukawsaw Gronniosaw*[14] is rich with resonances and cacophonous disharmonies that intersect along lines of class and gender that are heightened by the centrality of race. The narrator's invocation of his noble African history warrants further examination, beyond the traditional reading of it as a kind of displacement of *inferior Negro slave* with the *noble* and *superior black savage,* or, what scholars like Andrews describe as a "celebration [albeit critically examined] of the acculturation process" (*To Tell a Free Story,* 39). A deeper investigation into the African religions and spiritual practices in the Upper Volta region of Guinea is necessary to determine if Gronniosaw has been previously exposed to pre-Western Christian religions. Also, significant work remains to be done on Gronniosaw's experience of poverty and class oppression, which takes into account his interracial marriage and how that may have impacted his economic status.

Importantly, it is the fact that Gronniosaw's "albino" sister Logwy operates strategically as a foil to the association of whiteness and "fair" skin color with beauty. Logwy's "outsider/outcast" position as a colorless child in a colored society—white in a black world—parallels Gronniosaw's own position as outsider both in Bornou (Africa) and in the new worlds (Holland, England, Ivory Coast) he inhabits. It is important that Logwy is figured as an outsider based on her physical appearance—skin color—in her own culture, whereas it is Gronniosaw's actions—in direct conflict with his African society's customs and traditions—that ultimately mark him as outsider. However, there is culturally encoded meaning to be derived from understanding the nature of Gronniosaw's warm relationship with this younger sister—meaning that will allow a more far-reaching grasp of his future relationships with women inside and outside of his culture. Indeed, throughout his narrative we see signs of the inextricability of gender and racial oppression. If Gronniosaw's narration of his captivity and subsequent removes on the Gold Coast prior to his enslavement in the New World is any indication, patriarchy is an equally complex dilemma in Africa and in the West. It is through dialogues with or about women we gain insight into Gronniosaw's subversive and subtle resistance to slavery and oppression. Take, for example, Gronniosaw's invocation of his mother's anguish at his absence—and his need to proselytize to her and others as a key reason for his wanting to return to Bornou (Africa). The very sympathetic emotion he exhibits in this part of his text suggests a gendered performance of narrative pathos. Most important, like the faithful Logwy who loves and believes in him when others in his community shun him, the white slave mistress becomes a bridge to his Christian conversion.

Hence, his recounting of the "Old Ned" incident also becomes an indictment of white Christian masters' hypocrisy. Though scholars have tended to read this passage as Gronniosaw's signifying on his providential state, as Christian convert, they have looked less closely at the unknown gendered tongues through which Gronniosaw speaks. If Gronniosaw is less than direct about his own suffering as an enslaved African and nominally free black man who endures race and class prejudice, the white mistress's role as buffer between the white man and the black slave makes clear what it means to be black and Christian. Old Ned is punished for failure to properly "school" the new slave (James Albert) on the appropriate way to address one's mistress. Gronniosaw's assertion of (verbal and spiritual) authority over his masters (albeit through a missed act of translation) exposes yet another type of black conversion narrative. Like Gronniosaw's unheeded tearful plea to return home to Africa and spread the gospel, the excessively harsh punishment that Old Ned receives for interpreting and daring to pass on the Word of God suggests the harsh consequences that attend "Negroes Christians, Black as Cain," who hope to "join the Angelic train" (Wheatley, "On Being Brought from Africa to America" ll.7–8). Old Ned is severely whipped and banished from the house—demoted from house servant to field slave. The revelation of slave mistresses' relative power through Gronniosaw's narrative exchange enables a covert but meaningful dialogue about the dual nature of power with respect to race and gender.

Ironically, Marrant has a similar experience to Gronniosaw's with a Christian slave mistress, on a plantation where he taught slave children the Bible. However, the results are slightly different from those of Gronniosaw. In Marrant's narrative, the relative power of both the white female and the black preordained Christian convert demonstrate differently manipulated power structures. Like Gronniosaw, Marrant is spared the punishment reserved for other blacks—in this case the slave children—who, despite the brutal consequences, remain faithful to Christian teaching and continue in their lessons. However, unlike Gronniosaw's mistress, Marrant's white mistress's attempt to rely on her relative power—through her verbal request that her husband exact physical punishment on Marrant—is vetoed. The white slave master refuses to violate slave codes and whip "the free carpenter." Ultimately, the white slave master's conversion and the white slave mistress's subsequent "divine" punishment suggest a moment of race/gender dialogue that illustrates the limits of white female relative power and Christian patriarchal authority.

Clearly, while much work has been done on kinship with regard to mother-daughter and husband-wife relations in slavery, the repeated theme of mother-youngest sons, albinism, brother-sister relationships, and slave mistresses within precolonial West African families needs to be studied in the context of narratives like Gronniosaw's, Equiano's, and Smith's.

With regard to Venture Smith's *A Narrative of the Life and Adventures*[15] narrative, which is one of the most unique of all in terms of its use of myth and its almost wholly secular tone, further research needs to be done in the area of the interterritorial conflict to more fully study the underlying cause for capture and seizure of Africans from the continent. This part of his story relates to Equiano's reference to his watch in the tree for kidnappers. A closer examination of the cultural and historical circumstances on both sides of the Atlantic will enable a better understanding of the African self-presence and identification in a narrative like Smith's. Like Achebe's and Acholonu's corroboration of aspects of Equiano's story, additional studies in the area of the folklore which underlie the legends of Venture Smith need to be documented.

Ultimately, an approach to reading early African American literature in the way I suggested is not all-encompassing. (It certainly does not present the final answer; rather, it only produces more questions.) What my approach offers is a redirection of the trajectory from which such questions are proceeding. As promised, I have not merely had a conversation with not merely the text or its cultural representations, but I have also tried to present a clearer picture of the significance and the complex nature of eighteenth-century Afro-British American identification of, and with, the concept and reality of Africa.

CONCLUDING REMARKS

What Is African in African American?

I am.
Because I am African, I can
Because I am African American, I will
For those who cannot, for those who can but won't
For those whose struggle brought them to the grave
For them I'll be brave,
For all the memories and shards and tears I can't recover
For every mother, son, sister, papa, brother,
I've got to be, I've got to embrace forever and live within this
    eternity
For what I want to be but can't I'll be what I must
For those who don't know love or trust, for those who have lost all
    hope
I will love and trust, and forget my fears just long enough to be
    who I am
Because I am African, I can
Because I am African American, I will
I will, I will, I will, I will, I will, I will, I will

Be all that Phillis and Olaudah and Broteer Furro and Malcolm
   and Martin
and Angela and Assata and Lula and Ollie Brown put in me
For all they gave to me in my blood that's thicker than a thousand
   oceans Atlantic wider
         than any tears they cried,
Because I've no choice but to be beautiful and black and the
   woman my mother raised
         me to be
Because of those who died and bequeathed their legacy
For my loved ones who served in every war, every battle, every
   struggle
For those I could not or would not stand for or with,
For every breath that God has given me for everything and one I'll
   ever be
And for every child that's kin to me—and the village can't be num-
   bered with the sands of
         time
I remain African, I stand African and American against the viola-
   tors of the rights of those who made America at the expense of
   Africa and everything it should have been—and Africa will be
   AGAIN because WE Africans will, we will, we will, we will, we
   will, we
         will, we will
With worn bodies and torn lives, like our ancestors who adminis-
   tered broke but not broken, sick and tired but not too sick to
   fight, we will because we refuse to fail
Because I am African I must,
Because I am African American I will
For every land their peoples underdeveloped I will develop
I will mix my hand in dirt and sand and smell the water filled with
   blood and tears
And create with mud of time and ancestry and future destiny out of
   all that's left inside of
         me
A world where–nothing's wrong and everything is Right with being
   Black and Beautiful
         and claiming all it means within and without
Because every African American's soul cries out joyfully through
   the Middle Passage,

"We have returned, they said we wouldn't, but we've survived
    despite every chain, and
whip, and rope,
Despite the anger, and the hatred, and fear pressed upon us
Despite the blows we gave each other,
Despite the lost fathers and mothers and sisters and brothers,
Despite the maladies, starvation, hunger,
We will always be Africans together, we will stand and we will refuse
    those who say
We are not African, We are not American,
We are not anything but the slaves and peasants of the Universe"
For we know better, we think harder, we work longer, we get
    stronger
We will not forget whose we are, and we continue to steal ourselves
    back
As one goes out the front door two come in the back
As two go out the back, four come through the front
We are more than just a memory, a song, a drum, a solitary voice
    crying out
We are more than thousands gone, we are millions returned and
Because we are Africans,
Because we are African Americans
we will, We will, we Will, We will, we Will, We will, we Will

I want to contextualize this poem by way of capturing several intertextual moments that link Katherine Clay Bassard, Phillis Wheatley, and Maria Stewart with "Unbound." This poem, which returns to the question with which I began in the prefatory remarks of this book, refers to my own experiences in the summer of 2001 upon visiting—making a pilgrimage, really—Gorée Island in Senegal West Africa. Unlike Bassard, I was absolutely looking for a "positivistic search for 'roots'" (4). Moreover, I was looking for Wheatley's roots—I haven't found them yet (hers or mine). Nonetheless, Bassard's initial reactions to her 1994 visit to the Cape Coast Castle in Ghana ring uncannily familiar. Beyond echoing Bassard's expression of the sense of being suspended between Black Atlantic worlds, I would like to share something else about this experience. I found that the Atlantic Ocean from the African side of the Atlantic is so captivating—literally it takes your breath away—that once the sight of this water had impressed itself upon my memory, I could remember little else for a long time. Indeed, even when I reflect upon it for longer than a few moments I am magically carried back to Dakar. Thus, my experience of the water in Senegal provides yet another inter-textual link—to a memory of Wheatley's own mother pouring water each morning.

"A Song for Senegal" was penned on the occasion of my home-going back to Africa. I went to Dakar in Senegal West Africa looking for Phillis and found a piece of myself I had been mourning all my life. Having just returned from one of several visits to Gorée Island, I began reflecting on Wheatley's "On Being Brought from Africa to America." Standing at the entrance to the smallest space in which captured children were collected before being boarded onto ships to take the horrible journey of the Middle Passage, I began to wonder how Wheatley must have felt, frail, frightened, and just a small child in a dark, damp enclosure. This space seemed to me unbearable for even one adult to endure for more than perhaps an hour or two, at best, let alone several small children for an extended period. The dark space has little light except for the small crevices that permit a hint of sun. Yet, even this small relief of light was probably not there during the slavery era. Instead, it appears the result of hundreds of years of wear and weather eroding the surfaces enough to create even the small hole in the wall. I stood in dread and awe of what had happened, of what young Wheatley and millions of others—my ancestors—had endured. Mere feet away I approached the *door of no return*. I stopped there to proclaim a victory, to announce to my ancestors that I had returned with the blood of our captors in my veins to pay homage and respect. Even now I am reminded of the cautions given to African Americans who make the pilgrimage to slave forts. They say you shouldn't go alone—not at least the first time.

Thus, this occasional, elegiac myth of sufficiency is meant to honor Phillis Wheatley—whose creative urging prompted a search for her roots that uncovered shards of my own. I want to end with a final moment of unconscious intertextuality. When I was in Senegal writing this poem, I had not remembered Maria Stewart's nineteenth-century call of racial uplift for black people to turn the "I cans" into "I wills."[1] Thus, what intertextually links (consciously or unconsciously) Bassard, Wheatley, Stewart, and myself are our diverse responses to a "spiritual interrogation." For my part, as an African and an American I celebrate the enduring will and creative imagination of eighteenth-century African-descended writers like Wheatley who survived the Middle Passage and lived to tell about it. "Unbound" honors their imaginative and combative spirit, and extends their willingness to do battle with things seen and unseen to—to confront the dilemma of a ghost. I end with this poetic reflection and contextualization where I began—suspended between Black Atlantic worlds still looking for Phillis.

NOTES

Preface

1. Eulalie is a black American character in Christina Ama Ata Aidoo's play *Dilemma of a Ghost*. This character represents one of the significant dilemmas posed by Afro-Western notions of what it means to be "African." The subsequent marriage between this U.S.-born black woman from Harlem and Ato, an African-born man from Ghana, who meet at an American university and then move back to Africa after graduation, reveals just how entrenched such essentializing notions of Africa are in the mind of the black American. Aidoo captures the very complexity of the ways in which young black men and women of my generation—from both sides of the Atlantic—attempted to reclaim their African culture and identity.

Introduction

1. Hereafter referred to as Afro-British American writers. Although I follow the common practice of using African American and black interchangeably, Afro-British American refers to eighteenth-century blacks living in British colonies—to underscore the dilemma of self and identity during an era of nation building and race and class codification. African American will always refer to black Americans of the post–eighteenth century.

2. Throughout this study, African ways of knowing refer to various indigenously derived and syncretically constructed vernaculars, languages, utterances, and silences in African and African Diaspora cultures.

3. Hereinafter referred to as the *Interesting Narrative*. Unless otherwise noted, all references to this narrative will be from the ninth edition reprinted in *Olaudah Equiano: The Interesting Narrative and Other Writings*, edited with an introduction and notes by Vincent Carretta (New York: Penguin, 1995).

Chapter One

1. All references to this text are to the Macmillan edition: Christine Ama Ata Aidoo, *The Dilemma of a Ghost* (New York: Macmillan Company, 1971).

2. "African worldviews" throughout this study refers to "the epistemological [and ontological] differences inherent in both the origin and contradictions of knowledge and knowledge bases" (Kalu, "Women," 229). Further, my use of this term is informed by an understanding of its contested nature and its attendant "traditional aesthetics." (See Chidi Amuta, *The Theory of African Literature,* for outline of debates.)

3. One example of mourning/mooring can be seen in the link between Christian conversion and African burial. Albert Raboteau notes that "slaves customarily spoke of the period of seeking conversion as 'mourning' and thought of it as a time when the sinner should go apart, to a quiet place to struggle with his sins" (73). Raboteau points to examples from the Caribbean and the Sea Islands as "similar to initiation rites in Brazil, Trinidad, and West Africa." See Albert Raboteau, *Slave Religion: The 'Invisible Institution' in the Antebellum South* (Oxford: Oxford University Press, 2004).

4. I am grateful for John Saillant's apt use of this term to describe how "Black Nova Scotians refitted several elements of African religions in an effort to understand and to seek control of their situation" (28). See "John Marrant: Explaining Syncretism in African American View of Death, an Eighteenth-Century Example," *Culture and Tradition* 17 (1995): 25–41.

5. References to Blackamoor, Othello, and Moors are found throughout the culture and literature from at least the fourteenth century on—in fiction and nonfiction works (e.g., William Shakespeare and John Locke).

According to *The Concise Oxford English Dictionary,* ed. Catherine Soanes and Angus Stevenson (Oxford: Oxford University Press, 2004):

> "Moor" *n.:* a marsh, an area of unenclosed, uncultivated land . . . a region of wasteland. "Moor" *v.:* to secure (a ship, boat, or other floating object) in a particular place by means of one or more chains, ropes, or cables fastened to the shore or to the anchors. Of a ship: to be made secure in a particular place, esp. by means of anchors or cables; to take up a particular position. "Moor" *n.:* originally used to denote a native or inhabitant of ancient Mauretania, a region of North Africa, it was later used to refer to a member of a Muslim people of Berber and Arab descent in habiting north-western Africa. In the Middle Ages, and as late as the seventeenth century, the Moors were widely supposed to be mostly black or very dark-skinned, although the existence of 'white Moors' was recognized. "Blackamoor" *n.:* a black-skinned African, an Ethiopian, a Negro; any very dark-skinned person. Since at least the sixteenth century . . . the term [Moor] has been used interchangeably as both neutral descriptor and as that which [denotes] derogatory traits based on skin-color and region of descent.

6. Although psychoanalytic "mourning" (which denotes a simultaneous detachment from the binding traumatic psychical apparatus) parallels my claim of early African American literature's simultaneous mooring and mourning to dysfunctional ways of knowing, the cultural application of "mourning" I use here suggests a more complex and interrelated relationship between mourning and its psychical object. See Jean Laplanche and J. B. Pontalis, eds., *The Language of Psycho-Analysis,* trans. Donald Nicholson-Smith (New York: Norton, 1973).

7. In general, "our" refers to a diverse and admittedly rather loosely constructed community of writers, critics, and readers of black American literature, as well as those literary scholars and theorists for whom issues related to language and cultural appropriation of Blackness or Africanness remain at the heart of an identification of aesthetic value.

8. Arlene A. Elder explains that "The Bird of the Wayside of the Prologue . . . [who] represents the apparently meaningless . . . incomprehensive continuum of human life . . . is also . . . an interpreter who can 'furnish you with the reasons why / this and that and other things/Happened'" (Aidoo qtd. in "Ama Ata Aidoo: The Development of a Woman's Voice," *Emerging Perspectives on Ama Ata Aidoo,* ed. Ada Uzoamaka Azodo and Gay Wilentz (Trenton, NJ: Africa World, 1999), 159.

9. As the play develops, we realize that Eulalie is equally disenchanted with her new family and the unexpected outcome of her plans for a return to her African homeland. Unlike Ato, Eulalie, whose mother is dead, has no family. Therefore, she comes to Africa not only expecting a return to a mythic Africa filled with coconut palms and drums beating jazz rhythms, but also hoping that Ato's family will be hers. Instead, she finds herself surprisingly a stranger and an outcast in a place whose people, customs, rituals, and traditions appear as foreign to her as she does to them.

10. Esi Kom complains that she "cannot get a penny to pay the smallest debt . . . [because] Hureri must have . . . her machines" (70; Act 3). Similarly, the two village women claim that Eulalie "uses machines for doing everything" (74; Act 4)—"machines that cook and . . . machines that sweep" (75; Act 4). The machine that is most often held up to ridicule is the refrigerator. As an outsider, everyone naturally assumes that it is Eulalie who demands refrigerated beverages; however, both she and Ato make use of this machine. The village women remark that "her water must be colder than hailstone" and that "Monka's teeth were set on edge for drinking water in her house" (73–74; Act 4).

11. The "been-to" is a character in African literature that represents the Western-educated African-born man or woman. As a result of having "been-to" these non-African places, the African who returns home no longer values African cultures and traditions and has a difficult time recovering a former African self while appreciating the value of non-African experiences. Gay Wilentz argues, Aidoo "connects the situation of the educated African 'been to' with the dilemma of the diaspora" (269). Vincent Odamtten describes the been-to as "a paradox" symbolizing both "the possibility of surmounting the restrictions and limitations of their neocolonial reality" and "their oppression" as

one who is "envied and even despised or resented" (31). In terms of the value of highlighting the ambivalence of such a character, for understanding the dilemma of eighteenth-century self and identity, it might be helpful to think of "been-to" as embodying—being mourned/moored to—a kind of fractured consciousness struggling to dislodge dysfunctional remnants of black experiences of slavery and nominal (un)freedom in colonial Britain and the United States. Moreover, given the difficulty experienced by those characters who had not left Africa, but were determining where to place themselves in a newly independent African country (Ghana), it may also be useful to similarly consider enslaved Africans. Like formerly colonized African citizens, they exhibit and register similar anxieties about the nature of locating one's African self.

12. "In Aidoo's view, their eagerness to learn about and discuss the world around them transcends mere gossip . . . curiosity or voyeurism. The distinction implies a public educative function for storytelling that is made moral through the serious involvement of teller and listener, artist and audience" (Elder, 160).

13. Now, it might be objected, and rightly so, that I am attempting to draw a line of analogy between Ato Yawson and Kwame Nkrumah to argue for an understanding of Aidoo's *Dilemma* as a political allegory of sorts. I am most certainly not. Admittedly, Nkrumah was a complex figure whose politics and contributions to Africa are heavily debated. However, it is relatively safe to conclude that at the time of Aidoo's play Nkrumah symbolized (among other things) the seemingly insurmountable challenges posed by decolonization and Pan-Africanism, and what was at stake for a newly independent African country like Ghana. Consequently, I agree with Anthonia Kalu's assessment that "significant to the situation in *The Dilemma* . . . is that the Ghana in question is new to all the characters. In the new dispensation, the negotiations and transitions are no longer smooth as everyone strives for harmony, full participation and recognition" ("Women," 67–76).

14. Written, performed, and subsequently published when Aidoo was still an undergraduate student at the University of Ghana at Accra, Aidoo admits to her attempt to write a play addressing the Pan-African possibilities playing themselves out at the historical moment in the sixties when leader Nkrumah was attempting to build bridges between diasporic African communities. Historically and politically timely, this play's first unearthing of the historical and cultural divides that complicate dialogue among Africans of the Diaspora remains relevant in the more than forty years since it was first performed (1964 Ghana).

15. More certainty than possibility, once a splintered black consciousness enters, passes through, and recovers from such a reconstructed portal it will—as a necessary consequence—return differently and unrecognizably fragmented, on a quest to self-identify with new newly identified cultural shards.

16. My use of "rise" is meant to signify on the "bewildering combination of forces" to which Julian Mayfield refers in his description of Margaret Walker's poetry (qtd. in Gayle, 27). Specifically, I point here to black literature's historical engagement with the dilemma of transcendent and insurgent rising— the dilemma of responding to competing calls to both rise above and rise

up. Spanning an aesthetic continuum from the eighteenth to the twentieth century, from Lucy Terry and Phillis Wheatley to Walker, Maya Angelou, and beyond, African American history has been imagined within what John Charles Shields termed—in his description of Wheatley's poetry—a "poetics of ascent." Thus, to rise is to invoke an aesthetic continuum that builds bridges and sustains links between "a past rooted in pain" (Angelou) and a new life and a new vision of life that springs forth—unbounded, free, and continuously renewing. The early black writers in this book provide the seeds from which this type of aesthetic develops—in the space of active and ongoing engagement with the dilemma of rising up and rising above.

17. Diana Fuss points to productive uses and deliberate "abuses" of essentialism.

18. Equiano and other eighteenth-century Africans, as well as many other writers, have pointed out examples of such violations against African societies which include murder and adultery.

19. See also Gauthier's *Morals by Agreement* (Oxford: Clarendon Press, 1986) for a further analysis of social dilemmas as explored with regard to the limitations of American social contract and dilemma theory as models for exploration of dilemma within the context of this book.

20. Similarly, in his essay "Princes and Powers" in *Nobody Knows My Name,* Baldwin confronts the dilemma of simultaneously assuming and losing one's cultural identity. In response to Leopold Senghor's reading of Richard Wright's *Black Boy* as a text that would "undoubtedly reveal the African heritage to which it owed its existence" (Senghor, qtd. in Baldwin, *Collected Essays,* 154), Baldwin cautions that in "presenting Wright with his African heritage," Senghor risks at the same time "taking away his [American] identity" (154). While Baldwin concedes that "there was undoubtedly something African in *Black Boy,* as there was undoubtedly something African in all American Negroes, the great question of what this was and how it had survived, remained wide open" (154).

21. For example, in "Letter III" of *Letters from an American Farmer,* J. Hector St. John de Crevecoeur asks and attempts to answer the question: "What is an American?" Similarly, in "Heritage," poet Countee Cullen complicates Crevecoeur's unearthing of the "American Adam" by asking, and with less certainty about his position within the Crevecoeur's American melting pot theory, "What is Africa to me?" Between the white European-American Frenchman and the African American, Wheatley, an "Ethiop," and Equiano, an "Igbo," embrace the dilemma of becoming Afro-British American.

22. Although this issue of how much of Josiah Henson's life Stowe actually used as source material for *Uncle Tom's Cabin* is uncertain, the literary and cultural model of a docile black man remains. Henson's own words chillingly confirm this: "[Miss Stowe] referred to my published life-story, as an exemplification of the truth of the character of her Uncle Tom. From that time to the present, I have been called 'Uncle Tom.'"

23. Both black and white history have been misleading/misled in this regard. It is to this simultaneous call from the Thomas Jeffersons and the Redding Saunders, that this book in part responds.

24. See also Cerroni-Long, "Benign Neglect? Anthropology and the Study

of Blacks in the United States," *Journal of Black Studies* 17, no. 4 (1987): 438–69.

25. Herskovitz shares this concern as he notes that "accounting for the presence or absence of cultural survivals" must include "assessing the intensity" and "discovering how they have changed their form or . . . assumed new meaning" (*Myth*, 14). Similarly, David Evans argues that "*Africanism* . . . places the emphasis entirely on the African component of the cultural trait and fails to describe the process" (380).

26. I use this term "loopholes" in a similar manner as does Valerie Smith in her often-cited essay "'Loopholes of Retreat': Architecture and Ideology in Harriet Jacobs's *Incidents in the Life of a Slave Girl*," in *Reading Black, Reading Feminist: A Critical Anthology,* ed. Henry Louis Gates Jr. (New York: Meridian, 1990).

27. My invocation of the structural value of dilemma as a rhetorical and grammatical "tool" of empowerment and action rather than the converse, primarily because of its negative connotations and its pejorative valuation, is not (structurally) unlike reformulations of "dysfunctional" deconstructive "margin to center" theories such as those advanced by bell hooks, which provide highly instructive theoretical models. Rather than merely constituting the margin as a place from which to move to the center, the margin is constructed as place of power. Dilemma is similarly valuable. Much like the traditional Western view of African dilemma tales—as understood by William Bascom (and others) as having their primary (didactic) value in the realm of the ethical; for example, to teach societal values and mores though the application of judgment to the tale (story) presented—the significance of the tales' resistance to any simplistic aesthetic value is arguably what gives it value. The "riddle" stimulates not only the mind, but the soul as well. The beauty of its transcendent value, the ability to remove one from one's self as in traditional forms of poetry, suggest an aesthetic which has yet to fully be articulated, even as it subsumed under "didactic" as though this term—much like dilemma—always already disclaimed any value. The very premises upon which African dilemma tales are valued—for their ability to "tap into" and otherwise engage a reader's intellectual and moral power—are in fact what give them their aesthetic value and assign them to ethereal realms as well. See William R. Bascom, *African Dilemma Tales* (Paris: Mouton, 1975), for a fuller explanation of this genre.

28. Katherine Bassard reveals early black women writers' strategies for creating spaces of self-recovery through the use of "spirituals matrix [that] proceeds from the deconstruction of oppositions of sacred/secular, political/religious, social/spiritual that plague much thinking around spirituals even as it disrupts the binaries of African/Euramerican, functional/aesthetic" (*Spiritual Interrogations*, 27).

29. See Toni Morrison's *Playing in the Dark: Whiteness and the Literary Imagination* (New York: Random House, 1993). Morrison discourages "those totalizing approaches to African-American scholarship which have no drive other than the exchange of dominations—dominant Eurocentric scholarship replaced by dominant Afro-centric scholarship" (8). Engaging the dilemma of what Morrison terms "American Africanism," she exposes the imagery of Africanness in

white American literature. Such a concept is a large part of the dilemma that eighteenth-century black writers confronted.

30. Paul Gilroy has most recently coined this term in his 1993 text, *The Black Atlantic: Modernity and Double Consciousness*. However, Isodore Okpewho notes that "the phrase itself may be traced to Robert Farris Thompson . . . and the series of courses he taught at Yale University in the '70s on the subject of Black Atlantic civilizations" (*The African Diaspora*, xxi).

31. I am referring here to work of scholars such as Henry Louis Gates Jr. (1988), Houston A. Baker Jr. (1984), Chikwenye Okonjo Ogunyemi (1996), Mae Gwendolyn Henderson (1989), and others. Gates locates African ways of knowing at the nexus of a Yoruban-derived deity, Esu Elegbara, and his Pan-African derived cousin, the Signifying Monkey. Baker "[appropriates] the vastness of the [black] vernacular in the United States to a single [blues] matrix" (14), in order to contextualize African cultural resonances. Ogunyemi simultaneously recenters the African wo/man and child through mutable transformative dialogue known as *palava*. Henderson signifies the underlying simultaneity of African women's discourse through her introduction of African practice and cultural reorientation of the spiritual utterances of "speaking in tongues."

32. African scholars such as Chinua Achebe, Michael Echeruo, Ngugi wa' Thiongo, and numerous others have rigorously investigated issues of African "authenticity" as they relate to language and literature.

33. Even as I suggest the critical need for "unpacking," I recognize an equally important—perhaps more pressing—need in some circumstances (on social, political, economic levels, for example) to judiciously and responsibly "dispense" the contents of this very real "baggage," however metaphorically we as literary critics might abstract the powerful knowledge(s) it produces and reproduces.

34. Fox-Genovese points to the predicament of black women writers, who are caught between re-presentation and representation. "Is the black woman writer first a self, a solitary statue? Or is she first a woman and if so, in relation to whom? No dilemma could more clearly expose the condition of any self as hostage to society, politics, and language" (199–200).

35. In the American Adamic myth of New World origins, Adam is not African. Joanna Brooks interrogates this myth in *American Lazarus*. Further complicating this flawed ordering is the attempt to "refit" a continent into a country.

36. It should be noted here that the work of literary critics Houston A. Baker Jr. and Henry Louis Gates Jr., rather than reflect a use of a "system of conceptual thought generated [wholly or significantly] from the African deep structure . . . the African worldview" (Peters, 36), highlights the way in which Western epistemologies are reoriented through connection to indigenous and syncretized African worldviews to create hybridized African ways of knowing. For, even as their work is heavily laden with the discourse of European theory, it simultaneously engages in a *palava* with the hegemonic discourse in ways that reproduce Afro/Western critical structures of meaning of value for African-centered readings of literature. Indeed, it is the transformative power implied in such syncretized forms that is most valuable in these tools of analysis.

37. Such interpretive strategies and modes of analysis, whose underlying artistic and philosophical principles are grounded in progressive engagement with Africanisms, are sometimes referred to as Africentric. "Africentric" is a term that refers to a "foundational designation, bearing definite and precise grounding in indigenous African thought and customs . . . refer[ring] specifically to African cultural attributes, ontologies, epistemologies, and axiologies with respect to their purposeful, illuminative, and regenerative agency for Africa and the African Diaspora. A related term which describes similar methods of African recovery is Afrocentrism." "Afrocentric" is defined as a term that "designates[s] matters peculiar to the enslaved Africans and their descendants in the Americas, issues peculiar to the African American racial self and its manifold predicaments" (Peters, 35). This term has been both decried as a totalizing approach to designating Africa and applauded as a tool of empowerment. In "Afrocentricity: Problems of Logic, Method, and Nomenclature," the late Dr. Erskine Peters sheds light on regressive and progressive elements of these two African-centered methods—Afrocentric and Africentric.

38. Vincent Carretta suggests that a diverse "choice of identities [such as Afro-Briton and African American] was possible because both British and American identities were recent political constructions invented in the eighteenth century" (7).

39. Abiola Irele's work is an example of the type of self-conscious scholarly work to which I am referring. Notably, he adopts a self-interrogative posture when he questions the motives and position of a critic's overwhelming and overarching need to define Africa. In his questioning of the motives and position of the literary critic (qua investigator), he suggests that "however gratifying it may be . . . to arrive at a precise definition of African literature, the effort [misses] the point [of] plac[ing] the focus . . . the essential force of African literature—[on] its reference to the historical and experiential" (*The African Experience in Literature and Ideology*, 11). This type of critical force which has positively influenced literary scholarship since 1981 remains relevant to my integrative approach.

40. I refer here to those scholars mentioned in my introduction and the scholarship their work brings forward.

41. Wole Soyinka complicates and universalizes this notion of "complementarity" when he asserts that "the African world, like any other 'world' is [both] unique [and] possesses . . . in common with other cultures, the virtues of complementarity" (*Myth, Literature and the African World*, xii).

42. "African origins of the American self" signifies the conflicting worldviews operating within Wheatley's consciousness. For example, the "Puritan psychology [that] lies in contrast between personal responsibility and individualism" that Sacvan Berkovitch describes in *Puritan Origins of the American Self* stands in opposition to African ontologies that understand a less contentious relationship between personal and collective responsibility. In many African societies the "gift" rather than the "burden" of the assumption of responsibility is celebrated by means of initiation ceremonies. See also Mailidoma Patrice Some's *Of Water and the Spirit*. The community grants this gift because personal responsibility represents an investment in the development of the community,

even as it celebrates its understanding and respect for a particular person's gifts (talents) within a community. This particular African way of knowing has neither been wholly ruptured nor lost over time. Nor has it been maintained without significant mediation from Western resources. Culture and literature continue to contend with what DuBois has described as "double consciousness" (see W. E. B. DuBois's *Souls of Black Folk*).

43. An excellent example of this dilemma faced by the critical attempt to voice gender analysis within African-centered contexts is the way in which Holloway reads the difference between black women and white women's revision of the metaphors of childbirth and literary creation. "Creativity was a compromise of childbirth in the literature of the West. . . . For black women, babies were often neither realistic nor a matter of choice, and black women writers have reconstructed the issue into the figurative dimensions of their literary texts. In their works childbirth is often framed as a threat to survival rather than the (comparatively) benign worry that pregnancy will 'sabotage their creative drive'" (171). Hence, if feminist paradigms displaced the mother with the Father, and if Afrocentric paradigms displaced the black or African mother with the African Father, then the "depth of memory that black women's textual strategies are designed to acknowledge" permit a critical step toward a recovery—in Holloway's terms a (re)membrance—of African Mother/Father (Wo/Man) as central to dislodging dysfunctional Western paradigms. Indeed, Holloway's work is critical to understanding the depth of narratives that emerge from a text like Wheatley's "Niobe."

44. My reference to this African motif is directly related to early African American literature's simultaneous yearning for and objectification of literacy and orality as demonstrated in the "talking book" trope, as described earlier. It is important to note that the focus on literacy as an aesthetic value and therefore central theme occupying early black texts does not necessarily preclude a very practical understanding by the authors under study in this book that literacy was not synonymous with freedom—a type of freedom perhaps. Indeed, if anything, literacy, once acquired, gave these writers the tools with which to critique the underlying visions and implications of states and types of (un)freedom. John Saillant makes a compelling argument for this way of situating "freedom" in the context of the new republic and the narratives of nominally free men such as John Jea. See "Traveling in Old and New Worlds with John Jea, the African Preacher, 1773–1816," *Journal of American Studies* 33, no. 3 (1999): 471–90.

45. "Palava", as Ogunyemi describes it (a gendered mode of conversation that invites disagreement), is used to explore women's transgression and enactment of radical politics of gender, class, and culture conflicts while they simultaneously build a bridge between males and females in an attempt to rebuild African communities at various levels—familial, local, village, urban, and country.

46. Mae Gwendolyn Henderson, for example, appropriates biblical concepts and scriptural language to shed light on black women's inter- and intratexuality in her theory of "Speaking in Tongues."

47. Gabrielle Foreman's "histotextuality" offers important considerations of

"the multiple strands at work in" nineteenth-century "African-American women's literary tradition" (331).

48. See note 41, above.

49. For example, while Patricia Hill Collins's revised black feminist theory parallels the type of structure that Ogunyemi's more global context suggests, Ogunyemi uses definable African motifs and tropes that are grounded in an identifiable worldview. Her use of African-centered knowledge bases and her appropriation of European language into African contexts support an expanded vision of African women's thought conceived of in the *palava*. In her reworking of the concept of black feminist thought, Collins presents a complex analysis of empowerment such that the terms that define it no longer foreground her discussion. Rather, Collins's more inclusive "emphasi[s] [on the] particular dimensions that characterize it, but that are not unique to it" allow her to make connections to the African Diaspora in ways that abstractly explore both the similarities and differences. Her retaining of the "main ideas" of Afrocentrism without using the "loaded" term parallel Peters's use of the term. However, Peters's analysis and critique neither renders the "term" useless nor, in Collins's terms, "discredits" it.

50. See Kalu's conclusion concerning just such a need for "a systematic rearticulation of the female principle, whose agenda for continued advancement and progress is unequivocally mapped on Africa's cultural landscapes" ("Women and the Social Construction," 287). Platonic models—as illustrated, for example, in Gorgias—utilize similar European-centered, purposeful dialectic-dialogic discourse methods.

51. Sources for references to *mbari* are from Cole (*Mbari*) and Achebe ("African Literature").

Chapter Two

1. See Margaret Odell's biography on Wheatley and John Wheatley's letter (dated November 14, 1772) to the publisher of *Poems on Various Subjects Religious and Moral*. http://docsouth.unc.edu/neh/wheatley/wheatley.html#wheat9. Accessed July 9, 2007.

2. All references to Ovid's text, unless otherwise noted, will be the translation in the Loeb Edition. See Ovid, *Metamorphoses Books I–VIII,* ed. G. P. Goold, trans. Frank Justus Miller (Cambridge: Harvard University Press, 1999).

3. Michael Gomez uses this term to refer to "related yet distinguishable life-styles" (9) that differentiate between mere "synthesis of . . . European and African cultural forms" and the actual lifestyles African Americans maintained in the face of "culture[s] of coercion and . . . volition" (10). Thus, polycultural refers to both "forms of expression [and] the intent and meaning behind the slave's participation" (10).

4. E.g., "On Being Brought from Africa to America," "To the University of Cambridge, in New England," and "To the Right Honorable William, Earl of Dartmouth."

5. "Nation" refers to a group of persons related by common language,

descent (or origin) and history, country, as well as "a particular class, kind, or race of persons" (*OED* s.v.). Between the late seventeenth and eighteenth centuries, the community of colonial subjects gradually metamorphosed from a group of displaced English men and women with a common language and history into a race of white, male, propertied rational humans with a natural right to independence and ascendancy over those who were of other nations (race and gender). The evolution of the term by which colonists described themselves, from "Christian" to "free" to "white," illustrates this metamorphosis (Reich, 124).

6. My conceptualization of this term parallels Paul Gilroy's invention of "Africa" within the "rhizomorphic, fractal structure of the transcultural, international formation" (4) he calls the Black Atlantic.

7. See Glenn Hendler's work in the area of nineteenth-century sentimentality, gender, and the public sphere for additional insights into this phenomenon (see *Public Sentiments: Structures of Feeling in Nineteenth-Century American Literature* [Chapel Hill: University of North Carolina Press, 2001]).

8. The Great Commission commands Christians to "go ye therefore, and teach all nations . . . to observe all things whatsoever I have commanded you" (Matthew 28:19–20a). The understanding that Wheatley, as a devout Christian, could not have missed was "and lo, I am with you alway, even unto the end of the world" (Matthew 28:20b). This passage clearly links the Christian ethereal with the transient world. Finally, the word "life" (Greek: *zoe;* Hebrew: *nephesh*) in John 10:10 denotes that "abundant living" is promised both on earth and in heaven.

9. I describe Wheatley's work as a kind of marketplace because its synthesization of diverse Western and African ways of knowing creates a space of positive creative exchange and dialogue. Further, the role of the marketplace for African women as a center for cultural, commercial, and personal exchanges signifies on a feminized market space that does not exclude, but rather supports the entire community in West African cultures. According to Ogunyemi, "the marketplace [is] the site where . . . [many] purveyors thrive, each [with] a niche. The market combines, into one gigantic whole, what, in the Western world, has been compartmentalized and masculinized [or feminized] under capitalism into the departmental store, the bookstore, the grocery store, the hairdressing salon . . ." (*African Wo/Man Palava*, 49).

10. David Grimsted argues that "death is tied imagistically to slavery. To die in Christ is to be 'from bondage freed,' though death himself 'reigns tyrant o'er this mortal shore,' exercises his 'dire dominion,' and represents 'all destroying Power,' which vainly tries to 'chain us to hell, and bar the gates of light.' Wheatley addressed the 'grim monarch' in terms that should have touched the human slave drivers: 'Dost thou go on incessant to destroy, / Our griefs to double, and lay waste our joy?'" ("Anglo-American Racism and Phillis Wheatley's . . .," 357).

11. As a result, I will not find it necessary, for example, to identify Wheatley's employment of a bird trope. Nor will I make any claims about Wheatley's specific geographic origins on the continent of Africa. I have selected Senegal as a focal point of departure for African aesthetic influences in her work

because much of the historical evidence presented thus far suggests it is reasonable to do so.

12. See Luke 14:27–29 (King James Version): "And whosoever doth not bear his cross, and come after me, cannot be my disciple / For which of you, intending to build a tower, sitteth not down first, and counteth the cost, whether he have sufficient to finish it? / Lest haply, after he hath laid the foundation, and is not able to finish it, all that behold it begin to mock him."

13. See Antonio T. Bly, "Wheatley's 'To the University of Cambridge, in New-England,'" *Explicator* 55, no. 4 (Summer 1997): 205–9, for a less gendered reading of Wheatley's tactical employment of such religious themes to subvert dominant negative racial subscriptions and assert her own race pride.

14. Likewise, as critics we attempt to recover Wheatley from the fragmented remains of African, Western, and Afro-Western cultural and historical remains.

15. I am deeply indebted to Lucy Hayden's work (following John Shields), one of the first and still few scholars to suggest that Wheatley was "possibly drawing subliminally on the story-telling tradition of her African past when she wrote 'Goliath of Gath' as well as when she faced the challenge of recreating Ovid's passionate story of Niobe" (436). Necessarily, she acknowledges Shields's contribution—thinking along these lines—as I do here and elsewhere in this book. Importantly, however, she turns to Wheatley's Christian traditions for answers to the critical question she poses: "But why Book VI of The Metamorphoses and not another possibly one of those translated by Pope?" (436). See "Classical Tidings from the Afric Muse: Phillis Wheatley's Use of Mythology," *CLA* 34, no. 4 (June 1992): 432–47.

16. As of the Virginia Act of 1658, children followed the condition of their mother, thereby "demean[ing] the black mother because of her race and set[ting] her apart from white women" (Ashcraft-Eason, 70). This represents one of colonial America's earliest and most critical links between the naturalness of motherhood and the naturalness of slavery.

17. George Sandys's translation of the description of Niobe's children strikes an interpretive balance between Wheatley and Ovid: "Seuen beauteous daughters, and as many boyes. All these by marriage to be multiply'd." See Sandys's *Ovid's Metamorphoses Englished*.

18. "Seven" is "used symbolically, often denoting completion or perfection" (*OED* s.v.). Niobe's children and Zeus are both the children of Titans. Zeus is the son of Chronos and Niobe is the daughter of Tantalus (Smith, *Dictionary of Classical Reference in English Poetry*, 39–167). Niobe's and Latona's relative positions to divinity have to do with Zeus's usurping of his father's throne.

19. Like Bassard, I, too, "read Wheatley's memory of her mother's morning libations as [what Holloway terms] a '(cultural) mooring' that initiates a series of African American female '(spiritual) metaphors'" (37 passim). See also Holloway (passim). The version of Wheatley's memory I cite here (from Richmond) is actually an embellishment by her biographer. The embellished version appears on the page after this original version: "One circumstance alone, it might have been said, she remembered; and that was, her mother's custom of pouring out water before the sun at rising." See B. B. Thatcher,

Memoir of Phillis Wheatley, a Native African and Slave, 2nd ed. (Boston: Geo. W. Light, 1837), 2.

20. Robert Ferguson's elaboration of the significance of "metaphors of light" to "early republican problems of perception" is instructive. His work suggests yet another perspective from which discrete elements of eighteenth-century black aesthetics can be interpreted. If "to see is to know in eighteenth-century thought" and if sight—in its American Enlightenment context—is constructed within a "secular frame of reference" (28), then Wheatley's appropriation of the conventional use of metaphor of light creates a subtle but radical upheaval. Specifically, the black female poet dares to affirm her physical powers of observation alongside her mental and spiritual ones. Rising above the "sons of science," Wheatley ascends through her use of metaphors of light to "clarify" and redefine that which is simultaneously known and unknown—motherhood and nation. In so doing, she subtly and symbolically unveils and exposes the dilemma of a nation blinded and enslaved by its own view of freedom. As I elaborate on a bit more fully later, Wheatley's relationship to sight, seeing, and associated metaphors also links her to West African traditions of Sankofa and the Wayside Bird.

21. "Chi," according to Ogunyemi's interpretation, is "the quidditas inside the human body, the part that cannot be detected but that we know is there. It is essence, innateness, instincts, genetics, luck, endowment, destiny, empowerment; it is the caretaker and giver installed within" (36). She also points to the centrality of motherhood in the myth of Osun, who is the mother of Esu, the intermediary between the divine and human realm and one of the most important Yoruban deities.

22. Boubacar Barry notes that between 1681 and 1810 an estimated 304,330 to 500,000 slaves were exported from the Senegambia region alone. *Senegambia and the Atlantic Slave Trade* (Cambridge: Cambridge University Press, 1998), 61–80.

23. Wheatley, not unlike her contemporary Abigail Adams, is concerned about improved conditions for women in the newly imagined postcolonial society. More importantly, though, the poet understands that "all men [and women] would be tyrants if they could" (Adams qtd. in Adeola James, *In Their Own Voices,* 68).

24. Recent works such as David Goldenberg's *The Curse of Ham: Race and Slavery in Early Judaism, Christianity, and Islam* (Princeton, NJ: Princeton University Press, 2003), and Newell G. Bringhurst and Darron T. Smith's *Black and Mormon* (Urbana: University of Illinois Press, 2004) offer important insights on this topic. Of course, Werner Sollors's numerous works on ethnicity and mixed-race literature and culture and Winthrop Jordan's *White over Black* remain key texts for further study on this tradition.

25. Comparisons as well between Isaac and Ishmael were well known during this period with many eighteenth-century religious texts using Sarah and Hagar as examples of the "Two Covenants" Law and Grace, respectively.

26. The alternate spelling of Sarah's earlier name as Sarai is meant to signify on the drastically different biblical metamorphoses (cultural and spiritual conversions) that these two women experience. More important, the Genesis

narratives of name changing have important implications for reading national and natural identity in Wheatley. Specifically, from Genesis 16 to 17, there is a significant renaming of both Sarai and Abram. Abram becomes "Abraham, father of many nations" and Sarai becomes "Sarah, mother of many nations." Three chapters later after the promised birth of their son Isaac, the child through whom the covenant with God and lineage of the nation of Israel will be fulfilled, Hagar experiences a metamorphosis without name change. Sarah's complete transformation to natural versus stepmother sparks a monstrous transformation for Hagar, whose movement from bondswoman of the house of Abraham, and mother of a son of Abraham who is heir to his household and inheritor of a proud lineage, becomes "Hagar the Egyptian" outcast mother to Ishmael the wild man, who would become the ruler of an "other" kind of nation.

27. I conclude with a reference to displaced African fathers to signify the critical attention that remains to be paid to the multiple codings and balanced rendering of "gender" in Wheatley's works.

Chapter Three

1. Interpretations offered in this chapter on issues regarding Afro-Western recovery of African identities and worldview—especially within the context of the heavily contested site of Equiano's Igbo-American-British-West Indian identity—support my thesis: Afro-European American literature of the eighteenth century is situated squarely within the dilemma of a ghost—a dilemma I argue ought to be embraced by confronting head-on the question of "What is 'African' in African American literature?" Rather than simply locating or identifying African identity, it is more productive to complicate issues further by theorizing and unraveling the very dilemma itself that identity poses. In this way, we both reveal the richness of this literature and complicate any simple view of the construction of African identities in eighteenth-century Afro-British America.

2. African and African American literary scholarship (cited above) has been actively engaged in landscaping and remapping the critical terrain of African spaces within African American culture and literature. Their work has built upon African-centered scholarship outside the field of literary studies by such prominent figures as John Henrik Clarke, Yosef ben-Jochannan, Cheikh Anta Diop, Molefe Asante, Jacob Caruthers, and Ivan Van Sertima.

3. Roxann Wheeler, "Limited Visions of Africa: Geographies of Savagery and Civility in Early Eighteenth-Century Narratives," in *Writes of Passage: Reading Travel Writing*, ed. James Duncan and Derek Gregory (New York: Routledge, 1999), 14–48.

> The ordinary range of knowledge about Africa and Africans in the early eighteenth century was a combination of doubt and conviction, fact and fantasy. Although geographies were common in the libraries of the educated, it was through travel writing that

most Britons gained their ideas about Africans and Africa. Indeed, in England, travel literature was second only to theological texts in popularity during the eighteenth century, and although Africa was one of the least known places, it figured prominently in the many compendiums of travel published during the eighteenth century. In fact almost four times as many books about Africa appeared in the first half of the eighteenth century as all of the previous century. . . . Revisionist scholarship, such as Anthony Barker's history of the African image, has convincingly argued about this literature that "this period before about 1769 was a fruitful one, yielding the most influential descriptions of Negro society of any in the eighteenth century" (15).

Margaret Hunt, "Racism, Imperialism, and the Traveler's Gaze in Eighteenth-Century England," *Journal of British Studies* 32, Issue 4, *Making the English Middle Class, ca 1700–1850* (October 1993): 333–57. Hunt remarks on the "extremely derivative" quality of "most travel accounts, both published and unpublished . . . [that] bears witness to . . . the ceaseless need it seem[ed] to inspire in the traveler to reconfirm stereotypes about the people he or she encounter[ed]." In particular, "visitors to Africa remarked upon the nakedness and heathenish character of Africans" (339–40).

4. Edward W. Said, *Orientalism* (New York: Pantheon Books, 1978). See also the preface to the 2003 Penguin edition of *Orientalism*.

5. I am indebted to scholar Anthonia Kalu for this critical insight first presented at the 1998 American Society for Eighteenth-Century Studies (ASECS) Conference.

6. Quoted from Isaiah 12:2–4

7. Asante expresses the full import of *nommo* and the vital function it fulfills in its capacity to drive African structures of meaning, being, and analysis. This "word force" is an indispensable aspect of a society that understands the interconnectedness between the utilitarian or functional and the seemingly abstract nature of art (*The Afrocentric Idea*, 17). "Thus the African [artist] sees [his or her] discourse [or rhetoric] as the creative manifestation of what is *called to be.* That which is *called to be* . . . becomes the created thing; and the artist, or speaker, satisfies the demands of society by calling into being that which is functional" (75; emphasis in original).

8. Also, it is worth noting that the biblical recording of "the generations of Jacob" (Genesis 37:2) resonates in interesting ways as it relates to lost birthright (Abraham, Essau, and Jacob), slavery (Joseph as favored son of Jacob is sold into slavery by his brothers), and the legacy of Jesus, which comes through the legacy of Abraham.

9. I am grateful for Angelo Costanzo's clarification of a subtle but significant difference between at least two different ways of reading Equiano's use of Vassa. Whereas Carretta emphasizes Equiano's use of Vassa to also support his assertion that Equiano was born in South Carolina and not in Africa, it is equally plausible that Equiano's use of Vassa is a matter of necessary convenience—purely for legal and practical purposes.

10. Along similar lines, Irele has argued "that African letters in European languages were called into being in the first place primarily by a sense of historical grievance, and . . . sustained . . . by our continuing need to situate our collective existence—our very being as Africans" (*The African Imagination*, 46).

11. Elizabeth Alexander is an award-winning poet, essayist, and professor of African American studies at Yale University. The work I cite in this study is from her book of critical essays *The Black Interior*—an important contribution to contemporary black aesthetic theories.

12. Originally a title conferred upon Native Americans, eighteenth-century black writers such as James Albert Gronniosaw (1770), Venture Smith (1798), and Olaudah Equiano (1789) often appropriated the concept of the noble savage in an African context to assert their human rights vis-à-vis a noble and often royal African lineage.

13. A. E. Afigbo, *Ropes of Sand: Studies in Igbo History and Culture* (Ibadan: Oxford University Press, 1981). Afigbo argues that the "languages" to which Equiano refers are most likely different Igbo dialects.

> Sense of "country" was very narrow in precolonial Igboland, so narrow that it would at times be limited to the village group. With a young boy who had never traveled out of his village before and had not attended any of the large inter-group markets or fairs where speakers of many different Igbo dialects met, this narrowness of outlook would be even more pronounced. This would then explain why what must have been dialects of the same language were described by him as different tongues and how the young Equiano who was being hustled down the coast to be sold, could learn "two or three different tongues" within a space of about seen months even though no special efforts would have been made by his masters to teach him these tongues." (150)

14. Equiano's attention to the importance of his being "understood" with an Afro-Igbo context is relevant to his narrative act of African cultural reclamation. Specifically, the importance of community and conversation to an Igbo cannot be overstated, and the fact that he cloaks this replacement or African fragment within the context of eighteenth-century knowledge about language is especially clever—demonstrating his adroitness at maneuvering both Western letters and sentiments. See also Gretchen Holbrook Gerzina, *Black London: Life before Emancipation* (New Brunswick, NJ: Rutgers University Press, 1995) and Emmanuel M. P. Edeh, *Towards an Igbo Metaphysic* (Chicago: Loyola University Press, 1985).

15. While Carl Linnaeus's scientific scheme (*Systema Naturae*, 1735) classified man according to certain human racial characteristics, Georges Buffon's "anthropocentric" scheme (*Histoire Naturelle*, 1749) positioned man within the animal hierarchy dependent upon how near or far he was situated to the lower animals. Africans were placed at the bottom of both systems of classifications. The biologically based racism—vis-à-vis physical anthropology and environmentalism—of Virey, Rousseau, Blumenback, and other biological

determinists, anthropologists, and natural scientists—consciously and unconsciously—participated in developing such biocultural landscapes.

16. I offer a brief and contracted reading of this description in terms of Equiano's signifying in chapter 2. Also, Carretta has fittingly noted the significance of Equiano's reference to the "history of neither a saint, a hero, nor a tyrant" (31) with regard to traditional literary conventions of the period. First, such a reference "was increasingly seen in the seventeenth and eighteenth centuries as the proper subject for autobiography, biography, and the novel." Second, Equiano's "decision to use the name of Gustavus Vassa, the Swedish patriot king who overthrew a tyrannical usurper, certainly gives him an heroic cast" (xx).

17. Faction is a "form of literature that treats real people or events as if they were fictional or uses real people or events as essential elements in an otherwise fictional rendition . . . a mix of fact and fiction." *American Heritage Dictionary of the English Language* (4th ed., 2000). While I prefer "faction," other scholars consider "first novel by a person of African descent" to be more representative of "the path-breaking nature of Equiano's efforts" (Reader's Report on "Unbound").

18. Helena Woodard, *African-British Writings in the Eighteenth Century: The Politics of Race and Reason* (Westport, CT: Greenwood, 1999). Her analysis of the works of Defoe and Swift as two of the more prominent writers "that we can look back to find the African as an indelible fixture in English writings" explores the complexities of literature which offers "a popular culture symbol of human depravity [which] serves a polite readership and a cultivated intellectual establishment more purposefully when turned to didactic ends." Namely, such work "still leaves intact the problematical emblematic representation of depravity," which in the case of Swift was "black, female, and African" (110). James Baldwin, in *Notes of a Native Son*, explores similar risks with regard to the problematic nature of "black representativeness" as seen most prominently in the work of Stowe's *Uncle Tom's Cabin* and Richard Wright's *Native Son*.

19. Chikwenye Okonjo Ogunyemi, *Africa Wo/man Palava: The Nigerian Novel by Women* (Chicago: University of Chicago Press, 1996). Ogunyemi recuperates the homophone and feminine version of "palaver" as "palava," which means "trouble" or "quarrel." This critical linguistic move recenters the African wo/man and child (African woman, man, child) through mutable transformative dialogue known as *palava*. "Palava" is used to explore women's transgression and enactment of radical politics of gender, class, and culture conflicts while they simultaneously build a bridge between males and females in an attempt to rebuild African communities at various levels—familial, local, village, urban, and country. Thus, *palava* refers to "interpretation, both as textual analysis and as translation from one language to another . . . [and] misinterpretation through misreading or misunderstanding [that] generates palava or quarrel. The [role of the] critic as interpreter [is to] attempt to set the record straight, to resolve disputes through illumination to make a text more easily understood, especially as most are written in the language of the colonizer" (96). In *palava* a consensus is often achieved in the space of disagreement or difference. Having a conversation with an eighteenth-century slave narrative, for example, means

that the critic attempts to address questions the narrative poses by repeatedly questioning the multiple and diverse vistas from which the author speaks. I argue that Equiano uses his narrative to engage in just such dialogue as that implied by my use of the term.

20. While the extensive scholarship on Equiano's narrative repositioning of subjectivity and agency is too numerous to mention, Woodard's reading is representative. "Acting as a foreign observer of English culture . . . Equiano . . . both vilifies and esteems the European, ultimately challenging readers to view themselves as the objectified Other" (195). See also Winthrop Jordan, *White over Black: American Attitudes toward the Negro 1550–1812* (Chapel Hill: University of North Carolina Press, 1968). This historian's seminal and still relevant (though somewhat dated) argument provides one of the most cogent and rigorously defended analyses of what he terms "definition by negation."

21. Andrew Varney, *Eighteenth-Century Writers in Their World: A Mighty Maze* (New York: St. Martin's Press, 1999). Varney argues that the "tension generated between the contesting principles of familiarity and otherness, or of recognition and perplexity . . . is inscribed in early eighteenth-century writing cultures on alien cultures, irrespective of whether they are real or imaginary" (4). Further, "in terms of the very many narratives of the early part of the eighteenth century which record real or invented histories of—or voyages to—remote places, this opposition manifests itself in on the one hand discovering outlandish wonders in such places, and on the other in finding that they are in fact very like home" (4). Certainly, Equiano's critical analysis of "home" in his narrative suggests an attempt to explore familiarity and foreignness as coexisting cultural arenas.

22. Universal symbols include the serpent in the Garden of Eden who represents the Devil, a symbol of regeneration and immortality, and two references to Moses' use of the snake as a symbol of healing—when God told Moses to put snakes on a pole to cure snakebite and when God turned Moses' rod into a snake and then changed it back to demonstrate his power. Benjamin Franklin's image of the disjointed snake in his 1751 cartoon became the symbol of American unity, as well as classical images of Hermes' intertwined snakes with the staff of the healer Asclepius. Further, there are intertextual moments to be noticed between Equiano's references and Harriet Jacobs's *Incidents in the Life of a Slave Girl* and Frederick Douglass's *Narrative*. Douglass remarks that "such was his [Master Covey's] cunning, that we used to call him, among ourselves, 'the snake'" (61). This description of Covey lurking in the grass is indicative of his deceitful character and similarity to the serpent—devil—in the Genesis myth. Jacobs, like Equiano, recounts her tale of fleeing from her masters to a space of wilderness where the fear of snakes becomes equally menacing and analogously related to the fear of being recaptured.

23. While other aspects of Catherine Acholonu's *The Igbo Roots of Equiano* have been called into question—her cultural readings about snake lore in Igbo culture are useful. She argues that it is quite natural that an Isseke Igbo would use a parable involving a snake to illustrate something as significant as one's destiny in this world, as "the snake is the Igbo symbol of spirituality" (83). Thus, whether Elder Egwuatu Onwuezike is old enough to have first- or secondhand verifiable knowledge of Equiano's having lived in his village, as an Igbo elder

his knowledge of Igbo culture and ways of knowing are not questioned. On-wuezike confirms that "the python was beloved among our people. We did worship it as other villages did and we welcomed it. We lived with it, and its arrival is always seen as a good omen" (qtd. in Acholonu, 64).

24. Acholonu adds that Equiano was a "member of the Eseke ruling kin-dred," and his uncle "was the chief judge of the village and therefore the ruler." Moreover, "his father, Ekwealuo, was one of Isseke's great judges and titled men" (35).

25. In the Judeo-Christian tradition, one of the primary distinguishing factors in the hierarchy of divinity, humanity, and other subhuman forms of life is the ability to name. God first calls atmospheric conditions such as light and earth into existence from matter that is void and without substance through the act of naming. God said "let there be light" and so forth. His creation of man requires a bit more interconnection than mere name—the breathing of life into human form. However, immediately following the creation of man—named Adam—is humanity's naming of animals. Thus, the power to name, in a Judeo-Christian "Western" theology, connotes "dominance" over as supported by scriptural doc-trine. It is the divinity—God—who calls into existence, through an act of nam-ing, and humanity who is then given the authority of naming that which he has dominion over. From a Western perspective, an enslaved African's assertion of such "naming" power, through his connotative reference to the names of things already in existence, is tantamount to signifying a similar form of humanity, if not agency (as that of his white masters). From an Igbo or African perspective, *nommo,* or naming, is analogous—through coterminous identification and de-scription—to bring into existence a particular type of energy—to the very act of creation itself. The boundaries between divinity and humanity are not quite as delineated as in the Western traditions. Therefore, the value Equiano places on names and naming is quite significant to his narrative of progress and to his assertion of African humanity—from multiple vistas.

26. "Conventional eighteenth-century narratives by white travelers described the land, people, culture, and the experience of engaging such 'foreign' experi-ences, even if, as was often the case, the 'other' was within. Moreover, in order to fulfill their fundamental purpose of naming, defining, and describing 'oth-ers,' traditional travel narratives by whites employ such descriptive techniques as: (a) observations, which refer to 'specific descriptions of what [the traveler] saw'; and (b) reflections, which refer to 'the philosophical, aesthetic, moral, or political thoughts' these sights occasioned" (Langley, "Interesting Exchanges," 49–58).

27. Angelo Costanzo's *Surprizing Narrative* provides an excellent analysis of Equiano's use of biblical types such as Joseph and others.

28. William Andrews's *To Tell a Free Story,* in particular chapters 1 and 2 on the first fifty years, provides comprehensive analysis of the distinction between eighteenth-century slave narrative conventions.

29. I refer here to the multiple names: Olaudah (birth name in Africa), Michael (on board the *African Snow* on the way to the West Indies), Jacob (in Virginia), and Gustavus (on board the *Industrious Bee* on the way to Eng-land).

30. Equiano refers to these two different types of snakes and the multiple meanings they connote and denote.

31. Signifying is also relevant to resituation of the British antislavery debate within an African context.

32. Biblical exegesis that privileges figurative over purely literal has historically been—cogently and convincingly—argued by biblical scholars as the predominant characteristic and language especially as interpretations are applied to books of the Old Testament. Paradoxically—when applied to "others"—figurative and literal scriptural interpretations are liberally and flexibly applied, for the most part, as needed to support social, economic, and political aims.

33. Alexander argues that "[b]lack life is so consciously about presentation. Whether that image presented is church lady or thug, the sense that we are always being evaluated has everything to do with how we comport [or present] ourselves" (13). Notably, "if any one aphorism can characterize the experience of black people in this country, it might be that the white authored national narrative deliberately contradicts the histories our bodies know. There have always been narratives to justify the barbaric practices of slavery and lynching. African Americans have always existed in a counter-citizen relationship to the law; how else to contend with knowing oneself as a whole human being when the constitution defines you as 'three fifths'?" (179). Further, she refers directly to the "realistic [black] narrative" from which "the real world and the made world—made and imagined as art—flow" (14).

34. Jordan, *White over Black: American Attitudes toward the Negro 1550–1812*. In this seminal text Jordan argues that "for Englishmen, then, the heathenism of Negroes was at once a counter-image of their own religion and a summons to eradicate an important distinction between two people" (21). Further, "as with skin color, English reporting of African customs constituted an exercise in self-inspection by means of comparison" (Jordan, 25; my emphasis). Woodard, 100–101.

> Like Gronniosaw, Sancho, and Cugoano before, Equiano had to reconstitute himself on the Great Chain of Being, though always against hierarchical structures of dominance that is consistently European; further, he had to assert an identity independently of an ideological Chain. Equiano's position on the hierarchical Chain threatens to compromise his credibility as an author in a European literary marketplace. In other words, before he could authorize his commentary to (re)shape readers' conceptions about Africans, he first had to establish self-authorization. . . . In order to alter white perceptions about blacks and slave, Equiano thus contests those prevailing representations of Africans as Other which accompany a long history of European travel writings. (Woodard, 100–101)

35. See note 11 above.

Chapter Four

1. The speaker in Hughes's poem is a twenty-two-year-old "colored" college student from Winston-Salem, North Carolina, attending an all-white English class in Harlem. Through the young student's voice, Hughes considers whether being a black writer is synonymous with writing "black." "Will my page be colored that I write? . . . Being me, it will not be white" (ll.27–28).

2. This epigraph is taken from Robert Stepto's preface to the second edition of *From Behind the Veil,* his seminal text in the study of African American slave narratives and narrative form.

3. In this quotation taken from Vincent Carretta's noteworthy anthology of black British-American writers, *Unchained Voices,* he argues that "eighteenth-century authors of African birth or descent . . . continu[ed] to identify themselves as Afro-Britons rather than embracing the new political identity of African Americans." Carretta suggests that this choice between British and American identities has to do with the fact that "all [these authors] were subjects of the British monarch before the American Revolution" (1). I problematize Carretta's analysis of "national" primarily because even as he historicizes the fluidity of Western "national" and "cultural" identity, he denies (or excludes) such specificity with regard to African "cultural" and "national" identities. Here, he moves fluidly between the terms "Creoles," "Africans," and "blacks" without any contextualization or historicization. Hence, I argue, he names their African cultural identities while he simultaneously posits the choices possible for their Western "national" identities. Further, that this naming occurs—rather unconsciously—at the level of the sentence speaks directly to the dilemma of locating an always already essentialized "Africa" within Western systems of identification (the needle in the haystack to which Stepto refers).

4. In "Tracing Igbo into the African Diaspora," Douglas B. Chambers argues that the earliest attempts at cultural reconnection through "diasporic ethnogenesis, or the creation of new African derived ethnic identities outside the continent, seems to have been the first step in the historical creolization of these forcibly displaced populations" (55). Necessarily this type of reorientation suggests the possibility of sociohistorical and anthropological reconstructions of meaning and knowledge—in this case, as I suggest—within literature. For example, in the absence of their former African communities (known or unknown), early African authors such as Wheatley and Equiano begin to imagine (or remember) an African community.

5. At some level perhaps Gilroy might be seen to be a bit limited or restrictive in his failure to fully draw out the value of such early nationalist movements. Basically, eighteenth- and nineteenth-century Africans in America who consciously decide to construct their communities on the basis of "race" or "national" identity—which they name African—provide at least one viable model of productive essentialism. However, I fundamentally agree with a great many assertions in Gilroy's approach; perhaps the concept of Black Atlantic as it applies to the eighteenth century needs to be expanded across time as well as geographically—with a loosening of the "boundaries" of the Enlightenment.

6. Patricia Liggins Hill contends that "filled with rather comic irony, the poem must be recognized as the first symbolic portrayal portending race relations in the United Sates for the next two centuries: a battle between Native Americans and Euro-Americans as witnessed and recorded by an African American" (90). Erlene Stetson argues that "black women poets in the United States . . . driven into a compelling quest for [person and collective integration of] identity" used "subterfuge and ambivalence" as strategies of survival and expression based on "a [subconscious and subversive] perception of reality as unified and dialectic" (xvii).

7. Deerfield historian George Sheldon notes that the record of the death of "Robert Tigo, Negro Serv't to Mr. Jn Williams died yr 11th day of May 1695" is the "earliest evidence of negro servitude in Deerfield" (50). Ironically, in 1706 a prominent Deerfield citizen, Rev. John Williams, published what was up until then one of the most well-known captivity narratives in Deerfield, *The Redeemed Captive Returning to Zion, A Faithful History of Remarkable Occurrences, in the Captivity and the Deliverance of Mr. John Williams in 1706*. His narrative tells of the capture of "his family, and his neighborhood unto Canada," during which his wife, two of his five infant children, his two negro servants, and many other white settlers were killed. Rosalie Murphy Baum notes that Williams's narrative "is one of the New England Puritan accounts that is considered an example of the archetypal form" ("John Williams's Captivity Narrative: A Consideration of Normative Ethnicity," 61).

8. Descriptions of Terry's poetic form vary from Proper's doggerel to Sidney and Emma Kaplan's "rough-hewn verse" to Nellie McKay's "ballad" of "rhymed tetrameter couplets" designed to be sung. Such a diverse range of meter and style of her poem emphasizes the unique richness of the poet's inspiration and indicates the complexity of translating from oral to written form.

9. All references to "The Bars Fight" are quoted from David Proper's biography *Lucy Terry Prince, Singer of History* (Deerfield, MA: Pocumtuck Valley Memorial Association, 1997).

10. Mechal Sobel notes that because "blacks kept family history, made it their own, and returned it to the next generation . . . [they] played a very important role in preserving, magnifying, and disseminating family history . . . their own ideas of kin and kinship responsibility permeated this heritage" (*The World They Made Together,* 133–34).

11. It is worth considering Terry's representation of Native/Anglo conflict in relation to Rev. John Williams's captivity narrative written twenty-six years earlier. Although Williams uses the phrase "fight in meadow" to describe an English/French encounter in which a French ensign is killed, Williams's framing of his captivity within the context of "an incursion of the French and Indians" highlights his position as an innocent victim of the unwarranted circumstances of his captivity.

12. "Verily I say unto you. Whosoever shall not receive the kingdom of God as a little child shall in no wise enter therein" (Luke 18:14b). Ironically the Greek word for "child" as used in this passage is *paidion*, a diminutive of *pais,* which means "slave" or "servant," especially to a king; and by eminence to God. James Strong, ed., *The New Strong's Exhaustive Concordance of the Bible* (Nashville, TN: Thomas Nelson, 1990).

13. Unless otherwise indicated, all references are taken from *The Narrative of the Lord's Wonderful Dealings with John Marrant, A Black (Now going to Preach the Gospel in Nova Scotia) Born in New-York, in North-America.* The 1785 fourth enlarged edition as reprinted in *Unchained Voices: Anthology of Black Authors in the English-Speaking World of the 18th Century,* ed. Vincent Carretta (Expanded Edition) (Lexington: University Press of Kentucky, 2004).

14. Unless otherwise indicated, all references are taken from *A Narrative of the Most Remarkable Particulars in the Life of James Albert Ukawsaw Gronniosaw, An African Prince, As Related by Himself.* The 1772 edition as reprinted in *Unchained Voices: Anthology of Black Authors in the English-Speaking World of the 18th Century,* ed. Vincent Carretta (Expanded Edition) (Lexington: University Press of Kentucky, 2004).

15. Unless otherwise indicated, all references are taken from *A Narrative of the Life and adventures of Venture, A Native of Africa: But Resident Above Sixty Years in the United States of America. Related by Himself.* The 1798 edition as reprinted in *Unchained Voices: Anthology of Black Authors in the English-Speaking World of the 18th Century,* ed. Carretta.

Concluding Remarks

1. America's first black female public speaker, Maria Stewart, calls for black self-uplift. She begins by acknowledging white society's failure to "promote the cause" of African Americans, the "benighted sons and daughters of Africa, who have enriched the soils of America with their tears and blood." After which, on the basis of observing the "many able and talented ones among us," Stewart deduces the following: "'I can't,' is a great barrier in the way, I hope it will soon be removed, and 'I will' resume its place" (from *Religion and The Pure Principles of Morality, The Sure Foundation on Which We Must Build* [1831]).

BIBLIOGRAPHY

Achebe, Chinua. "African Literature as Restoration of Celebration." In *Chinua Achebe: A Celebration*. Edited by Kirsten Holst Petersen and Anna Rutherford. Portsmouth, NH: Heinemann, 1990.

_____. "'Chi' in Igbo Cosmology." In Eze, *African Philosophy*, 67–72.

_____. *Hopes and Impediments: Selected Essays*. New York: Doubleday, 1990.

_____. "The Igbo World and Its Art." In Eze, *African Philosophy*, 435–37.

Acholonu, Catherine Obianuju. *The Igbo Roots of Olaudah Equiano: An Anthropological Research*. Owerri, Nigeria: AFA Publications, 1989.

Afigbo, A. E. *Ropes of Sand: Studies in Igbo History and Culture*. Ibadan: Oxford University Press, 1981.

Aidoo, Ama Ata. *The Dilemma of a Ghost*. London: Longman, 1980.

Alexander, Elizabeth. *The Black Interior: Essays*. Saint Paul, MN: Graywolf, 2004.

Amadiume, Ifi. *Male Daughters, Female Husbands: Gender and Sex in African Society*. London: Zed, 1987.

American Heritage Dictionary of the English Language. 4th ed. New York: Houghton Mifflin, 2000.

Amuta, Chidi. *The Theory of African Literature: Implications for Practical Criticism*. Atlantic Highlands, NJ: Zed, 1989.

Anderson, Benedict. *Imagined Communities: Reflections on the Origin and Spread of Nationalism*. London: Verso, 1991.

Anderson, Victor. *Beyond Ontological Blackness: An Essay on African American Religious and Cultural Criticism*. New York: Continuum, 1995.

Andrews, William L. *African American Autobiography: A Collection of Critical Essays*. Englewood Cliffs, NJ: Prentice Hall, 1993.

_____. *To Tell a Free Story: The First Century of Afro-American Autobiography, 1760–1865*. Urbana: University of Illinois Press, 1986.

Angelou, Maya. "And Still I Rise." In *Phenomenal Woman: Four Poems Celebrating Women*. New York: Random House, 1994.

Appiah, Kwame Anthony. *In My Father's House: Africa in the Philosophy of Culture.* New York: Oxford University Press, 1992.

Asante, Molefi Kete. *The Afrocentric Idea.* Revised and expanded edition. Philadelphia: Temple University Press, 1998.

Ashcraft-Eason, Lillian. "Freedom among African Women Servants and Slaves in the Seventeenth-Century British Colonies." In *Women and Freedom in Early America,* edited by Larry D. Eldridge, 62–79. New York: New York University Press, 1997.

Azodo, Ada Uzoamaka, and Gay Wilentz, eds. *Emerging Perspectives on Ama Ata Aidoo.* Trenton, NJ: Africa World, 1999.

Baker, Houston A. *Blues, Ideology, and Afro-American Literature: A Vernacular Theory.* Chicago: University of Chicago Press, 1984.

Baldwin, James. *Collected Essays.* New York: Library of America, 1998.

———. *Nobody Knows My Name.* In *Collected Essays.*

———. *Notes of a Native Son.* Boston: Beacon, 1983.

Barksdale, Richard K., and Kenneth Kinnamon, eds. *Black Writers of America: A Comprehensive Anthology.* Upper Saddle River, NJ: Prentice Hall, 1972.

Bascom, William R. *African Dilemma Tales.* Paris: Mouton, 1975.

Bassard, Katherine. *Spiritual Interrogations: Culture, Gender, and Community in Early African American Women's Writing.* Princeton, NJ: Princeton University Press, 1999.

Batten, Charles L., Jr. *Pleasurable Instruction: Form and Convention in Eighteenth Century Travel Literature.* Berkeley: University of California Press, 1978.

Baum, Rosalie Murphy. "John Williams's Captivity Narrative: A Consideration of Normative Ethnicity." In Shuffelton, *A Mixed Race,* 56–76.

Barry, Boubacar. *Senegambia and the Atlantic Slave Trade.* Cambridge: Cambridge University Press, 1998.

Benezet, Anthony. *Some Historical Account of Guinea, Its Situation, Produce and the General Disposition of Its Inhabitants, With an Inquiry Into the Rise and Progress of the Slave Trade, its Nature, and Lamentable Effects.* London: Cass, 1968.

Bercovitch, Sacvan. *The Puritan Origins of the American Self.* New Haven, CN: Yale University Press, 1975.

Bhabha, Homi K. "The Other Question: Difference, Discrimination, and the Discourse of Colonialism." In *Black British Cultural Studies: A Reader,* edited by Houston A. Baker Jr., Manthia Diawara, and Ruth H. Lindeborg, 87–106. Chicago: University of Chicago Press, 1996.

Bly, Antonio T. "Wheatley's 'To The University of Cambridge, in New-England.'" *Explicator* 55, no. 4 (Summer 1997): 205–9.

Block, Sharon. "Rape without Women: Print Culture and the Politicization of Rape, 1765–1815." *Journal of American History* 89, no. 3 (2002): 47 pars. http://www.historycooperative.org/journals/jah/89.3/block.html (accessed January 10, 2007).

Bordman, Gerald, and Thomas S. Hischak, eds. "Othello." In *Oxford Companion to American Theater.* Oxford: Oxford University Press, 2004.

Bosman, William. *A New and Accurate Description of the Coast of Guinea: Divided into the Gold, The Slave, and The Ivory Coasts.* 1704. Reprint London: Frank Cass, 1967.

Brooks, Joanna. *American Lazarus: Religion and the Rise of African American and Native American Literatures*. New York: Oxford University Press, 2003.

———. "John Marrant's *Journal:* Providence and Prophecy in the Eighteenth-Century Black Atlantic." *North Star: A Journal of African American Religious History* 3, no. 1 (Fall 1999). http://northstar.edu/volume3/brooks.html. Accessed January 10, 2007.

Brooks, Joanna, and John Saillant, eds. *"Face Zion forward": First Writers of the Black Atlantic, 1785–1798*. Boston: Northeastern University Press, 2002.

Brooks, Otis. *Ovid as an Epic Poet*. Cambridge: Cambridge University Press, 1966.

Carretta, Vincent. *Equiano the African: Biography of a Self-Made Man*. Athens: University of Georgia Press, 2005.

———, ed. *Olaudah Equiano: The Interesting Narrative and Other Writings*. New York: Penguin, 1995.

———. *Unchained Voices: An Anthology of Black Authors in the English- Speaking World of the 18th Century*. Lexington: University Press of Kentucky, 1996.

Cerroni-Long, E. L. "Benign Neglect? Anthropology and the Study of Blacks in the United States." *Journal of Black Studies* 17, no. 4 (1987): 438–69.

Chambers, Douglass B. "Tracing Igbo into the African Diaspora." In *Identity in the Shadow of Slavery*, edited by Paul Lovejoy, 55–70. New York: Continuum, 2000.

Chinweizu, Onwuchekwa, and Jemie and Ihechukwu Madubuike. *Toward the Decolonization of African Literature*. 2 vols. Washington, DC: Howard University Press, 1983.

Clarke, John Henrik. "African Cultural Responses to Slavery and Oppression in the Americas." In *African Presence in the Americas*, edited by Carlos Moore, Tanya R. Sanders, and Shawna Moore, 73–95. Trenton, NJ: Africa World, 1995.

Cole, Herbert M. *Mbari, Art and Life among the Owerri Igbo*. Bloomington: Indiana University Press, 1982.

Costanzo, Angelo. *Surprizing Narrative: Olaudah Equiano and the Beginnings of Black Autobiography*. New York: Greenwood, 1987.

Cullen, Countee. "Heritage." In Hill, *Call and Response*, 910–13.

Davis, Angela. *Blues Legacies and Black Feminism: Gertrude "Ma" Rainey, Bessie Smith, and Billie Holiday*. New York: Vintage, 1999.

Davis, Brion David. *The Problem of Slavery in the Age of Revolution 1770–1823*. Ithaca, NY: Cornell University Press, 1975.

Davis, Thomas J. "Emancipation, Rhetoric, Natural Rights, and Revolutionary New England: A Note on Four Black Petitions in Massachusetts, 1773–1777." *New England Quarterly* 62, no. 2 (June 1989): 248–63.

De Crevecoeur, Hector St. John. *Letters from an American Farmer: describing certain provincial situations, manners, and customs, and conveying some idea of the state of the people of North America. / Written to a friend in England, by J. Hector St. John, a farmer in Pennsylvania*. Philadelphia: From the press of Mathew Carey, March 4,—MDCCXCIII [1793].

Desrochers, Robert E., Jr. "'Not Fade Away': The Narrative of Venture Smith, an African American in the Early Republic." *Journal of American History* 84, no. 1 (June 1977): 40–66.

Diop, Cheikh Anta. *The African Origin of Civilization: Myth or Reality.* Chicago: Lawrence Hill, 1974.

Douglass, Frederick. *Narrative of the Life of Douglass, an American Slave Written by Himself.* Boston: Anti-Slavery Office, 1945. http://docsouth.unc/neh/douglass/menu.html. Accessed July 12, 2007.

DuBois, William Edward Burghardt. "The Conservation of Races." In *The Thoughts and Writings of W. E. B. DuBois The Seventh Son,* vol. 1, edited by Julius Lester, 176–87. New York: Random House, 1971.

———. *The Souls of Black Folk: Essays and Sketches.* Chicago: A. C. McClurg, 1922.

Dunbar, Paul Laurence. "Sympathy." In Hill, ed., *Call and Response,* 614–15.

Echeruo, Michael J. "An African Diaspora: The Ontological Project." In Okpewho, Bavies, and Mazrui, *The African Diaspora,* 3–18.

———. "Theologizing 'Underneath the Tree': An African Topos in Ukawsaw Gronniosaw, William Black, and William Cole." *Research in African Literatures* 23, no. 4 (Winter 1992): 51–58.

Edeh, Emmanuel M. P. *Towards an Igbo Metaphysics.* Chicago: Loyola University Press, 1985.

Edwards, Paul, and Rosalind Shaw. "The Invisible *Chi* in Equiano's *Interesting Narrative.*" *Journal of African Literature* 19 (1989): 146–56.

Elder, Arlene A. "Ama Ata Aidoo: The Development of a Woman's Voice." In Azodo and Wilentz, *Emerging Perspectives on Ama Ata Aidoo,* 157–69.

Equiano, Olaudah. *The Interesting Narrative of the Life of Olaudah Equiano, or Gustavus Vassa, The African, Written By Himself.* 9th ed., 1794. In Carretta, *Olaudah Equiano.*

Erkkila, Betsy. "Phillis Wheatley and the Black American Revolution." In Shuffelton, *A Mixed Race,* 225–40.

Evans, David. "The Reinterpretation of African Musical Instruments in the United States." In Okpewho, Davies, and Mazrui, *The African Diaspora,* 379–90.

Eze, Emmanuel Chukwudi, ed. *African Philosophy: An Anthology.* Malden, MA: Blackwell, 1998.

Fabricant, Carole. *Swift's Landscape.* Notre Dame, IN: University of Notre Dame Press, 1995.

"Faction." *American Heritage Dictionary of the English Language.* 4th ed. New York: Houghton Mifflin, 2000.

Fatunmbi, Fá'lokun Awo. *Eşu Elegba: Ifà and the Divine Messenger.* New York: Original Publications, 1992.

Felkins, Leon. "The Prisoner's Dilemma." http://perspicuity.net/sd/pd-brf.html (September 5, 1995; last revision on March 12, 2001).

Ferguson, Robert A. *The American Enlightenment, 1750–1820.* Cambridge, MA: Harvard University Press, 1997.

Fliegelman, Jay. *Prodigals and Pilgrims: The American Revolution against Patriarchal Authority, 1750–1800.* Cambridge: Cambridge University Press, 1982.

Foreman, Gabrielle P. "'Reading Aright': White Slavery, Black Referents, and the Strategy of Histotextuality in *Iola Leroy.*" *Yale Journal of Criticism* 10, no. 2 (1997): 327–54.

Foucault, Michel. *The Archaeology of Knowledge.* Translated by A. M. Sheridan. New York: Harper & Row, 1972.

Fox-Genovese, Elizabeth. "My Statue, My Self: Autobiographical Writings of

Afro-American Women." In *The Private Self: Theory and Practice of Women's Autobiographical Writings.* Edited by Shari Benstock. Chapel Hill: University of North Carolina Press, 1988.

Fuller, Hoyt. "The New Black Literature: Protest or Imagination?" In Gayle, *The Black Aesthetic,* 327–48.

Fuss, Diana. *Essentially Speaking: Feminism, Nature and Difference.* New York: Routledge, 1989.

Gabler-Hover, Janet. *Dreaming Black/Writing White: The Hagar Myth in American Cultural History.* Lexington: University Press of Kentucky, 2000.

Galinsky, G. K. *Ovid's Metamorphoses: An Introduction to the Basic Aspects.* Berkeley: University of California Press, 1975.

Gates, Henry Louis, Jr. "James Albert Gronniosaw and the Trope of the Talking Book." *Southern Review* 22, no. 2 (1986): 252–72.

———. *The Signifying Monkey: A Theory of African American Literary Criticism.* New York: Oxford University Press, 1988.

Gates, Henry Louits, Jr., and William L. Andrews, eds. *The Pioneers of the Black Atlantic: Five Slave Narratives from the Enlightenment 1772–1815.* Washington, DC: Civitas, 1998.

Gates, Henry Louis, Jr., and Nellie Y. McKay, eds. *The Norton Anthology of African American Literature.* New York: Norton, 1997.

Gauthier, David. *Morals by Agreement.* Oxford: Clarendon, 1986.

Gayle, Addison. *The Black Aesthetic.* Garden City, NY: Doubleday, 1972.

Gerzina, Gretchen Holbrook. *Black London: Life before Emancipation.* New Brunswick, NJ: Rutgers University Press, 1995.

Gilroy, Paul. *The Black Atlantic: Modernity and Double Consciousness.* Cambridge, MA: Harvard University Press, 1993.

Gomez, Michael A. *Exchanging Our Country Marks: The Transformation of African Identities in the Colonial and Antebellum South.* Chapel Hill: University of North Carolina Press, 1998.

Gould, Philip. *Barbaric Traffic: Commerce and Antislavery in the Eighteenth-Century Atlantic World.* Cambridge, MA: Harvard University Press, 2003.

———. *Covenant and Republic: Historical Romance and the Politics of Puritanism.* Cambridge: Cambridge University Press, 1996.

———. "Free Carpenter, Venture Capitalist: Reading the Lives of the Early Black Atlantic." *American Literary History* 12, no. 4 (2000): 659–84.

Grimsted, David. "Anglo-American Racism and Phillis Wheatley's 'Sable Veil,' 'Length'ned Chain,' and 'Knitted Heart.'" In *Women in the Age of the American Revolution,* edited by Ronald Hoffman and Peter J. Albert, 338–446. Charlottesville: University Press of Virginia, 1989.

Gronniosaw, James Albert. *A Narrative of the Most Remarkable Particulars in the Life of James Albert Ukawsaw Gronniosaw, An African Prince, As Related By Himself.* In Carretta, *Unchained Voices,* 32–58.

Habermas, Jurgen. *The Structural Transformation of the Public Sphere: An Inquiry into a Category of Bourgeois Society.* Translated by Thomas Burger. 6th ed. Boston: MIT Press, 1994.

Hale, Thomas A. *Griots and Griottes: Masters of Words and Music.* Bloomington: Indiana University Press, 1998.

Hammon, Briton. *A Narrative of the Uncommon Sufferings, and Surprizing*

Deliverance of Briton Hammon, a Negro man,–servant to General Winslow, of Marsh-field, in New-England . . . . In Carretta, *Unchained Voices,* 20–25.

Harris, Sharon M., ed. *American Writers to 1800.* New York: Oxford University Press, 1996.

_____. *Executing Race: Early American Women's Narratives of Race, Society, and the Law.* Columbus: The Ohio State University Press, 2005.

Hayden, Lucy K. "Classical Tidings from the Afric Muse: Phillis Wheatley's Use of Greek and Roman Mythology." *College Language Association Journal* 35, no. 4 (June 1992): 432–47.

Henderson, Mae Gwendolyn. "Speaking in Tongues: Dialogics, Dialectics, and the Black's Writer's Literary Tradition." In Smith and Watson, *Women, Autobiography, Theory,* 343–51.

Hendler, Glenn. *Public Sentiments: Structures of Feeling in Nineteenth-Century American Literature.* Chapel Hill: University of North Carolina Press, 2001.

Herskovitz, Melville. *The Myth of the Negro Past.* New York: Harper & Brothers, 1941.

_____. "A Preliminary Consideration of the Culture Areas of Africa." *American Anthropologist* 26, no. 1 (January–March 1924): 50–63.

_____. "The Significance of West Africa for Negro Research." *Journal of Negro History* 21, no. 1 (January 1936): 15–30.

Heusch, Luc de. *Sacrifice in Africa: A Structuralist Approach.* Translated by Linda O'Brien and Alice Morton. Bloomington: Indiana University Press, 1985.

Hill, Patricia Liggins. *Call and Response: The Riverside Anthology of the African American Literary Tradition.* Boston: Houghton Mifflin Company, 1998.

Holloway, Joseph E. "The Origins of African-American Culture." In *Africanisms in American Culture,* edited by Joseph E. Holloway, 1–18. Bloomington: Indiana University Press, 1990.

Holloway, Karla F. C. *Moorings and Metaphors: Figures of Culture and Gender in Black Women's Literature.* New Brunswick, NJ: Rutgers University Press, 1992.

hooks, bell. *Yearning: Race, Gender, and Cultural Politics.* Boston: South End, 1990.

Hudson-Weems, Clenora. "The African American Literary Tradition." In *The African American Experience: An Historiographical and Bibliographical Guide,* edited by Arvah E. Strickland and Robert E. Weems Jr., 116–43. Westport, CT: Greenwood, 2001.

_____. "Africana Womanism: An Overview." In *Out of the Revolution: The Development of Africana Studies,* edited by Delores P. Aldridge and Carlene Young. Lanham, MD: Lexington, 2000.

_____. *Africana Womanism: Reclaiming Ourselves.* Troy, MI: Bedford, 1993.

Hughes, Langston. "Theme for English B." *The Prentice Hall Anthology of African American Literature,* edited by Rochelle Smith and Sharon L. Jones, 446. Saddle River, NJ: Prentice Hall, 2000.

Hunt, Margaret. "Racism, Imperialism and the Traveler's Gaze in Eighteenth-Century England." *Journal of British Studies* 32 (1993): 333–57.

Irele, Abiola. *The African Experience in Literature and Ideology.* Bloomington: Indiana University Press, 1990.

_____. *The African Imagination: Literature in Africa and the Black Diaspora.* Oxford: Oxford University Press, 2001.

Isani, Mukhtar Ali. "'Gambia on My Soul': Africa and the African in the Writings of Phillis Wheatley." *MELUS* (Society for the Study of the Multi-Ethnic Literature of the United States) 6, no. 1 (1979): 64–72.

James, Adeola. *In Their Own Voices: African Women Writers Talk.* London: James Curry, 1990.

James, Janet Wilson. *Changing Ideas about Women in the United States, 1776–1825.* New York: Garland, 1981.

Jefferson, Thomas. *Notes on the State of Virginia.* Chapel Hill: University of North Carolina Press, 1982.

Jones, James M. "Psychological Knowledge and the New American Dilemma of Race: Race-neutral vs. Race-conscious Social Policies." *Journal of Social Issues* (Winter 1998): 64–662.

Jordan, June. "The Difficult Miracle of Black Poetry in America; Or, Something Like a Sonnet for Phillis Wheatley." *Massachusetts Review* 27, no. 2 (Summer 1986): 252–62.

Jordan, Winthrop. *White over Black: American Attitudes toward the Negro 1550–1812.* Chapel Hill: University of North Carolina Press, 1968.

Kalu, Anthonia C. "African/African American Dialogue: Toward a New Diaspora." *Pan-Africanism and Cross-Cultural Understanding: A Reader,* edited by François N. Muyumba and Esther Atcherson, 275–88. Needham Heights, MD: Ginn, 1993.

_____. "Reader's Notes." In Langley, "*The Dilemma of a Ghost.*"

_____. "Those Left Out in the Rain." *African Studies Review* 37, no. 2 (September 1994): 77–95.

_____. "Traditional Narratives in the African Novel: African Literary Theory Reconsidered." *Orality, Literacy and the Fictive Imagination: African Diasporan Literatures,* edited by Tom Spencer-Walters, 21–44. Troy, MI: Bedford, 1998.

_____. "Women and the Social Construction of Gender in African Development." *Africa Today* 43, no. 3 (1996): 269–87.

_____. "Women in African Literature." *African Transitions* 490 (2000): 67–76.

_____. *Women, Literature, and Development in Africa.* Trenton, NJ: Africa World Press, 2001.

Kaplan, Sidney, and Emma Nogrady, eds. *The Black Presence in the Era of the American Revolution.* Rev. ed. Amherst: University of Massachusetts Press, 1989.

Kazanjian, David. *The Colonizing Trick: National Culture and Imperial Citizenship in Early America.* Minneapolis: University of Minnesota Press, 2003.

Kazanjian, David, and David L. Eng, eds. *Loss: The Politics of Mourning.* Berkeley: University of California Press, 2003.

Kristeva, Julia. *Strangers to Ourselves.* New York: Columbia University Press, 1991.

La Pin, Deirdre. "Tale and Trickster in Yoruba Verbal Art." *Research in African Literatures* 11, no. 3 (Fall 1980): 327–41

Langley, April. "*The Dilemma of a Ghost:* Eighteenth-Century African American

Literature and Its Mournings/Moorings." PhD diss., University of Notre Dame, 2001.

_____. "Interesting Exchanges: Cultural Expeditions and Rhetorical Acquisitions in *The Interesting Narrative of Olaudah Equiano, or Gustavus Vassa the African*." *BMa: The Sonia Sanchez Literary Review* 9, no.1 (Fall 2003): 49–58.

Laplanche, Jean, and J. B. Pontalis. *The Language of Psycho-Analysis*. Translated by Donald Nicholson-Smith. New York: Norton, 1973.

Lewis, R.W.B. *The American Adam: Innocence, Tragedy, and Tradition in the Nineteenth Century*. Chicago: University of Chicago Press, 1955.

Lionnet, Françoise. *Autobiographical Voices: Race, Gender, Self-Portraiture*. Ithaca, NY: Cornell University Press, 1989.

_____. *Postcolonial Representations*. Ithaca, NY: Cornell University Press, 1995.

Locke, John. *An Essay Concerning Human Understanding*. Oxford: Clarendon, 1924.

Lorde, Audre. *Sister Outsider*. Trumansburg, NY: Crossing, 1984.

Marrant, John. *A Journal of the Rev. John Marrant, from August the 18th, 1785 to the 16th of March, 1790. To Which Are Added, Two Sermons; One Preached on Ragged Island on Sabbath Day, the 17th Day of October, 1787; The Other at Boston, in New England, on Thursday, the 24th of June, 1789*. London, 1791.

_____. *A Narrative of the Life of John Marrant of New York, in North America: Giving an Account of His Conversion When Only Fourteen Years of Age*. Leeds: Davies and Co. at the Stanhope Press, 1810.

_____. *A Narrative of the Lord's Wonderful Dealings With John Marrant, a Black (Now Going to Preach the Gospel in Nova-Scotia) Born in New York, in North-America*. In Carretta, 110–33.

_____. *A Narrative of the Lord's Wonderful Dealings With John Marrant, a Black (Now Going to Preach the Gospel in Nova-Scotia) Born in New York, in North-America*. In *Black Atlantic Writers of the 18th Century*, edited by Adam Potkay and Susan Burr, 75–105. New York: St. Martin's Press, 1996.

Marren, Susan M. "Between Slavery and Freedom: The Transgressive Self in Olaudah Equiano's Autobiography." *PMLA* (Publications of the Modern Language Association of America) 108 (1993): 94–105.

Mason, Ernest D. "Black Art and the Configurations of Experience: The Philosophy of Black Aesthetic." *College Language Association* 27, no. 1 (1983): 1–17.

Martin, Reginald. "'Total Life Is What We Want': The Progressive Stages of the Black Aesthetic in Literature." *South Atlantic Review* 51, no. 4 (November 1986): 49–67.

Mather, Cotton. *The Negro Christianized: An Essay to Excite and Assist the Good Work, the Instruction of Negro-Servants in Christianity*. Boston: B. Green, 1706.

Mayfield, Julian. "You Touch My Black Aesthetic and I'll Touch Yours." In Gayle, *The Black Aesthetic*, 23–30.

McBride, David. "Medical Experimentation, Racial Hygiene and Black Bodies." *Debatte: Review of Contemporary German Affairs* 7, no. 1 (May 1999): 63–80.

McKay, Nellie. "The Narrative Self: Race, Politics, and Culture in Black American Women's Autobiography." In Smith and Watson, *Women, Autobiography, Theory: A Reader*, 96–107.

McNee, Lisa. *Selfish Gifts: Senegalese Women's Autobiographical Discourses*. Albany: State University of New York Press, 2000.

Miller, Johanna Lewis. "Women and Economic Freedom in the North Carolina Back Country." *Women and Freedom in Early America*, edited by Larry D. Eldridge, 191–208. New York: New York University Press, 1997.

Montgomery, Benilde. "Recapturing John Marrant. Ethnicity." In Shuffelton, *A Mixed Race*, 105–18.

Mudimbe, V. Y. *The Invention of Africa: Gnosis, Philosophy, and the Order of Knowledge*. Bloomington: Indiana University Press, 1988.

Mullane, Deirdre. *Crossing the Danger Water: Three Hundred Years of African-American Writing*. New York: Anchor, 1993.

Murphy, Geraldine. "Olaudah Equiano Accidental Tourist." *Eighteenth-Century Studies* 27 (1994): 551–68.

"Nation." *Oxford English Dictionary*. New York: 2nd ed. Oxford University Press, 1989.

Neal, Larry. "The Black Arts Movement." In Gayle, *The Black Aesthetic*, 257–74.

Nwapa, Flora. *Efuru*. London: Heinemann, 1966.

Odamtten, Vincent A. *The Art of Ama Ata Aidoo: Polylectics and Reading against Neocolonialism*. Gainesville: University Press of Florida, 1994.

Ogundipe, Ayodele. "Esu Elegbara, the Yoruba God of Chance and Uncertainty: A Study in Yoruba Mythology." PhD diss., Indiana University, 1978.

Ogunyemi, Chikwenye Okonjo. *Africa Wo/man Palava: The Nigerian Novel by Women*. Chicago: University of Chicago Press, 1996.

Ohadike, Don C. *Anioma: Asocial History of the Western Igbo People*. Athens: Ohio University Press, 1994.

Okpewho, Isidore, Carole Boyce Davies, and Ali A. Mazrui, eds. *The African Diaspora: African Origins and New World Identities*. Bloomington: Indiana University Press, 1999.

Olupona, Jacob K. "The Study of Yoruba Religious Tradition in Historical Perspective." *Numan* 40, no. 3 (1993): 240–73.

Orban, Katalin. "Dominant and Submerged Discourses in *The Life* of Olaudah Equiano (or Gustavus Vassa?)." *African American Review* 27 (1993): 644–64.

Ostriker, Alicia Suskin. *Stealing the Language: The Emergence of Women's Poetry in America*. Boston: Beacon, 1986.

Ovid. *Metamorphoses*. Edited by G. P. Goold and translated by Frank Justus Miller. Cambridge, MA: Harvard University Press, 1984.

Peters, Erskine A. "Afrocentricity: Problems of Logic, Method and Nomenclature." *Twenty-first Century Afro Review* 2 (Winter 1996): 1–44.

Prince, Lucy Terry. "The Bars Fight." In Proper, *Lucy Terry Prince*, 18–19.

Proper, David R. *Lucy Terry Prince: Singer of History*. Deerfield, MA: Pocumtuck Valley Memorial Association, 1997.

Raboteau, Albert J. *Slave Religion: The "Invisible Institution" in the Antebellum South*. New York: Oxford University Press, 1978.

Reich, Jerome R. *Colonial America*. 2nd ed. Englewood Cliffs, NJ: Prentice Hall, 1989.

Richmond, M. A. *Bid the Vassal Soar: Interpretative Essays on the Life and Poetry* of Phillis Wheatley (ca. 1753–1784) and George Mores Horton (ca. 1797–1883). Washington, DC: Howard University Press, 1974.

Said, Edward W. *Orientalism.* New York: Pantheon Books, 1978.

Saillant, John. *Black Puritan, Black Republican: The Life and Thought of Lemuel Haynes, 1753–1833.* New York: Oxford University Press, 2003.

_____. "Hymnody and the Persistence of an African American Faith in Sierra Leone." *Hymn* 48, no. 1 (January 1977): 8–17.

_____. "John Marrant: Explaining Syncretism in African American View of Death, an Eighteenth-Century Example." *Culture and Tradition* 17 (1995): 25–41.

_____. "Traveling in Old and New Worlds with John Jea, the African Preacher, 1773–1816." *Journal of American Studies* 33, no. 3 (1999): 471–90.

Samuels, Wilfred D. "Disguised Voice in the *Interesting Narrative of Olaudah Equiano, or Gustavus, The African.*" *Black Literature Forum* 19 (1985): 64–69.

_____. "Making Crooked Paths Straight: Crossroads and Conversion in the Interesting Narrative of the Life of Olaudah Equiano." Unpublished manuscript.

Sandys, George. *Ovid's Metamorphoses Englished.* 1632. Reprint, New York: Garland, 1976.

Scheick, William J. "Subjection and Prophecy in Phillis Wheatley's Verse Paraphrases of Scripture." *College Literature* 22, no. 3 (October 1995): 122–31.

Scheub, Harold. *Story.* Madison: University of Wisconsin Press, 1998.

Sekora, John. "Black Message/White Envelope: Genre, Authenticity, and Authority in the Antebellum Slave Narrative." *Callaloo* 32 (Summer 1987): 482–515.

_____. "Red, White, and Black: Indian Captivities, Colonial Printers, and the Early African American Narrative." In Shuffelton, *A Mixed Race,* 92–104.

Shakespeare, William. "Othello, the Moor of Venice." *The Complete Works of Shakespeare,* edited by David Bevington, 1117–66. New York: Harper Collins, 1992.

Sheldon, George. "Negro Slavery in Old Deerfield." *New England Magazine* (March 1893): 49–60.

Shields, John C. *The American Aeneas: Classical Origins of the American Self.* Knoxville: University of Tennessee Press, 2001.

_____. "Phillis Wheatley's Poetics of Ascent." PhD diss., University of Tennessee Press, 1975.

_____. "Phillis Wheatley's Use of Classicism." *American Literature* 52, no. 1 (1980): 97–111.

Shields, John C., ed. *The Collected Works of Phillis Wheatley.* New York: Oxford University Press, 1988.

Shuffelton, Frank, ed. *A Mixed Race: Ethnicity in Early America.* New York: Oxford University Press, 1993.

Singleton, Theresa A., ed. *"I, Too, Am America": Archeological Studies of African-American Life.* Charlottesville: University Press of Virginia, 1999.

Sinopoli, Richard C. *From Many, One: Readings in American Political and Social Thought.* Washington, DC: Georgetown University Press, 1997.

Smith, Eric. *A Dictionary of Classical Reference in English Poetry.* Woodbridge, Suffolk: D. S. Brewer, 1984.

Smith, Mark M. "Time, Sound, and the Virginia Slave." In *Afro-Virginian History and Culture,* edited by John Saillant, 29–60. New York: Garland, 1999.

Smith, Sidonie, and Julia Watson, eds. *Women, Autobiography, Theory: A Reader.* Madison: University of Wisconsin Press, 1998.

Smith, Valerie. "'Loopholes of Retreat': Architecture and Ideology in Harriet Jacobs's *Incidents in the Life of a Slave Girl.*" In *Reading Black, Reading Feminist: A Critical Anthology.* Edited by Henry Louis Gates Jr. New York: Meridian, 1990.

Smith, Venture. *A Narrative of the Life and Adventures of Venture, a Native of Africa: But Resident Above Sixty Years in the United States of America; Related by Himself.* In Carretta, *Unchained Voices,* 369–87.

Smitherman, Geneva. *Talkin' That Talk: Language, Culture and Education in African America.* London: Routledge, 2000.

Sobel, Mechal. *Trabelin' On: The Slave Journey to an Afro-Baptist Faith.* Westport, CT: Greenwood, 1979.

———. *The World They Made Together: Black and White Values in Eighteenth-Century Virginia.* Princeton, NJ: Princeton University Press, 1987.

Some, Malidoma Patrice. *Of Water and the Spirit: Ritual Magic, and Initiation in the Life of an African Shaman.* New York: Jeremy P. Tarcher/Putnam, 1994.

Soyinka, Wole. *Myth, Literature and the African World.* Cambridge: Cambridge University Press, 1976.

———. *This Past Must Address Its Present: The 1986 Nobel Lecture.* New York: Anson Phelps Stokes Institute for African, Afro-American, and American Indian Affairs, 1988.

Spivak, Gayatri Chakravorty. "Can the Subaltern Speak?" In *Marxism and the Interpretation of Culture,* edited by Cary Nelson and Laurence Grossberg, 271–313. Urbana: University of Illinois Press, 1988.

Stepto, Robert B. *From Behind the Veil: A Study of Afro-American Narrative.* Urbana: University of Illinois Press, 1991.

Stetson, Erlene, ed. *Black Sister: Poetry by Black American Women, 1746–1980.* Bloomington: Indiana University Press, 1981.

Strong, James. *The New Strong's Exhaustive Concordance of the Bible.* Nashville, TN: Thomas Nelson, 1990.

Stuckey, Sterling. *Slave Culture: Nationalist Theory and the Foundations of Black America.* New York: Oxford University Press, 1987.

Sudarkasa, Niara. "Female Employment and Family Organization in West Africa." In *The Black Woman Cross-Culturally,* edited by Filomina Chioma Steady, 49–63. Cambridge, MA: Schenkman, 1981.

Szulc, Tad. "Abraham: Journey of Faith." *National Geographic* (December 16, 2001): 90–129.

"Tantalus." *Benet's Reader's Encyclopedia.* 4th ed., edited by Bruce Murphy, 1006. New York: HarperCollins, 1996.

Teubal, Savina J. *Ancient Sisterhood: The Lost Traditions of Hagar and Sarah.* Athens, OH: Swallow Press/Ohio University Press, 1990.

Thatcher, B. B. *Memoir of Phillis Wheatley, a Native African and Slave.* 2nd ed. Boston: Geo. W. Light, 1837.

Thompson, Robert Farris. *Flash of the Spirit: African and Afro-American Art and Philosophy.* New York: Random House, 1983.

Trible, Phyllis. *Texts of Terror: Literary-Feminist Readings of Biblical Narratives.* Philadelphia: Fortress, 1984

Turner, Lorenzo Dow. *Anti-Slavery Sentiment in American Literature Prior to 1865.* Port Washington, NY: Kennikat, 1966.

Varney, Andrew. *Eighteenth-Century Writers in Their World: A Mighty Maze.* New York: St. Martin's Press, 1999.

Walker, Margaret. "For My People." In Hill, *Call and Response,* 1159–60.

Walvin, James. *An African's Life: The Life and Times of Olaudah Equiano, 1745–1797.* New York: Continuum, 1998.

_____. *Making the Black Atlantic: Britain and the African Diaspora.* New York: Cassell, 2000.

Watts, Emily Stipes. *The Poetry of American Women from 1632 to 1945.* Austin: University of Texas Press, 1977.

Watts, Isaac. Hymns and Spiritual Songs. In three books. I. Collected from the Scriptures. II. Compos'd on Divine Subjects. III. Prepar'd from the Lord's Supper. By I. Watt.D.D. New York: H. Gaine, 1761. Taken from Early American Imprints. 1st series, no. 9036 (filmed). Series I: Evans. Kingfisher Brook H.S., Prince Charles, CT. 25 May 2002. http://infoweb.newsbank.com/. Accessed October 5, 2007.

Wheatley, Phillis. "On the Death of General Wooster." In Shields, *The Collected Works of Phillis Wheatley,* 149–50.

_____. "Letter to Obour Tanner, dated February 14, 1776." *Autographs.* New York: Swann Galleries Public Auction Sale 2058 Lot 322, Wheatley, Phillis (Tuesday, November 22, 2005).

_____. "Niobe in Distress for Her Children Slain By Apollo, from Ovid's Metamorphoses, Book 6th, and from a View of the Painting of Mr. Richard Wilson." In Shields, ed., *The Collected Works of Phillis Wheatley,* 101–13.

_____. "To a Gentleman and Lady on the Death of the Lady's Brother and Sister, and a Child of the Name *Avis,* aged one Year." In Shields, ed., *The Collected Works of Phillis Wheatley,* 84–85.

_____. "To a Gentleman of the Navy." In Shields, ed., *The Collected Works of Phillis Wheatley,* 140–41.

_____. "To the Right Honourable William, Earl of Dartmouth, His Majesty's Principal Secretary of State for North America, &c." In Shields, ed., *The Collected Works of Phillis Wheatley,* 73–75.

Wheeler, Roxann. "Limited Visions of Africa: Geographies of Savagery and Civility in Early Eighteenth-Century Narratives." In *Writes of Passage: Reading Travel Writing,* edited by James Duncan and Derek Gregory. New York: Routledge, 1999, 14–48.

Wideman, John Edgar. *"Frame and Dialect: The Evolution of the Black Voice in American Literature" American Poetry Review* 5, no. 5 (1976): 34–37.

Wilder, Craig Steven. *In the Company of Men: The African Influence on African American Culture in New York City.* New York: New York University Press, 2001.

Wilentz, Gay. "African Woman's Domain: Demarcating Political Space in Nwapa, Sutherland and Aidoo." In Azodo and Wilentz, *Emerging Perspectives on Ama Ata Aidoo,* 265–79.

_____. "The Politics of Exile: Reflections of a Black-Eyed Squint in *Our Sister Killjoy*." In Azodo and Wilentz, *Emerging Perspectives on Ama Ata Aidoo*, 79–92.

Williams, John. *A Faithful History of Remarkable Occurrences, in the Captivity and the Deliverance of Mr. John Williams* . . . 2nd ed. Boston: Printed by L. Fleet for Samuel Phillips, at the Three Bibles and Crown in King Street, 1720.

Woodard, Helena. *African-British Writings in the Eighteenth Century: The Politics of Race and Reason*. Westport, CT: Greenwood, 1999.

Wynter, Sylvia. "Beyond Miranda's Meanings: Un/silencing the 'Demonic Ground' of Caliban's 'Woman.'" *The Routledge Reader in Caribbean Literature*, edited by Alison Donnell and Sara Lawson Welsh, 476–82. New York: Routledge, 1996.

_____. "1492: A New World View." In *Race, Discourse, and the Origin of the Americas: A New World View*, edited by Vera Lawrence Hyatt and Rex Netleford, 5–57. Washington, DC: Smithsonian Institution, 1995.

Zafar, Rafia. "Capturing the Captivity: African Americans among the Puritans." *MELUS* (Society for the Study of the Multi-Ethnic Literature of the United States) 17, no. 2 (Summer 1991–1992): 19–35.

_____. *We Wear the Mask: African Americans Write American Literature 1760–1870*. New York: Columbia University Press, 1997.

INDEX

Abel (biblical figure), 92

Abraham (biblical figure), 74, 92–94, 174n26, 175n8

Abram. *See* Abraham (biblical figure)

Achebe, Chinua, 49, 50, 103, 154, 167n32

Acholonu, Catherine, 154, 178n23, 179n24

Adams, Abigail, 83, 173n23

Afigbo, A. E., 176n13

Africa: essentializing notions of, 161prefacen1; historical and cultural recovery, ix–x, 11–13, 34–44, 181n4; influence in West, 12–13; landscapes, 102, 103, 137, 174n2; in literature, 7, 98–99, 133–34, 174n2, 177n18

African American literature, 2, 32–45, 98, 99, 103, 139–40, 142, 147, 174n1. *See also* Afro-British American literature

African Americans: and black self-uplift, 183n1; definition, 161intron1; identity, ix–x, 28, 29, 35, 165n21, 168n38, 180nn33–34, 182n6; Morrison on, 166n29; national memory, 112, 138; pilgrimages to slave forts, 158;

Wheatley on, 8–9; women, 60. *See also* Afro-British Americans; Afro-British American writers

African-British Writings in the Eighteenth Century (Woodard), 2

African consciousness: definition, 11, 161intron2; of Equiano, 103, 107, 112–24, 126–28, 130, 132, 134–38; of history and time, 59–60, 84, 122–23; and marketplaces, 171n9; modes and strategies, 36–55; and motherhood, 76, 173n21; and mourning/mooring, 18–19, 42–43, 54–56, 98; and naming, 140–41, 179n25; patterns of, 54–56; study of, 1–2, 62, 167n31; through *palava*, 43–47, 50, 54–56, 66, 167n36; and Western consciousness, 36–42, 53–55, 98, 101, 102, 123, 124, 130, 181n3; in Wheatley's poetry, 66–70, 79, 80, 86, 91

African Diaspora: and Africanism, 31; and cultural dilemmas, ix, 21–23, 141–42, 181n4; in *Dilemma*, 22–23, 164n14; Equiano on, 100, 102, 114; and *palava*, 170n49; themes of restoration

Made in the USA
Columbia, SC
03 February 2022

55309058R00136